BETRUMPED

BETRUMPED

THE SURPRISING HISTORY OF 3,000 LONG-LOST, EXOTIC AND ENDANGERED WORDS

EDWARD ALLHUSEN

AMBERLEY

This book is typeset in the Caslon typeface, the same that was used in Samuel Johnson's dictionary. William Caslon (1692–1766), a contemporary of Johnson, created the typeface that bears his name in 1734 and it was used for many publications in the eighteenth century. It also crossed the Atlantic, where it was used to typeset the American Declaration of Independence in 1776.

First published 2018

Amberley Publishing
The Hill, Stroud
Gloucestershire, GL5 4EP

www.amberley-books.com

British Library Cataloguing in Publication Data.
A catalogue record for this book is available from the British Library.

ISBN 978 1 4456 7867 2 (paperback)
ISBN 978 1 4456 7868 9 (ebook)

Typesetting and Origination by Amberley Publishing.
Printed in the UK.

Contents

Dedicated to all the explorers, inventors, scientists, authors and scriveners who, over the last 1,600 years, have sensitively enhanced the dialect of a small north European tribe into the most widely spoken language in the world – and to you, the reader, for perpetuating the use of the English language.

Introduction

What is the greatest invention of all time?

If you stop people in the street and ask them to make their choice they usually say the wheel. Certainly a deserving candidate, and it is doubtful that any of us get through a day without travelling by courtesy of a wheel or turning a knob on an appliance. There are many others – penicillin, concrete, telephones, petrol engines, sliced bread – the list is endless. Yet one invention is seldom even shortlisted despite all of us using it every day, just as you are doing right now. Surely the greatest invention is language, which is seldom considered as people take it for granted. But it certainly is an invention, for no new-born child comes equipped with a vocabulary. All the words in all of the world's estimated 6,912 languages and countless dialects were invented by man. Samuel Johnson defined 42,773 words in his famous dictionary published in 1755 but now it is believed that there are in excess of 600,000 words in the English language. Where did they all come from?

Many are made up by scientists with a sense of humour – words like pneumonoultramicroscopicsilicovolcanokoniosis, which is a disease of the lungs. Many are made up by joining words together, such as bedridden. Ridden means filled with something unpleasant.

So bed is where you go when you are ridden with pneumonoult... etc. etc.

Far more were borrowed from other languages and in Part One we will look at the origins of the very welcome immigrants who have done so much to enhance the pages of our dictionaries.

Before the fifth century, the languages spoken in Britain were Latin [*Domino, Mantelpiece, Refrigerate*] and Celtic [*Butcher, Glass, Lukewarm*][1], but they were swept aside when the Anglo-Saxons invaded. The Angles, from the south of present-day Denmark, brought with them the language which became the foundation of the English we speak today. Since there were no dictionaries there is no way of knowing the full extent of their language, but many words we use today date back to that period. [*Bishop, Daisy, Earwig*]. Over the next 500 years it developed steadily, being spoken by the Venerable Bede (although he wrote in Latin) plus King Alfred and other Anglo-Saxon kings. Then came the Vikings and many words came to English from their Norse language [*Acre, Awkward, Ski*].

When the Normans invaded in 1066, Norman-French became the language of government while English continued to be spoken by the subjugated Saxons. It was not until three centuries after the invasion that English was used in the law courts and government. Throughout this time English continued to acquire words from further afield, for this was the age of the crusades when knights and pilgrims returning from the Holy Land brought home exotic items and ideas never before seen in the west, thus introducing words that originated in China, India and Persia. [*Ivory, Oranges, Pyjamas, Satin, Sugar, Shampoo*].

English continued to glean words from other languages during military campaigns throughout the Middle Ages, but it was not until the close of the Plantagenet era that an event occurred that was to mark the beginning of the standardisation of the language. William Caxton set up his printing press at Westminster in 1476 and most of

---

[1]*Words bracketed in italic can be found listed in the text.*

the books that he produced were in English. For the first time the mass production of the printed word provided a reference for spelling and grammar. Shortly afterwards, with the arrival of the Tudors, the language went through drastic changes, particularly in pronunciation, and that in turn led to further modification of spellings and so Modern English was born. A few years later it became the language of Shakespeare and the authorised King James version of the Bible.

This was also the dawn of the great era of exploration, and travellers returning from distant lands introduced a plethora of new foods, ideas and items for which they retained the native names. [*Anorak*, *Avocado*, *Barbeque*, *Hooch*, *Potato* and *Tobacco*].

As the Industrial Revolution gained momentum and scientific research progressed, many new words were needed to describe inventions and discoveries. It was towards the Greek and Latin, in which languages the new subjects had first been studied, that those who coined the new words invariably turned [*Anatomy*, *Bacteria*, *Factory*, *Inoculate*, *Vaccine* and *Vitamin*].

So we, the English, have appropriated words from all over the globe and it is this willingness of our language to accept these incomers that gives it strength. Its constant ability to adapt has been the cornerstone of its success. Other languages such as French have been more concerned with purity than progress. While lovers of the English language tend to sneer at Americanisms and bad usage, spare a thought that maybe you are witnessing the type of change that has strengthened English to the point at which it is now an unstoppable global language. Quite the opposite to Cornish, which served an area too small to survive as anyone's first language but thankfully not before it contributed words such as *Bludgeon* and *Puffin* to English.

Mandarin [*Char*, *Kowtow*, *Typhoon*], Arabic [*Algebra*, *Artichoke*, *Chemistry*, *Coffee*], Spanish [*Alcove*, *Boot*, *Castanets*, *Dagger*] and Hindi [*Bungalow*, *Chutney*, *Dinghy*] vie with English for the accolade of being spoken by the most people as their first language. But it is English that is spoken by far more people as a second language, and they do so all over the world. English is the international language of commerce and government and the one in which two people from different linguistic backgrounds are most likely to converse. Over half of everyone living in the EU has English as a first or second language.

So then what happens? Once words have arrived and become established as the building blocks of English do they remain unchanged in spelling, meaning and pronunciation until the end of time? No, they do not! They drift in and out of popularity. Many have already been consigned to the literary scrapheap, while others are tottering on the edge of oblivion suffering from lack of use.

What better way to see how things have changed than to go back 250 years to take a stroll through the pages of Dr Johnson's dictionary? In Part Two we seek out words that have moved on with time. Some gems have disappeared from our vernacular altogether, and really ought to be brought back. Others are well known to us but seem to have slid sideways into totally different meanings.

Finally, in just the same way that we become increasingly perturbed by species of animals edging their way towards extinction, so also should we show concern for words that appear to be nearing their demise simply because we do not use them enough. Their future is in our mouths and on our keyboards. Part Three therefore contains words that seem not to be around as much as they used to be. These are words that most people are aware of but, for no discernible reason, they have chosen to retire them into the inner recesses of their vocabulary through lack of use.

Changing fashion has understandably seen off bombazine and spats, while idleness on the part of authors and speechifiers has giving undeserved life to shockers such as nice. That is the one word that should be scrapped for it threatens so many others. How can a meal, a walk and a hat all be described by the same adjective? How much better to describe a meal as delicious, a walk as invigorating and a hat as chic?

Some words understandably slip away as situations change. Tanner, for instance, the nickname of that attractive little slip of a coin worth six old pence that disappeared with decimalisation. It is most unlikely that we would ever require a two-and-a-half-new-pence coin, but there is no reason why its neighbour in the dictionary piggy bank, the florin, could not be used to describe the ten-pence piece. They are both one tenth of a pound.

A lessening of demand for literary perfection in the eye of the reader has allowed us to tolerate previously unacceptable laziness as we hurtle towards a one-size-fits-all world. Here, in this graveyard of language, where Chaucer and Shakespeare once plied their art, these gems of the English language will soon be forgotten for we live in an age when pronouncements, even from the higher echelons of the world stage, are reduced to 280 characters. Where will it end?

All that needs to happen for these waifs and strays of the language to be restored to their former glory is for them to be used, so here is the challenge. Each day pick any one of these that has remained dormant in a hidden crevice of your vocabulary and use it before nightfall. If you do not and other people do not, then they must be considered endangered. Please help them.

Abbreviations: adj. adjective; adv. adverb; excl. exclamation; interj. interjection; n. noun; prep. preposition; v. verb.

PART ONE
Arrivals

Adopted words and where they came from

Words emigrate and immigrate, they arrive with invading armies and embrace changing fashions. They amend their spellings as they roam across centuries, languages and cultures. English has never minded picking up linguistic newcomers. Here you will find over 1,300 words from 100 different languages, from Cornish to Tibetan and from Inuit to Tongan, that have enhanced English. As British explorers discovered previously unknown items such as *Amethysts* and *Asbestos*, *Budgerigars* and *Banjoes*, *Catamarans* and *Coffee* they brought them home with the name they had learnt overseas. In times of conflict we gained *Rifle*, *Turncoat* and *Sapper*, while developments in the medical world brought us *Quarantine*, *Stethoscope* and *Vertebra*.

A

ABACUS Hebrew *Abaq* Dust.

> The predecessor of the abacus, sliding beads on a series of wires, were round pebbles laid in grooves drawn in the sand or dust. English usage of the word dates back to the fourteenth century. *See also Calculus.*

ABANDON Latin *Ab* From and *Bandum* Flag.

> If you move away from the flag you abandon the colours. The colour was the flag of the regiment that defined the rallying point on the field of battle. The ceremony of Trooping the Colour, now ceremonial, was to show the regimental flag to the troops so they could more easily locate it.

ABATTOIR French *Abattre* To strike down.

> A chilling reference to the fate of animals in a slaughterhouse.

ABBOT Syriac *Abba* Father.

ABDICATION Latin *Abdicatio* To disown.

> The act of renouncing or disowning a permanent office, such as that of a monarch, as opposed to one to which you are appointed, was previously also applied to the disinheritance of a child by someone in the permanent position of a parent.

ABORIGINE Latin *Ab* From and *Origine* Beginning.

> The term now most associated with the early inhabitants of Australia can correctly be applied to any people who have been somewhere since the 'beginning'.

ABRUPT Latin *Abruptus* Broken off.

> An abrupt action invariably involves the breaking off of a situation. Rupture is from the same source.

ABSINTHE Syriac *Ab-sintha* The author of sleep.
Absinthe is a very alcoholic, aniseed-flavoured spirit.

ABSTEMIOUS Latin *Ab* Away and *Temus* Strong drink.
A drink strong enough to make you drunk. So to be abstemious is to keep away from strong drink.

ABSURD Latin *Ab* From and *Surdus* Deaf.
The cruel allusion is to the reply given by a deaf man to a question he has not heard distinctly.

ACADEMY Greek *Academeia* was the name of an olive grove outside Athens.
Academus, the owner of the land, was a farmer who helped Castor and Pollux search for their sister, Helen, who had been taken away by Theseus. From then on, as Athens expanded around it, the grove was protected and it was here that Plato came to hold his symposiums.

ACCOLADE Italian *Accolata* To embrace.
Denoting the ancient ceremony of the monarch conferring accolades, such as knighthoods, by laying his arms around the new knight's neck and embracing him.

ACCOST Latin *Costa* Side, rib.
If you accost someone the chances are that you are standing at their side, next to their ribs. *See also Coast.*

ACCUMULATE Latin *Cumulus* A heap or pile.
When we say that a man has made his pile we mean that he has accumulated a fortune. A large and billowing pile of cloud is called cumulus.

ACCURATE Latin *Cura* Pains.
If you take pains your work is likely to be accurate.

ACE Latin *As* A unit.

ACRE Norse *Aker* An open field.
An acre is an area of 10 square chains, and although it can now be any area of that size it was originally a long, thin strip of open ground measuring 1 chain (66 feet) wide by 10 chains (660 feet or one furlong) long. A chain was a unit of measure invented by clergyman Edmund Gunter (1581–1626) which consisted, quite literally, of a chain made of 100 links. The chain is now scarcely used except as the length of a cricket pitch between the wickets. *See also Furlong*.

ACROBAT Greek *Akrobates* To run on tiptoe or to climb aloft.

ACUPUNCTURE Latin *Acus* Needle and *Pungere* To prick.

ADAGIO Italian *Ad Agio* At ease.
Music to be performed slowly.

ADIEU French *A Dieu* To God.
To God I commend you as you set out on your journey.

ADJECTIVE Latin *Ad* To and *Jacere* To throw.
An adjective is a word that throws extra detail to a noun.

ADJUTANT Latin *Adjutans* To assist.
An adjutant is an army officer who assists his superior by completing administrative tasks. The word also refers to two types of large, carrion-eating storks, although this is supposedly due to their military bearing and has nothing to do with the word's Latin root.

ADMIRAL Arabic *Amir-el bahr* Ruler of the sea.

ADVENT Latin *Ad* To and *Venio* To come.
As applied to the coming of Christ.

AFFLUENCE Latin *Affluo* To flow to.
Wealth may be said to flow to the rich.

AFRICA Latin *Afri*.
The Afri tribe occupied the ancient city of Carthage on the North African coast near present-day Tunis. They were named after Aphroi, meaning 'sea-foam', the icthyocentaur King of Lybia in ancient Greek mythology. As an icthyocentaur, or marine centaur, he was typically depicted as having the upper body of a man, horse's hooves for hands and the tail of a fish instead of legs, as well as lobster-claws for horns.

AGGRAVATE Latin *Ad* To and *Gravis* Heavy.
To aggravate a trouble is to make it heavier to bear. *See also Gravity*.

AGHAST Anglo-Saxon *Gast* Ghost.
To stand aghast is to stand as though frightened by a ghost.

AGNOSTIC Greek *A* Without and *Gnomi* To know.
The word, coined as recently as 1869 by Professor Thomas Huxley, refers to anyone who claims that without material evidence knowledge is impossible.

AHOY Norse *Aoi*.
The battle cry of the Vikings as they ran their galleys onto the enemy shore. Now used by people on ships to attract the attention of others rather than to intimidate them.

ALARM Norman-French *Larum* A thief.
Bells were rung to warn of the presence of a thief. The cry went up to rouse sleepers *A larum!*

ALBATROSS Arabic *Al Gattas* A Pelican via Portuguese *Alcatraz* Gannet.

These large white birds were found by early Portuguese explorers visiting Alcatraz island in San Francisco bay and gave their name to the notorious prison there.

ALBUM Latin *Albus* White.

An album is a book which has unprinted white pages. *See also Blank.*

ALCOHOL Arabic *Alkohl* Spirit or essence.

ALCOVE Spanish *Alcova* from Arabic *Al-Kubbah* A vaulted building such as is often the shape of an alcove.

ALDERMAN Anglo-Saxon *Ealdorman* Elder man.

An alderman is a senior member of a council or assembly. The title of *Ealdorman* was originally used by Anglo-Saxon nobles, who governed shires. *See also Sheriff.*

ALGEBRA Arabic *Al-Jabr* Transposition.

Algebra is the branch of mathematics in which numbers are transposed into letters for the purpose of calculation.

ALIMONY Latin *Alimonia* Nourishment.

Alimony is the nourishment given to a divorced party. It does not refer to payment as is indicated by not being spelt alimoney.

ALLIGATOR Spanish *Lagarto* Lizard.

A Spanish sailor on an English ship is said to have cried '*A lagarto*' when he saw an alligator. Being unfamiliar with the creatures, the English assumed that this was the correct name for the species.

AIOLI Latin *Allium* Garlic and *Oleum* Oil.

Aioli is a sauce made by mixing garlic and oil.

ALLSPICE Derived from the dried fruit of the pimenta plant that grows in the Caribbean. The name of this spice is an example of overenthusiastic marketing by the early importers who claimed that it contained the flavours of all known spices when only nutmeg, cloves and cinnamon are discernible.

ALMA MATER Latin *Alma Mater* Nourishing mother.
A term of affection used by students to describe their university.

ALMANAC Either Arabic *Al* The and *Manah* Diary, or Anglo-Saxon *All Monath* All the months – or, as is the way with word origins, very likely both.

ALOFT Norse *A* In and *Lopt* Air.
Assimilated into the English language in the twelfth century, this term also referred to heaven, atmosphere and the upper floor of a house, all of which are above us. It is also the origin of the word loft.

ALP Latin *Albus* White, a reference to the snow-covered peaks or Latin *Altus* High.

ALPHABET Greek *Alpha* A and *Beta* B.
A combination of the first two letters of the Greek alphabet, *alpha* and *beta*. The Greeks took these letters from the Phoenician for ox and house which represented the first two letters of their alphabet. *See also Camel.*

ALTAR Latin *Altus* High.
A raised table positioned higher than the congregation so that they could watch sacrifices and later religious ceremonies. It has a similar root to altimeter, a device for measuring height and alto, a high voice.

ALZHEIMER Named after the German neurologist Alois Alzheimer (1864–1915), who first identified the disease. *See also Dementia.*

AMARETTO Italian *Amaro* Bitter.
A liqueur flavoured with bitter almonds.

AMATEUR Latin *Amator* A lover.
One who pursues an interest for love rather than for money.

AMAZON Greek *A* lack of and *Mazos* Breast.
A reference to the supposed practice of the mythological female warriors who are reputed to have had their right breasts removed so that they could more easily draw their bow strings.

AMBASSADOR Latin *Ambactus* A slave or servant.
An ambassador is a servant of his country.

AMBIDEXTROUS Latin *Ambo* Both and *Dexter* Right.
An ambidextrous person is someone who can make skilful use of both hands in the way that the majority of people can only use their right hand. *See also Awkward, Dexterity and Gawky.*

AMBITIOUS Latin *Ambio* To go round.
Alluding to the practice of ambitious Romans 'going round' to canvas votes when seeking election to high office.

AMBUSH French *En* In and *Bois* Wood.
Indicating where most ambushes occurred.

AMEN Hebrew *Amen* So be it.

AMERICA The dominant theory is that America is derived from Amerigo Vespucci (1454–1512), a native of Florence who crossed the Atlantic shortly after Columbus and published maps upon his return to Europe arrogantly proclaiming the New World as Tierra da Amerigo. Another theory, albeit one that has not gained much support, is that Welsh fishermen had been travelling to the coast of America for centuries before Columbus and Vespucci and that the name is derived from one Richard Amerike, a Welsh merchant from Bristol who funded a voyage of exploration to Newfoundland.

AMETHYST Greek *A* Opposite to and *Methyein* To make drunk.
It was once thought that the blue gemstone was able to prevent drunkenness.

AMMONIA Named after The Temple of *Ammon* in Egypt near which ammonia was first made by burning dung from the numerous camels bringing pilgrims to worship there. *See also Ammonite.*

AMMONITE The ancient Egyptian god Ammon was usually depicted with ram's horns. The fossilized cephalopod is so named because it has a coiled cell structure resembling a ram's horn. *See also Ammonia.*

AMOK Malay *Amoq* Frenzied.
To rush about in a frenzied state is to run amok. The original Malay adjective referred to frenzied combat.

AMPHITHEATRE Greek *Amphi* On both sides and *Theatron* A theatre.
An amphitheatre has seats on all sides.

AMPHORA Greek *Amphi* On both sides and *Phoreus* A bearer.
An amphora is a jug that is carried by handles on both sides.

AMPUTATE Latin *Amputare* To prune.
Before its surgical use became commonplace, pruning was a horticultural term.

ANACHRONISM Greek *An* Backwards and *Chronos* Time.
An anachronism is something from a time in the past.

ANARCHY Greek *An* Backwards (or against) and *Arche* Government.
Anarchy occurs when a society revolts against its government.

ANATOMY Greek *Ana* Up and *Tomnein* To cut.
Anatomy, the study of an organism's structure, is learned by dissection or cutting up.

ANECDOTE Greek *Ekdotos* To publish.

ANGEL Greek *Angelos* A messenger.

ANGLE Old English *Angul* A hook.
An angle joins two parts such as the two sides of a fish hook.

ANIMALS The English names of domestic animals are nearly all Anglo-Saxon: cat, dog, pup, horse, mare, hound, hog, sow, pig, sheep, cow, ox, bull, ram, ewe, lamb, calf, colt, foal, ass, drake, duck, cock, hen, chick and goose. The names of wild beasts, on the contrary, are mainly Norman-French: lion, tiger, elephant, leopard, panther, etc. It is also interesting to note that although the names of living domestic animals are Saxon, we use Norman names for their meat: beef, mutton, veal and pork. This would suggest that, after the conquest, Saxons were retained as farmhands and thus the language retained their names for the stock they tended. When the animals became meat, however, they were consumed by the Normans who applied their own names to their food. *See also Humble Pie.*

ANORAK Kalaallisut (a dialect of the Inuit language spoken on the western side of Greenland) *Anoraq* A seal skin hooded coat that is regularly coated with fish oil to maintain water resistance. *See also Parka.*

ANTEDILUVIAN Latin *Ante* Before and *Diluvium* Flood.
Someone or thing that is very old, perhaps even predating Noah's flood.

ANTIBIOTIC Greek *Anti* Against and *Bios* Life.
An antibiotic is a substance that acts against the life of harmful bacteria. The word was coined in 1942.

ANTIMACASSAR Oil of Macassar is a hair lotion made from coconut and palm oil that traders purchased in the Indonesian port of Macassar in the Celebes, now known as Sulawesi. Much in vogue during the Victorian era and the first half of the twentieth century, it had the unfortunate tendency to rub off the back of the head on to chairs. The antimacassar, a washable cloth often embroidered like a doily, was positioned to preserve the upholstery.

ANTIPODES Greek *Anti* Opposed to and *Podos* A foot.
This word was introduced by Plato to describe the other side of the earth, the literal translation being a reference to those who stand with feet opposite to our own. Interestingly no one from Europe had been anywhere near the other side of the world when Plato thought about this. The Antipodes Islands are 500 miles (800 kilometres) south-east of New Zealand and are so called because they are the closest land to the true antipodes of London.

ANTISEPTIC Greek *Anti* Against and *Sepsis* Putrefaction.
The word was coined in the mid-eighteenth century.

APARTHEID Afrikaans *Apartheid* Apartness.
Apartheid can mean either separation of different races or of different sexes.

APOCRYPHAL Greek *Apo* From *Krupto* To hide.
An apocryphal story is one of such uncertain origin that the author is now quite hidden.

APPLAUD Latin *Plaudere* To clap.

APRICOT Latin *Praecoqua* Early ripening fruit.
Apricots, formerly known as apricocks, were introduced to Europe from Armenia at the time of Alexander the Great (356–323 BC). *See also Precocious.*

APRIL *See Months of the Year.*

ARABLE Latin *Arare* To plough.
Arable land is ploughable land.

ARCHIPELAGO Greek *Archos* Chief and *Pelagos* Sea.
This is the name the Greeks gave to the Aegean, a sea that abounds with small islands. It is now used to describe any group of islands.

ARCTIC Greek *Arktikos* Bear.
The Great Bear constellation Ursa Major, otherwise known as the Plough, is always visible in the Arctic.

ARENA Latin *Harena* Sand.
A name given by Romans to that part of an amphitheatre where gladiators fought and where Christians were thrown to the lions. It was strewn with red sand to conceal from the view of spectators any blood that might have been spilled. As such, the word should not really be used to describe an area without sand.

ARISTOCRACY Greek *Aristos* The best and *Kratos* Power or strength.
Aristocracy therefore refers to rule by people able to show that they are the most powerful. *See also Democracy.*

ARMISTICE Latin *Arma* Weapons and *Statium* Stopping.

ARITHMETIC Greek *Arithmetike* To count.

ARMADILLO Spanish *Armado* Armed.
A South American animal armed with a hard, shell-like protection.

AROMA Greek *Aroma* A spice.

ARRIVE Latin *Ad* To and *Ripa* River bank.
The allusion is to arriving by landing from a boat or ship. Riparian rights are those of the owner of the river bank such as are enjoyed by a fisherman.

ARROWROOT So called because the Arawak speaking people of the Caribbean and the north east coastal areas of South America applied the root of the plant to wounds inflicted by poisoned arrows. *See also Toxic.*

ARTERY Greek *Arteria* Windpipe.
Arteries and veins are pipes that enable blood to carry 'wind' or oxygen around the body.

ARTESIAN French *Artois* A town in France where Europe's first known artesian well was sunk.
The Chinese had discovered centuries before that wells constructed in certain areas were able to drive water to the surface with pressure generated by the surrounding strata.

ARTICHOKE Arabic *Al-harshuf* Rough-skinned.
The Globe Artichoke, a member of the thistle family, originated in North Africa where they may still be found growing in the wild. *See also Jerusalem Artichoke.*

ARTISAN Latin *Artitus* Skilled.

ASBESTOS Greek *Sbestos* Extinguished.

Asbestos, since it does not burn, is ideal for extinguishing fires.

ASPARAGUS Latin *A* Intensive and *Sparasso* To tear.

A reference to the strong prickles on some species of the plant that tear the hands when harvesting.

ASPIRIN Greek *A* Without and *Spiraea* The Latin name of the meadowsweet plant.

Acetylsalicylic acid, which is the effective ingredient of aspirin, occurs naturally in the leaves of the plant and they have been used for medicinal purposes all over the world for centuries. But aspirin is manufactured by a chemical process that takes place without using spiraea.

ASSASSIN Arabic *Hashishiyyin* Hashish eaters.

Members of this military and religious sect in eleventh-century Persia carried out secret murders using *hashish* or Indian hemp as a stimulant to nerve themselves for their horrible work.

ASSET French *Assez* Sufficient.

An asset was originally the property of a deceased person sufficient to pay his debts and legacies.

ASSIZE Latin *Ad* To and S*edere* To sit.

When judges conduct an assize they are said to be sitting.

ASTERISK Greek *Asteriskos* A small star.

A similar root to asteroid from the Greek *Asteroeides* Star-like.

ASTHMA Greek *Asthma* To breathe with open mouth.

ASTONISH Anglo-Saxon *Stunian* To stun or Latin *Attonitus* Thunderstruck.

ASTROLOGY Greek *Astron* Star and *Logos* Discourse.

ASTRONAUT Greek *Astron* Star and *Nautes* Sailor.
An astronaut is someone who voyages to the stars.

ASTRONOMY Greek *Astron* Star and *Nomos* Law.
Astronomy is the study of the laws of the stars.

ATHLETE Greek *Athlos* To contest.

ATOLL Dhivehi (The Maldives) An atoll is a coral reef that circles a lagoon partially or completely. Since coral reefs are organic it may be said that they are the world's largest living organisms.

ATMOSPHERE Greek *Atmos* Vapour and *Sphaira* A sphere.
Atmosphere is the vapour that surrounds the sphere that is the earth.

ATOM Greek *A* Not *Tomos* Cutting.
This word was used in ancient Greek philosophy and then brought back in 1805 to refer to something so small that it could not be cut, let alone split.

AUCTION Latin *Auctum* To increase.
An auction is a sale where the price increases.

AUDIENCE Latin *Audire* To hear.
The word audience originally referred to the act of hearing a performance, not watching it.

AUGUST *See Months of the Year.*

AUTOCRAT Greek *Autos* Self and *Kratos* Power.
An autocrat is someone who maintains power in his own hands.

AVAST Italian *Basta* Enough.

Avast is the nautical term for stop, as in 'That's far enough.'

AVOCADO Nahuatl (Aztec) *Ahuacatl* Testicle.

Avocados were supposed to be an aphrodisiac, but this belief was probably due more to the similarity of the avocado's shape to a giant testicle than to any proven effects. *See also Orchid.*

AWKWARD Middle English *Awk* Back-handed or left-handed, from Old Norse *Afugr* Turned the other way round.

A left-handed man was considered an awkward man since he found it awkward to do things with his right hand in the way that most people – those who were right handed – were able to. Anything clumsily done was said to be awkwardly done, i.e. done as though with a left hand. *See also Ambidextrous, Dexterity, Gawky and Southpaw.*

AZURE Farsi *Lazvard* A place in Afghanistan where the blue stone lapis lazuli has been mined since 4,000 BC. Many other languages, notably in southern Europe, have a word similar to azure for blue but the word blue originates from the Frankish *Blao* Shining and variations of that are used for blue in most northern European languages.

B

BABOON Old French *Baboue* Grimace.

The baboon has a particularly ugly face.

BACHELOR Latin *Baculum* Stick.

A bachelor was a young man training for knighthood and before they were allowed to use real swords they perfected their fighting skills with sticks. *See also Bacteria.*

BACON Anglo-Saxon *Boc* Beech tree.

Pigs are often found feeding on beech nuts, a diet that was once believed to produce the best bacon. *See also Book.*

BACKGAMMON Danish *Bakke* A tray and *Gammen* A game.

The fast-moving game of counters and dice thrown into a wooden tray was introduced to England by invading Danes.

BACTERIA Greek *Baktron* Staff.

When bacteria were first observed under the microscope (*c.* 1847) it was noticed that they resembled little sticks or staffs. Some time later (*c.* 1883) another form of tiny organism was discovered and, pursuing the same theme, these were named bacillus from Latin *Baculus*, Rod. *Baculum* is Latin for a stick and *Baculine* was punishment by beating with a stick. *See also Bachelor.*

BALANCE Latin *Bi* Two and *Lanx* A dish.

Balance scales have two dishes suspended from either end of a beam.

BALLAD Latin *Ballare* To dance.

A ballad is a story set to music that was invariably performed with dancing. A ball, as in a dance party, has the same origin.

BALLAST Dutch *Bag læs* Back load.

When a ship had to return back home without a cargo it was necessary to load stones or other worthless weighty material as ballast to maintain the ship's stability.

BALLISTICS Latin *Ballista* A machine used by the Roman army to hurl stones during sieges from Greek *Ballistes* To throw.

BANJO Kimbundu (Angola) *Manza*.

The stringed instrument travelled to the United States with slaves from Africa. Since it has a relatively straight forward construction it was a natural choice for them to make on arrival. *See also Calypso*.

BANK Latin *Banco* A table.

Visitors to ancient Rome were only allowed to use the local currency and had to visit money changers who set up tables where they transacted their business.

BANKRUPT Latin *Banco* A table and *Rotto* Broken.

In the Middle Ages it was customary for tables belonging to insolvent money changers to be broken up to prevent further trading.

BANTAM The name of these small chickens was taken from Bantam formerly a major seaport of Indonesia where European sailors took poultry on board for the voyage home.

BAPTISE Greek *Baptien* To dip.

BARACK Swahili *Barack* One who is blessed. *See also Obama*.

BARBARIAN Sanskrit *Barbara* Stammering.

An onomatopoeic word indicating babbling and incoherent speech in the same way that we say blah blah. A term applied to the language of tribes whose speech was unintelligible to the Greeks. Someone who spoke like this was labelled a barbarian.

BARBER Latin *Barba* Beard.

BARBEQUE Taíno (the language of the Bahamas) *Barbacoa* Sacred fire pit.

A traditional Caribbean method for cooking meat involved placing an entire goat into a specially dug hole in the ground and covering it with maguey leaves and coal, before setting it alight and leaving it to cook for a few hours.

BARGE BOARD *Verge board*, an architectural term for a decorative edge to an eave which, due to its elevated position, was clearly nothing to do with canal boats. In fact, it is a corruption of verge board, that is a board on the edge or verge of the house.

BARITONE Greek *Bary* Heavy and *Tonos* Tone.
Deep-sounding.

BARN Old English *Bern* from *Bere* Barley and *Ern* A house.
A building in which grain is stored.

BAROMETER Greek *Baros* Weight and *Metron* Measure.
A barometer measures atmospheric pressure, the weight of the air above it.

BARLEY SUGAR French *Brûle* Burnt and *Sucre* Sugar.
There is no barley in the sugary sweet. Barley is a corruption of *brûle*.

BARRACK Italian *Barraca* Temporary housing and Celtic *Barro* Clay, mud.
A barrack was a simple hut made of branches and mud that could be constructed to provide adequate shelter for soldiers on campaign and the word is now used for any military accommodation.

BATTLEDORE, SHUTTLECOCK AND BADMINTON Provençal *Batedor* A beater or striker.
The original name of this game, battledore and shuttlecock, derives from the equipment required: the racquet or beater held

by the players and the shuttlecock, the latter being derived from the two words shuttle and cock. A shuttle is something that travels back and forth such as the shuttle on a loom and cock refers to the feathers of a shuttlecock, which resemble the tail feathers of a strutting cockerel. The game was played in ancient Greece but the rules of the modern sport were first defined in 1873 at Badminton in Gloucestershire, the home of the dukes of Beaufort.

BAYONET French *Bayonne* A French town where it is said that bayonets were either first made in 1640 or first used at a siege in 1665. However, there is earlier mention of 'a great knife to hang at the girdle' made at Bayona, near Toledo in Spain, which was noted for 'the excellent temper of the swords made there' and this may contradict the French origins of the word.

BAZAAR Persian *Bazar* A market.

BEAR MARKET A falling market in which a trader sells shares in the hope of being able to buy them back at a lower price before payment is due. The name is derived from the story of a man who sold a bear's skin before he had caught or killed the bear. *See also Bull Market.*

BEDLAM A corruption of *Bethlehem*, the name of a religious house in London that was converted into a lunatic asylum in 1546. It has become synonymous with chaos or madness.

BEDRIDDEN Anglo-Saxon *Bed* Bed and *Rida* Rider.
One who rides on or who is permanently carried on a bed.

BEDSTEAD Anglo-Saxon *Stead* or *Sted* A place, as in homestead, farmstead, etc.
We also use this word when we say 'Someone went in his stead (or instead of him)' meaning in place of him.

BEE-LINE American. Their way of saying 'in a straight line' as in 'as the crow flies', which originated in Europe. Bees and crows fly in straight lines between nests or hives and their feeding grounds.

BELFRY Norman-French *Berfroi*, from High German *Bercfrit* Tower.
These tall buildings often contained bells which were rung to warn of approaching enemies. The English believed that the word was connected with the bells and adapted it to belfry. In fact, it referred only to the tower and not, as is popularly assumed, a place where bells are hung. So a tower without bells can still be a belfry.

BELLADONNA Italian *Bella donna* Fair Lady.
This poisonous plant was used as a cosmetic and also to dilate the pupils of the eyes, a popular cosmetic practice with all fair ladies.

BELLOWS Anglo-Saxon *Boelig* A bag.

BENEATH Old English *Neath* Under.

BEQUEATH Anglo-Saxon *Becwethan* A will or testament expressed in words.

BERSERK Icelandic *Bern* Bear and *Serkr* Coat.
A warrior clad in either wolf or bear skin who fought in a state of uncontained fury.

BETTER Persian *Behter* Better.

BEVERAGE Italian *Bevere* To drink.

BICYCLE Latin *Bi* Two and Greek *Kyklos* A circle.
So a bicycle is two circles. *See also Encyclopaedia and Tandem.*

BID Anglo-Saxon *Beodan* To invite.

When we invite people to come to our house we bid them to do so. If we do not want to see them we forbid them to come.

BIGAMY Latin *Bi* Two and Greek *Gamos* Marriage.

BIGWIG In a British court the barristers and judges wear wigs. The more important you are, the larger the wig. Barristers' wigs are short and kept above the ears and a senior judge has a full-bottomed wig that drops down below the shoulders. The big wig is therefore worn by the bigwig.

BIKINI The Bikini Atoll in the Marshall Islands of Micronesia was chosen as an atomic bomb-testing site in 1946. Accordingly, the name bikini was chosen for the newly designed minimal bathing suit because it was intended to cause a similarly explosive reaction in men. The bikini was not the first garment of its kind, however; indeed, they have been found illustrating ancient Greek urns dating back as far as 1400 BC.

BILLIARDS Old French *Bille* Tree trunk and *Billard* A more slender stem of wood such as a billiard cue.

BINOCULAR Latin *Bini* Double and *Oculus* Eye.

BINT Arabic *Bint* Daughter.

BISCUIT Old French *Bis* Twice and *Cuit* Baked.

A biscuit is bread that has been baked twice to harden and preserve it for the duration of long voyages.

BISHOP Old English *Biscop* from Latin *Episcopus* Overseer.

BISTRO Russian *Bistro* Quick.

A restaurant where food is served quickly. The word entered the French language in 1814 via the occupying Cossacks who would shout 'Bistro!' when they wanted to be served quickly.

BLACKMAIL Old English *Mail* An obsolete term for payment of money.

Therefore blackmail is a black or dark and sinister demand for payment.

BLADE Anglo-Saxon *Blæd* A leaf of grass.

A blade can be a blade of grass or the blade of a sword due to the similarity in shape. *See also Gladioli.*

BLANCMANGE French *Blanc* White and *Manger* Food.

The milk dessert thickened with cornflour is simply white food.

BLANK French *Blanc* White.

A blank page is a white page. *See also Album.*

BLUDGEON Cornish *Blugon* Mallet.

BOBBY This slang term for policemen makes reference to Sir Robert Peel (Prime Minister 1834–35 and 1841–46), who introduced the first police force. At one time police were also nicknamed 'Peelers'.

BODY Anglo-Saxon *Bode* Box.

The body is a box or container for the organs. Another name given to the body by the Anglo-Saxons was *Sarvol-hus*, a house for the soul.

BOFFIN An inventor with a passion or obsession for his subject, noted for creating gadgets and gizmos. Named after Nicodemus Boffin, a character in *Our Mutual Friend* by Charles Dickens, his last completed novel.

BOLLOCKS Old English *Beallucas* Testicles.

BOLSHEVIK Russian *Bolshevik* Majority, from *Bolshoi* Great.
Before the Russian Revolution the fledgling Communist Party split in half, with Lenin leading the hard-line faction. Since they were in the majority, his followers became the Bolsheviks and the softer supporters became the *Mensheviks* (Russian *Mensh* Less).

BONFIRE Middle English *Bane-fyr* Bone fire.
Animal bones were ceremonially burnt at the Celtic festival of Samhain to ward off evil spirits. This word was erroneously believed by Dr Johnson to be derived from the French word *bon*, meaning good.

BONNET Gaelic *Bonaid* A head dress.

BONSAI Japanese *Bon* Basin or bowl and *Sai* To plant.
Bonsai is the art of growing miniature trees in shallow containers.

BOOK Anglo-Saxon *Boc* Beech.
Gothic tribes used slips of wood for writing tablets and found that the wood of the beech tree was most suitable. As slips of wood could not be rolled they were gathered together, becoming the leaves of a book. *See also Bacon and Volume.*

BOOT Spanish *Bota* Leather bag.
In Spain a *bota* was also used to describe a skin for carrying wine and this gives us the word bottle. A boot might also be described as a leather bag to contain a foot.

BOOTLEG Liquor that was sold illegally during the American prohibition of alcohol from 1920 to 1933. In order to transport alcohol without attracting the attention of the authorities, smugglers created bottles that were slim enough to slip into high-sided boots.

BOOZE Old English *Bousen* To drink in excess.

BOOTY Gothic *Botyan* To profit, such as a soldier would do when collecting the spoils of war.

BOUDOIR French *Bouder* To sulk.
A boudoir, the private quarters of a lady, was originally a place where she could go to sulk and is largely attributed to the practice of the mistresses of French kings retiring to their rooms when the monarch's amorous attentions were elsewhere.

BOY Middle English *Boie* Servant, knave. *See also Girl.*

BOYCOTT Charles Boycott was an agent for a number of absentee landlords in Co. Mayo, Ireland during the oppressive years of the nineteenth century. He acquired a reputation of dispossessing tenants who fell behind with their rent, eventually inspiring them to retaliate by uniting under a pact to have nothing to do with him – to boycott him – until he fled back to England.

BRACE Anglo-Saxon *Braceur* To bind or tie up.
A brace, such as a brace of pheasants, has come to mean two because they are usually tied together in pairs. However, it more correctly refers to the way in which they are fastened together, so three or four pheasants fastened together could also be described as a brace. We still use brace to describe a variety of fixings, particularly in architecture.

BREN GUN These light machine guns take their name from the first two letters of each of the two towns in which they were originally made: Brno in Czechoslovakia and Enfield in England.

BROCADE Latin *Brocco* Small spike, referring to the awl or needle used in the production of this fabric.

BROCK Old English *Brokkos* Badger.
In *The Tale of Mr Tod* Beatrix Potter named her disagreeable badger Tommy Brock. Mr Tod was the fox and tod is a northern name for a fox.

BROGUE Gaelic *Brog* A shoe.

BRONZE Persian *Berenj* Brass.
Bronze is an alloy of copper and tin whereas brass is an alloy of copper and zinc, so it seems at some stage the meanings of bronze and copper became muddled. Brass is derived from the Friesian *Bres*, copper. The Frisian Islands, best known for their high-yielding black-and-white milking cows, are strung out along the North Sea coast of Europe from Holland north to Denmark.

BROTHEL Middle English *Breothan* To go to ruin.

BUDDHA Sanskrit *Buddha* Awakened one.

BUDGERIGAR Gamilaraay (or one of the other Aboriginal languages of south-east Australia) *Betcherry* Good and *Gah* Eating.

BUDGET French *Bougette* A small bag.
The Chancellor of the Exchequer brings his all-important budget speech to the House of Commons in a leather briefcase and invariably pauses for a photo opportunity on his doorstep holding up the small bag before doing so.

BULB Greek *Bolbos* An onion.

BULL MARKET A market in which prices are rising, thus perpetuating yet more buying as traders attempt to acquire stocks at improving rates. The intense competition and frenetic activity has been compared to the fast-moving and sometimes ill-considered behaviour of a herd of bulls. *See also Bear market.*

BUMPF Slang for tedious and unimportant paperwork. A contraction of bum fodder, that is, paper for use in lavatories.

BUMPKIN Middle Dutch *Bommekijn* Little barrel.
Used in English as a term of reproach for rustics from the countryside, it was originally a derogatory allusion to the dumpiness of Dutchmen.

BUNGALOW Gujarati and Hindi *Bangla.* A low, thatched, one-storey house common in Bengal.

BUNKUM Buncombe is a town in North Carolina whose representative in Congress in 1820 was noted for delivering long, tedious speeches invariably filled with irrelevances.

BURGLAR Gaelic *Buar glacair* A cattle lifter.

BURROW Anglo-Saxon *Burgh* Stronghold, fortification.
The same word gives us borough, which meant a shelter or fortress around which settlements were established. Hence also its usage to refer to the home of the humble rabbit.

BUSTLE Icelandic *Bustla* To splash with water.
The word is derived from the rapid motion produced by the bubbling of a boiling liquid such as is found in the natural hot springs in Iceland.

BUTCHER French *Boucher* and Provençal *Bochier* from Celtic *Bouc* He-goat.
The word butcher is derived from 'the slaughterer of goats'.

BUTTER Bavarian *Buttern* To shake backwards and forwards as in the making of butter in a butter churn. Alternatively, Greek *Bous* Cow and *Turos* Cheese.

BUTTERFLY German and Dutch *Butterfleige* A large moth that infests dairies and lives on butter and milk that gave its name to the entire species.

BUXOM Anglo-Saxon *Boga* A bow and *Sum* Some.
The Old English word *Boughsome* referred to someone or something that easily bent to one's will like an archer's bow, therefore buxom was originally applied to that which was obedient or pliant and letter writers often signed off with 'your buxom servant'. The transition from obedience to the current meaning of a generously proportioned female form may be more to do with wishful thinking on the part of male admirers.

BY JINGO Basque *Jainko* God.
The term jingoism meaning military blustering derives from a patriotic, anti-Russian music hall song from the Victorian era that featured the expression 'By Jingo'. It was sung at a time when many people wanted a British fleet to sail through the Bosporus to engage with Russia.

BYE-LAW Danish, Norwegian, Old Norse *By* Town or borough.
A bye-law is therefore a local law 'of the town'. The Danes renamed many English settlements by incorporating their word for town, as is the case with Grimsby, Derby and Whitby.

C

CAB French *Cabrioler* To Prance or caper from Latin *Caper* Goat.

A cabriolet is a light carriage such as a Hansom cab pulled by one horse and noted for being able to swiftly weave in and out of heavier traffic *See also Caper and Taxi.*

CACOPHONY Greek *Kaktos* Bad and *Phone* A sound.
See also Telephone.

CADDY Malay *Kati* A unit of weight equivalent to 1 pound 3 ounces (600 grams).

A small packet of tea weighed one *kati*. Early travellers asked for a *kati* of tea believing it to be a packet or container of tea without realising that they were buying it by weight.

CALCULUS Latin *Calculi* Pebble.

The earliest aids to calculation were pebbles laid in rows on the ground. *See also Abacus.*

CALENDAR Latin *Calendae* The Romans called the first day of each month calends, which had particular significance since they marked a new moon. They were also the days on which debts had to be settled and on which important announcements were made.

CALICO A corruption of *Calicut*, the seaport on the coast of India where the unbleached, coarse woven textile originated.

CALLIGRAPHY Greek *Kallos* Beauty and *Graphein* Writing.

CALLISTHENICS Greek *Kallos* Beauty and *Sthenos* Strength.
These exercises promote strength through elegant movement.

CALORIE Latin *Calor* Heat.

A calorie is the amount of heat or energy required to raise the temperature of one gram of water by 1° Centigrade.

CALYPSO West African *Kaiso* Song.

Now more associated with the West Indies, where the practice of singing rhythmic songs and playing on simple instruments was the only form of entertainment available to slaves after their voyage across the Atlantic. *See also Banjo.*

CAMEL Phoenician *Gamel* Camel.

The Phoenician alphabet consisted of words for key everyday items that represented different letters. *Gamel* was the third character, the previous two being the words for ox and house. Other letters were named after hook, weapon, arm, fish, eye, mouth, head and perhaps most interestingly papyrus. *See also Alphabet, Library and Paper.*

CAMELLIA The beautiful flowering garden plant was introduced to Europe from Japan by a Spanish Jesuit called *Kamel.* There are over 200 species of camellia, the best known of which is the tea plant, Latin name *Camellia sinensis.*

CANCEL Latin *Cancellus* Lattice work.

Deeds were once cancelled by being marked with lines that crossed the writing in both directions, forming a lattice.

CANDIDATE Latin *Candidus* White.

It was the custom for Romans seeking to be elected to offices of state to wear white togas.

CANISTER Greek *Kanna* Cane, *Kanastron* Wicker basket and Latin *Canistrum* Basket.

Canisters were made from woven cane.

CANNIBAL Arawak (Northern South America and Caribbean) *Caniba* was the name of a human flesh-eating tribe encountered by early Spanish explorers, but the Europeans gave them the name Carib, from which Caribbean is derived.

CANOPY Greek *Conopeum* Net and *Konops* Mosquito.
A canopy was originally a mosquito net.

CANTER A Canterbury trot was the hurrying speed at which pilgrims travelled while on their way to pay homage at the tomb of Archbishop Thomas à Becket (1118–1170) in Canterbury.

CAPER Latin *Caper* Goat.
Meaning to skip about in a frolicsome manner, the word is an allusion to the habit that goats have of suddenly jumping about for no apparent reason. The symbol of the Zodiac sign Capricorn is a goat. *See also Cab.*

CAPSIZE Catalan *Capusa* To sink.

CAPUCHIN Latin *Caput* Head.
A capuchin monk wears a light-brown monastic habit with a prominent hood that covers the head. A cappuccino is a light brown drink with a prominent 'head' of foam. The capuchin monkey has light-brown colouring similar to the monk's habits and was given its name by early explorers.

CAR, CART Latin *Carra, carrum* Two-wheeled wagon.
This root also gives us the words carry, carrier and carriage. Automobile derives from two Greek words *Auto* Self and *Mobilis* Moving since they were the first vehicles to move without being pulled or pushed by a separate source of power such as a man, a horse or a railway engine.

CARAFE Arabic *Gharfa* Vessel, *Gharafa* To pour and Persian Q*arabah* A large flagon.

CARAVAN Persian *Kārwān* A company of travellers journeying through a desert or other hostile region.

CARDIGAN, BALACLAVA AND RAGLAN
These three garments all had military origins. The 7th Earl of Cardigan, who led the charge of the Light Brigade, wore the woollen cardigan that later bore his name to keep out the cold during the Crimean War (1854–56). So cold was it during the campaign that a request for woollen headgear was made and thousands of knitted garments were sent to the British army serving at Balaclava. The Raglan sleeve, in which the material of the sleeve extends over the shoulder as far as the collar, was devised for Lord Raglan's coat after he had an arm amputated following an injury sustained at the Battle of Waterloo.

CARNIVAL Italian *Carne* Flesh and *Vale* Farewell.
Carnivals were festivals held just before the commencement of Lent, during which period the eating of meat was forbidden.

CAROL Old French and Breton *Carole* A circle dance.
Before becoming Christmas songs carols were accompaniment for dancers.

CARPENTER Latin *Carpentarius*. A maker of wooden carriages.

CARTE BLANCHE French *Carte* Card and *Blanche* Blank.
A blank sheet of paper. Giving a man *carte blanche* means that he has no written instructions and is at liberty to act as he pleases.

CASH Tamil *Kasu*, from Sanskrit *Karsa* A weight of gold or silver.
The word cash has a variety of meanings in relation to south-east Asian currencies but the word originated in the South of India.

CAST Norse *Kasta* To throw. If you cast a fishing line you throw it onto the water.

CASTANETS Spanish *Castana* Chestnut.
The allusion is to the cracking sound of chestnuts bursting as they are roasted being similar to the sound of castanets.

CATAMARAN Tamil *Kattu Maram* Tied wood.
A catamaran is a vessel with two hulls that are fixed together. Originally it would be constructed by tying two tree trunks together.

CATHEDRAL A *Cathedra* was a chair in which Greek and Roman philosophers sat to deliver their orations. The name was then taken up by early Christian bishops, and the buildings in which they installed their *cathedra* became known as cathedrals, the seats of bishops. A bishop's diocese is also called his see from the Latin *Sedes* Seat.

CELSIUS An alternative name for the Centigrade scale that divides temperature into 100 *(centi)* grades between the freezing and boiling points of water. The first person to suggest this simple scale was Swedish astronomer Anders Celsius (1701–1744) in 1742. The less straightforward Fahrenheit scale, with 32 for freezing and 212 for boiling point, had been proposed three decades before by a German physicist named Daniel Fahrenheit (1686–1736).

CEMETERY Greek *Koimeterion* and Latin *Coemeterium* A sleeping place.

CENOTAPH Greek *Kenos* Empty and *Taphos* Tomb.
A cenotaph is erected to the memory of someone whose body is buried elsewhere.

CEREALS Latin *Ceres* The Roman goddess of agriculture has lent her name to corns such as wheat and barley.

CHAPEL Latin *Cappa* A cloak.

The first chapel was a sanctuary where the cloak of St Martin of Tours (316–397) was kept after he died. He is the patron saint of France.

CHARM Latin *Carmen* A song portraying grace, loveliness and beauty that lent its name to items and actions with the same qualities.

CHARWOMAN Anglo-Saxon *Cyre* To turn.

A charwoman was originally someone who would take a turn at doing any odd job. But it was not her task to make tea. *See also Char.*

CHAR Mandarin *Char* Tea.

Now English slang as in 'Would you like a cup of char?'

CHAUFFEUR French *Chauffer* To heat.

The boilers of early steam-powered vehicles had to be heated before they could be used and the chauffeur was the person responsible for doing this. Later they also became responsible for driving the vehicles. *See also Limousine.*

CHAV Romani *Charvorse* Boy.

CHEAP Anglo-Saxon *Caepian* To buy.

An article, if well bought, was said to be a good-cheap as in a good buy. If too much had been paid for it, it was a bad-cheap or as we would now say a bad buy. Cheap is now most usually used for 'good-cheap' and the prefix 'good' has been dropped as superfluous. But its derogatory meaning is not lost and cheap can still be used in a manner unrelated to cost to describe something inferior or ill-thought of, this being the successor to bad-cheap, albeit with a slightly varied meaning.

CHECKMATE Arabic *Shah* King and *Mata* Is dead.
The winner of a game of chess is the one who captures and kills his opponent's king.

CHEESE Anglo-Saxon *Cwysam* To squeeze.
Curds are squeezed to form cheese.

CHEMISTRY Arabic *Kimia* Something hidden.
The precursor to chemistry was alchemy, an ancient science that aimed to achieve ultimate wisdom as well as find a means of converting metals such as copper and lead into gold. Since much of the latter involved what we would now call chemistry, alchemists became chemists without forgetting that their original occupation was to find something that was hidden, most notably the still elusive process for converting other metals into gold.

CHIMPANZEE Angolan *Kivili-chimpenze* Ape.

CHIPOLATA Italian *Cipolla* Onions and *Cipollata* A dish of onions.
So the small sausages we know today took their name from a quite different wholly vegetarian dish.

CHIROPODIST Greek *Cheir* Hand and *Podos* Foot.
Now only concerned with ailments of the feet, chiropodists were once also concerned with the hands.

CHIT As in a slip of paper. Marathi (Central India) *Chit* Receipt.

CHOCOLATE Nahuatl (Aztec) *Xocolli* Bitter and *Atl* Water.
The Aztecs combined the two words to form *xocolat* and have been producing it for over 3000 years. The Spanish introduced chocolate, a product of the cacao tree that grows in Central and South America, to Europe during the sixteenth century.

CHUM Armenian *Chom* To live together.

CHUTNEY Hindi *Chatni* A portion of food.

CIGAR Spanish *Cigarro*, from Mayan *Siyar* Tobacco.

CLUMSY Icelandic *Klumsa* Hands stiffened or frozen so that they are incapable of grasping anything.

COAST Latin *Costa* A rib or side.
    The side of a country. The term sea coast shows that the word coast was not originally confined to the sea margin of a country. The side of anything may also be called its coast. For instance, there was a time when the side of a hill was called its coast. We retain a reference to that when we say 'to coast downhill' meaning to travel down the side of a hill. *See also Accost.*

COBALT German *Kobald* A devil.
    Silver miners named ores of this metal after the devil before its value was discovered because it was so hard as to be almost unworkable, the hardness being attributed to the malice of the devil.

COCAINE This stimulant is made from the leaves of the *Coca* tree most commonly found in the northern parts of South America. It has no connection to the *Cacao* tree from which cocoa is obtained.

CODSWALLOP In 1870 Hiram Codd (1838–1887) patented a method of retaining the fizz in a bottle of drink by inserting a glass marble in the neck that was forced up against a rubber washer by the pressure. The slang term wallop, meaning any poor-quality drink, was added to his name by competitors who were keen to discredit him after the popularity of his device threatened their businesses. It seems they were successful as codswallop now means nonsense or rubbish. Most of his bottles have not survived as children would break them to acquire the marble.

COFFEE Arabic *Qahweh* Coffee, from *Qahwat al būnn* Wine of the bean.
The word could also be related to the *Kaffa* region in Ethiopia, where coffee was grown.

COFFIN Greek *Cophinus* A basket.
In England corpses were once buried wrapped in sheets and laid in baskets, but in the sixteenth century wooden coffins were introduced. The vestry minutes of St Helens, Bishopsgate on 5 March 1564 recorded 'that none shall be buried within the church unless the dead corpse be coffined in wood'.

COLUMBINE Latin *Columba* Pigeon.
It is said that when the outer petals are pulled off the columbine flower, Latin name *Aquilegia*, the remainder resembles a pigeon.

COMMITTEE Old English *Committen* To entrust.
A committee is a group of people entrusted to carry out a task.

COMRADES Spanish *Camarades* Chamber.
A military term describing men who sleep in the same *camera* or chamber.

CONCLAVE Latin *Con* Together and *Clavis* A key.
A room that can be locked such as where cardinals meet in secret to elect a new pope.

CONCUBINE Latin *Con* Together and *Cubare* To lie down.
Concubines lie down with the men they live with.

CONDOM The name of the contraceptive device is not derived from the town of the same name in south-west France but from a member of the court of King Charles II, Colonel Cundum, who introduced the device at a time when the upper classes were given to a degree of high living quite unknown in the puritan Cromwellian years that preceded their own.

CONFLICT Latin *Con* Together and *Fligere* To strike.

CONGER Icelandic *Kongr* A king. The conger eel is the king eel.

CONGREGATE Latin *Con* Together and *Gregis* A flock.
See also Gregarious and Segregate.

CONJUGAL Latin *Con* Together and *Jugum* Yoke.
A husband and wife joined in marriage are therefore yoked together.

COOK Anglo-Saxon *Coc* Cook. Cook is not derived from the French *Cuisine*.
Similarly, kitchen is from the Anglo-Saxon *Cycene*.

COOPER German *Küpe* Tub, barrel or vat and *Küpfer* One who makes tubs.

COPY Latin *Copia* Abundance.
Creating a copy of something makes it more abundant.

CORE French *Coeur* The heart.

CORNET Latin *Corn* A horn and *Et* a diminutive.
Thus a cornet is a small horn.

COTTON Arabic *Koton* Cotton.

COUPLE Latin *Copula* from Hebrew *Kebel* Fetter, that is two items fixed together.

Thus two people who have been fixed together in marriage may be described as a couple but an unmarried couple who are yet to tie the knot should not be.

COUPON French *Couper* To cut.

A coupon is a portion that is cut off the main article.

COWARD Norman-French *Coue* A tail.

Most animals, when running away frightened, put their tails between their legs.

COXSWAIN Scandinavian, Dutch *Kog* A boat.

A swain is a young man and thus a coxswain is a young man in charge of a boat.

CRAYON French *Craye* Chalk.

A crayon was originally a writing implement made of chalk. This also gives us the name for the River Cray, which rises in the chalk hills of Surrey and runs through Croydon and Foot's Cray.

CRESCENT Latin *Crescens* To grow.

This word originally had no reference to a shape but to a moon that was growing or waxing, Frisian *Waxa* To increase, as opposed to one that was reducing or waning (Norse *Wan* To Lessen).

CREW CUT American oarsmen in university rowing eights adopted the habit of short hair in the belief that a crew with short hair met less wind resistance.

CRICKET Saxon *Crice* A staff or stick.

The ball was originally struck by a *criccette*, a short staff or stick. *See also Rugby and Soccer.*

CRINOLINE Latin *Crinis* Hair.

The elaborate skirts were originally stiffened with a coarse cloth made of horse hair.

CRIPPLE Anglo-Saxon *Creopare* A creeper.

Without assistance cripples were forced to creep along the ground.

CROCHET French *Croc* A hook.

A crochet is therefore a little hook as used in this method of knitting wool and thread together.

CROCKERY Welsh *Crochan*, Manx *Crocan*, Gaelic *Crogan* Pot or Icelandic *Krukka*. All words for earthenware pot or pitcher.

CRONE Anglo-Norman *Carogne* A ewe that has lost her teeth.

The term that is now applied to cantankerous old women was once used in a much less derogatory manner to describe women who had entered the last phase of their lives and had begun to embody the attributes of wisdom, maturity and spirituality that go with it.

CROUCH Old English *Couch* To lie down, to conceal.

A tiger crouches in long grass to conceal itself.

CROWBAR Old English *Cro* A curve.

A crowbar is a metal tool with a curve at one end designed to increase leverage.

CROWD Old English *Crudan* To press, to crush and Norwegian *Kryda* To swarm.

CRUMPET German *Krump* Bent or crumpled.

The holes on the surface of a crumpet, created by the use of extra baking powder, give an uneven or crumpled appearance.

CUPBOARD English *Cup* and Norman-French *Boor* Parlour.

A cupboard is therefore a room in which cups are kept, not a shelf behind a door.

CURFEW Norman-French *Couvre de feu* Cover the fire.

A law enforced by William the Conqueror but previously instituted by King Alfred. The curfew bell was rung each evening when cooking fires had to be extinguished. The most famous case when this regulation was ignored was on 1 September 1666, when the baker Thomas Farynor, of Pudding Lane, went to bed without covering his fire and a spark from the oven he left burning set fire to some wood stacked nearby, thus starting the Great Fire of London.

CURMUDGEON Old English *Corn mudgin* Corn trader.

Mudgins were merchants and those who traded in corn were invariably unpopular due to accusations of hoarding grain in order to keep the price up. Hence the word came to mean an avaricious monopolist. Samuel Johnson, however, when compiling his dictionary, could not find the word's derivation so he inserted a query seeking advice on the matter. An anonymous reply advised him that curmudgeon was formed by combining French *Cœur* Heart and *Méchant* Bad, thus taken literally to mean 'bad heart'. Johnson added that his explanation was from 'an unknown correspondent'.

CURRANT Greek *Corinth* The province where the seedless grapes were first cultivated and dried.

CYNICAL Greek *Kunikos* Dog-like.

The term first appeared in ancient Greece as the name for a new school of philosophers who rejected wealth and power in favour of a lifestyle without possessions, in keeping with virtue and nature. They were often to be found begging on the streets of Rome from the first century AD and were considered wild and dog-like. Passers-by became sceptical of their motives and the word evolved to mean any person who was unconvinced by another's thinking.

CZAR, TZAR Latin *Caesar* To Cut and later Emperor.
So dangerous was the caesarean section operation, the cutting of the mother to give birth to the baby, that it was only performed when the mother had died. Julius Caesar could not have been born by this method since we know his mother lived long after his birth, but one of his ancestors was probably born in this way and the name Caesar became something of a family name. After Julius Caesar became the Roman leader his name became synonymous with the title of Emperor, even though his successors were not of the same family. The word Czar, used to describe the supreme ruler of Russia and its sovereign states between 1547 and 1917, as well as the rulers of Bulgaria and Serbia at various times, derives from Caesar. *Kaiser*, the title given to the rulers of the Austrian, Austro-Hungarian and German Empires between 1804 and 1918, is also from Caesar.

D

DAB Middle English *Dabben* To strike.
To dab was originally to deliver a heavy blow with a weapon but with time it has reduced in ferocity to no more than a gentle pat. Dab is slang for a finger print, evidence of the gentle touch of the hand.

DACHSHUND German *Dachs* Badger and *Hund* Dog.
The mummified remains of similar dogs have been found in ancient Egyptian burial chambers but more recently they were bred in Europe to hunt badgers and rabbits. Their short legs are more to do with modern fashion than by-gone pursuits.

DAGGER Spanish *Daga* A sword.

DAISY Old English *Daeges* Day and *Eage* Eye.

The daisy closes its petals at night so the eye is only seen in the day.

DAIRY Old English *Dey* A farm servant, usually a female, whose duty was to make cheese and butter and tend to the calves. The *deyry* was the department under her care.

DALLY French *Dalier* To chat.

To dally now means to dawdle but it derives from the common practice of chatting while doing so. Dilly Dally, as in the old music hall song *'My old man said "Follow the van and don't dilly dally on the way'* means the same thing as dally.

DAM The *Dam* was a small Indian coin thus 'I don't care a dam' or 'I don't give a dam' is not swearing but means 'I don't care a penny'.

DAMASK This linen takes its name from Damascus in Syria, from where it was first imported to Europe by returning crusaders, having been carried there by camel trains from the east. Before the name of the city at which they bought the cloth gave its name to the material it was called diaper, as that word means a geometric pattern of alternating colours such as was often woven into the cloth. From there the word went in two directions. As a pattern, diaper is still applied to walls made of bricks of varying colours arranged into intricate designs. As a cloth it travelled across the Atlantic to be used to describe what in Europe is called a nappy.

DANDELION French *Dent de Lion* Lion's tooth.

The petals are said to resemble the teeth of a lion.

DATE The fruit. Greek *Daktylos* Finger.

The slender leaves of the date palm resemble fingers.

DAYS OF THE WEEK With the exception of Saturday, the names for the days of the week are all derived from northern European sources, whereas the months of the year are all of Greek or Latin origin. *See also months of the year.*

SUNDAY: The day of the Sun, a celebration of the importance of the Sun. Most northern European languages, including the lesser known Saxon, Norse and Frisian, have a similar name for the day that was always considered the first day of the week until it was consumed by the weekend.

MONDAY: The day of the Moon. Before the standardisation of the calendar the moon played a far more significant role in people's lives, indeed as long ago as the Stone Age time was measured in moons and it is from the moon that the word month is derived.

TUESDAY: Old English *Tiwes dæg* A day in honour of Tyr who was the Norse god of war, their equivalent of the Roman Mars. In other words, both Tuesday and March have similarly martial roots.

WEDNESDAY: Old English *Wēdnes dæg* The day of Woden or Odin, the foremost god of the Norsemen who remained an important god in England until the arrival of Christianity and was god of wisdom, battles and hunting.

THURSDAY: Thor's day. Thor was the Norse god of thunder. In some parts of the country, up until relatively recently, the derivations of Wednesday and Thursday were preserved in their pronunciation. For example, in Northumbria as late as 1900, Wednesday was known as Wodensday and Thursday was known as Thorsday.

FRIDAY: Named after Frigg or Freya, the wife of Woden. She is the Norse equivalent of Venus, the Roman goddess of love and beauty, after whom the day is named in other European languages. *Vendredi* in French and *Venerdi* in Italian.

SATURDAY: Saturn's day. Saturn was the Roman god of agriculture and this day is the only one without a northern European origin. In Scandinavian languages Saturday is called *Lordag* or *Loverdag* (from *lauther* foam) meaning bath day, since it was customary for the Vikings to wash themselves at the end of the week. As bathing was not popular with Anglo-Saxons they adopted a name from elsewhere.

D-DAY The D stands for Day, and is used to refer to military operations that have not yet had a specific date set for them, or when secrecy is necessary. In such situations, an H is also designated for Hour (H-Hour). The most famous D-Day was 6 June 1944, the Allied invasion of Normandy, but the notation had also been used in World War I.

DEADLINE Originally referred to a line seventeen feet from the inner enclosure of military prisons during the American Civil War which if crossed by prisoners would result in death.

DEBACLE French *Débâcle* Unleash.
This was particularly used to describe the melting of ice on a river, leading to a flood. Hence in English usage it refers to a flood – or, now, to any disaster.

DEBUT French *Débuter* To lead, to take the first turn such as in a game of billiards or bowls.
Nowadays it is more commonly associated with a new musician's first performance. A debutante is, or was, a young girl taking her first turn in adult social life.

DECEMBER *See Months of the Year.*

DECOY Dutch *Kooi* A cage.

Decoys were camouflaged basket ware tunnels of diminishing width into which ducks were driven by specially trained dogs. Nowadays a decoy can be used for any device or plan that distracts someone while another action such as entrapment is carried out.

DECREPIT Latin *De-* Down, and *Crepare* To break or creak.

DEFECATE Latin *Defaecare* To cleanse, to purify. Not typically considered to be an act of cleanliness, defecation does nonetheless cleanse the body.

DEFENCE Middle English *Fens* A fence, from Old French *Defens* Protected.

A fenced city is one that is well defended.

DEFINE Old French *Definir* To end, to terminate, to limit.

To define something is to terminate any uncertainty.

DELIRIOUS Latin *De* From and *Lira* A furrow.

Delirious people do not travel in a straight line such as they would if they remained in a furrow. *See also Furlong.*

DELTA Greek. The fourth letter of the Greek alphabet the capital style of which is written as a triangle. This is also the shape of the land that is reclaimed when a river, slowing as it reaches its final destination, deposits sediment that has been carried along in its water. *See also Meander.*

DEMENTIA Latin *De* Away from and *Mens* The mind.
See also Alzheimer.

DEMIJOHN French *Damejeanne* Lady Jane.

This large bottle with a short neck, often used in small-scale alcohol production, has nothing to do with a man named John, but rather with the image of a stout French lady. But who she was has been forgotten.

DEMOCRACY Greek *Demos* The people and *Kratos* Strength and power.
A democracy is government by the people who exercise their power through the ballot box. *See also Aristocracy.*

DENIM The cloth now used to manufacture jeans was originally made in France and takes its name from the town of Nimes where it was sold as *Serge de Nimes.*

DEPLETION Late Latin *Depletionem* Bloodletting.
Nowadays used rather broadly, the term once had a very specific meaning and referred only to the depletion of blood.

DERRICK Any crane or device for lifting something invariably has a rope hanging from it that resembles a gallows. Thomas Derrick was a hangman at the time of Queen Elizabeth I (reigned 1558–1603) and is reputed to have despatched 3,000 people, most of them at Tyburn.

DEVIL Old English *Deofol* Evil spirit from Greek *Diabolos* an accuser, slanderer.

DEVIOUS Latin *Devius* Out of the way, as in deviant.
The word did not come to mean deceitful until the seventeenth century, before which time it meant hidden away from the main stream, such as something lying beside the road rather than being on it.

DEVOUT Latin *Devotus* Devoted. The devout are devoted to a cause.

DEXTERITY Latin *Dexter* Right, as opposed to left.

A right-handed man who works skilfully with his hand is said to be dexterous. It is therefore inappropriate to describe an equally skilled left-handed person as dextrous. *See also Ambidextrous, Awkward and Gawky.*

DIAMOND Middle Latin *Diamantem*, from Latin *Adamantem* Hardest metal.

Diamond is the hardest known naturally occurring mineral.

DIET Greek *Diaita* A restricted way of life.

Originally the word could refer to any restriction, not just to food. The other meaning of Diet, a meeting of a governing assembly, has quite a different origin and is from Latin *Dieta* Day's work. The most famous was the Diet held in the German town of Worms in 1521 when the Holy Roman Emperor, carrying out the wishes of the Pope, issued an edict requiring Martin Luther's arrest.

DIG Anglo-Saxon *Dician* To make a ditch.

DILAPIDATE Latin *Dis* Apart and *Lapis* A stone.

Signifying the disintegration or decay of stone as in a ruined building. So it is improperly used when applied to the disintegration of anything other than stone.

DINGHY Hindi *Dingi* A little boat.

DINOSAUR Greek *Deinos* Awesome and *Saura* Reptile.

The term was coined as *Dinosauria* by English palaeontologist Richard Owen in 1842. *See also Stegosaurus.*

DIPLOMA Greek *Diploma* Folded double.

A diploma was originally the passport of a messenger that was folded in half for convenience of carriage.

DIPHTHERIA Greek *Diphthera* Leather.

This infectious disease causes a leathery membrane to form inside the throat.

DIPSOMANIA Greek *Dipsa* Thirst and *Mania* Madness.

A dipsomaniac is someone who has an uncontrollable, some might say mad, craving for alcohol.

DISASTER Greek *Dus* Unfavourable, bad and *Astron* Star.

Stars were thought to influence all human actions. The word disaster conveys the notion that calamities are caused by the unfavourable position of planets or stars.

DISCOUNT Latin *Dis* Away and *Compter* To count.

A discount may be said to be counting away from a price.

DISCOVER Latin *Dis* Away and *Couvrir* To cover.

Discoveries are made by taking away a covering to reveal something that was previously undiscovered.

DISPARAGE Latin *Dis* Away, *Par* Equal and French *Parage* Equality of birth.

To suggest that a person is some distance away from being equal is to disparage them.

DISTURB Latin *Dis* Completely and *Turbare* To throw into disorder.

DITTO Italian *Detto* As aforesaid, from *Dicere* To say.

DIVA Italian *Diva* Goddess.

Now applied mainly to opera singers, the word can describe any highly respected woman. The same origin as divine. Water divining, the ability to locate a source of water below the ground using the branch of a hazel bush, remains such a mystery that it has a name which suggests divine intervention.

DIVEST Latin *de Vestio* To undress, hence to deprive of. Divest is the opposite of invest.

DOCK Flemish *Dok* Cage.
That part of court reserved for the accused. At one time the prisoner would have been held in a cage while being tried.

DOCTOR Middle Latin *Doctor* Teacher, scholar.
It was only in the sixteenth century that the term started to be mostly used by the medical profession. The old meaning is still retained and a doctorate is usually non-medical.

DODO Portuguese *Doudo, doido* Fool.
The flightless dodo, endemic to Mauritius, was deemed to be foolish by Portuguese explorers because it approached humans without fear and was thus easily slaughtered. The species was extinct by 1700.

DOG DAYS Latin *Caniculares Dies*.
Named after the 'dog-star' Sirius (*Canicula*), which rises with the sun between 3 July and 11 August and ushers in the hottest time of the year.

DOLCELATTE Italian *Dolce* Sweet and *Latte* Milk.
A soft blue cow's milk cheese.

DOLLAR German *Thaler* Valley.
Bohemian silver coins were minted at Joachimsthal – St Joachim's Valley – in what is now the Czech Republic. When production moved to other locations the coins lost their association with St Joachim and became known simply as thalers, or 'valleys'. Dutch settlers in the New World took with them their guilders (also derived from *thaler*) and so was born the mighty dollar albeit with a slight variation in its name. There are two theories as to the origin of the dollar sign. One is that it was taken from the Spanish

coat of arms, which depicts two pillars bound by an S-shaped ribbon; the other maintains that it evolved from the way in which money bags were marked by banks, first with a U superimposed on top of an S and then in a more simplified form with an S struck through with two lines, i.e. the U without its curved base.

DOLPHIN Greek *Delphys* Womb.
Dolphins, which are mammals, are among a small group of marine creatures with wombs.

DOMINO Latin *Domino* Master.
The game using tiles with different numbers of spots was named by monks who cried '*Domino* I am the master' when they won, but its origins are thought to be related to the Chinese tile game of Mahjong. *See also Tiddlywinks.*

DOOLALLY British soldiers in India who were affected by the heat and showed signs of madness were housed in a sanatorium at *Deolali* near Bombay (Mumbai), while they waited for transportation home. Doolally, a corruption of the town's name, became slang for madness.

DOOM Old English *Dom* Judgment, condemnation.
In its original sense, the word was very closely associated with religion, or the intervention of some higher outside authority.

DORMER WINDOW Latin *Dormire* To sleep.
A dormer window is one in a sloping roof that provides light to a dormitory or sleeping place.

DORMOUSE Latin *Dormire* To sleep and English Mouse.
The dormouse can hibernate for six months at a time, surviving on fat deposits accumulated during their waking summer months. Lewis Carroll's dormouse at the Mad Hatter's Tea Party kept dropping off to sleep. *See also Treacle.*

DOWDY Scandinavian *Dawdie* A dirty, slovenly woman.

DOZEN Teutonic *Deux* Two and *Zen* Ten.
A simple explanation unlike eleven and twelve. *See Eleven and Twelve.*

DRACONIAN Draco was a very strict Greek legislator in the seventh century BC. Draconian laws are those that are unnecessarily strict and severe.

DRUG Low German *Droge–vate* Dry barrels or vats, vessels used to store drugs, which usually consisted of dried herbs.

DRUID Old Celtic *Dru* Tree, Oak, and *Wid* To know.
Druids were the teachers of Celtic society who had a vast knowledge of the natural world and worshipped oak trees.

DUFFEL Duffel is a town near Antwerp in Belgium where the thick cloth much used to make weatherproof hooded duffel coats was first woven.

DUM DUM Dum Dum is the town in India where the soft-headed bullets that expand on impact, thus causing a greater wound, were first made. They are now banned by international convention.

DUNGAREE Hindi *Dongari* A region near Bombay where the calico overalls were first used.
Being cheap to make, they were most frequently used by labourers and navvies. *See also Navvy.*

DYNAMITE Greek *Dynamis* Power.

E

EAGER French *Aigre* Rough, severe or harsh.

In the first scene of *Hamlet* Horatio says, 'It is a nipping and eager air.' His meaning is cold and harsh. *See also Vinegar.*

EARN Teutonic *Ernte* Harvest.

To earn is to harvest the fruit of one's labours.

EARWIG Old English *Ear* An undeveloped flower bud as in an ear of corn and *Wic* A hiding place or dwelling.

The favoured hiding place of these insects was an *earwic*, that is a flower bud. The popular notion that this insect has a propensity to crawl into the human ear is entirely erroneous brought about by there being two quite unconnected meanings of the word ear.

EAST Germanic *Austra* Toward the sun.

Hence Australia takes its name, being in the easternmost part of the world from the point of view of the European explorers who first visited it. *See also North, South and West.*

EASTER Old English *Eastre* The name of an Anglo-Saxon pagan goddess whose feast day was in the spring at around the same time as the modern day Christian festival.

ECHO Greek *Echo* A sound.

EDDY Norse *Yda* A whirlpool.

EDUCATE Latin *Educo* To lead forth.

Properly used, the word educate means to bring out the latent faculties of the mind rather than to instruct by imparting knowledge.

ELBOW Old English *Ell* The length of the forearm and Latin *Ulna* the bone in the forearm.

The length of the forearm, defined precisely as that of King Henry I (reigned 1100–1135), was used as a unit of measure. (A successor of the cubit, 300 of which were the length of Noah's Ark.) A bow is something that bends as in archery and an elbow is the bow or bend of the ell or forearm.

ELECTRICITY Greek *Elektron* Amber. The first research into static electricity was conducted in 650 BC by the Greek philosopher Thales of Miletos, who studied the electrical properties of amber.

ELEVEN AND TWELVE Teutonic. Eleven derives from the German *Ainlif* One left, that is after counting to ten you have one left over. Similarly twelve comes from the Gothic *Twa-lif* Two left. Our higher numbers, thirteen and fourteen etc., are from Three ten and Four ten etc. *See also Dozen and Numbers.*

EMANCIPATE Latin *Ex* Away from and *Mancipare* To transfer property.

So rather than referring to the act of giving something, such as an emancipated slave being given his freedom or an emancipated woman being given the vote, the word actually refers to what was transferred away from them i.e. the slavery and the lack of suffrage.

EMBRACE Latin *In* In and *Bracchia* Arms.

EMBRYO Greek *En* In and *Bryein* To swell.

The embryo develops into a foetus whilst inside the swelling uterus.

EMMET Old English *Aemette* Ant.

The word *emmet* is used by the Cornish to describe the tourists that descend on their part of the country every summer. *See also Grockle.*

END Old English *Ende* The opposite side.

To travel 'to the ends of the Earth' does not imply that the Earth is flat, but in fact requires it to be round.

ENDORSE Latin *In* In and *Dorsum* The back as in dorsal fin.

The word originally meant anything carried on the back; elephants were said to be endorsed with heavy loads. Its meaning is now limited to signing the back of documents and expressing approval of something.

ENCYCLOPAEDIA Greek *En* In, *Kyklos* Circle and *Paideia* Education.

An encyclopaedia provides an all-round education. *See also Bicycle.*

ENEMY Latin *E* From, indicating a negative and *Amicus* A friend.

An enemy is therefore a negative friend.

ENERGY Greek *En* In and *Ergon* Work.

ENGLAND The Angles were a tribe from Angeln in the southern part of present-day Denmark who migrated to the British Isles during the fifth and sixth centuries AD.

The word has become slightly corrupted to Engle Land, but the French still use the original spelling *Angleterre* Angle Land.

ENIGMA Latin *Aenigma* and Greek *Ainissesthai* To speak secretly or mysteriously.

An enigma is a riddle with a secret meaning and so perfectly described the coded messaging system devised by the Germans but intercepted by the British during the Second World War.

ENORMOUS Latin *Ex* Out of and *Norma* The rule, the norm.

This implies that something needn't be of great size in order for it to be accurately described as enormous, but merely unusual in some way.

ENTANGLE Anglo-Saxon *Tangle* A small bough or twig.
Twigs were smeared with birdlime to catch birds which, when caught, were said to be entangled. Hence the modern usage meaning an inability to disengage.

ENTHUSE Greek *En* In and *Theos* God.
Originally enthusiasm referred only to a passion for religious matters, but it has since come to refer to any area of interest.

ENTRY Latin *Intrare* To go into.

ENUNCIATE Latin *E* From and *Nuntius* A messenger.
Someone bringing a message takes particular care to speak clearly.

ENVOY French *Envoyer* To send.
An envoy is someone sent elsewhere to perform a task.

EPHEMERA Greek *Epi* For and *Hemera* A day.
An ephemeral item is one that lasts for a brief period of time perhaps for only one day. There is a species of mayfly whose Latin name is *Ephemera* on account of their lives lasting no longer than one day.

EPIDEMIC Greek *Epi* Among and *Demos* The people.
An epidemic is something that spreads among the people.

EPISTLE Greek *Epi* On the occasion and *Stellein* To send.
Originally the word referred to the occasion on which a message was sent, as opposed to the message itself.

EQUATOR Latin *Æquator diei et noctis* Equaliser of day and night.
Originally this was an imaginary line in the sky marking the passage of the sun on days when the day and night were of equal

length. It was later applied to the same place on the surface of the earth.

EQUINOX Latin *Aequus* Equal and *Nox* Night.
The equinox is when the length of the day is the same as that of the night and takes place in the spring as daylight increases and in the autumn as it diminishes.

ERADICATE Latin *E* From and *Radix* A root.
To permanently remove as when a plant is dug up by its roots.

ERMINE The pure white fur of the stoat is so called from it having originally been brought from Armenia.

EROTIC Greek *Eros* The god of love, lust and intercourse.
The famous statue in Piccadilly Circus, London is not of Eros at all but of the Angel of Christian Charity, a far more appropriate subject to commemorate Lord Shaftesbury (1801–1885), the Victorian reformer who did much to improve working conditions in Britain.

ERROR Latin *Erro* To wander.
Error has come to mean to wander from accuracy, but previously it simply meant to wander. For example, Ben Jonson wrote of a voyage as 'an error by sea'.

ERUDITE Latin *E* From and *Rudis* Rude.
An erudite person is one whose learned manner is without any vulgarity or rudeness.

ETHIOPIA Greek *Aithein* To burn and *Ops* Face.
The Greeks referred to all inhabitants of sub-Saharan Africa as Ethiopians believing the colour of their skin was due to burning by the sun.

ETYMOLOGY Greek *Etumon* True sense and *Logia* A study of.
You are reading a book of etymology that studies the true sense of words.

EUNUCH Greek *Eune* Bed and *Echein* To have charge of.
Castrated men were put in charge of the beds within harems since they could be trusted not to perform sexual indiscretions. The word therefore refers to the occupation rather than to the person who had undergone the operation.

EVIL Old English *Yfel* Bad, wicked.

EXAGGERATE Latin *Agger* To heap or pile up.
Nowadays it still means to pile it on but in terms of speech rather than physically. *Agger* also meant earthwork fortification, something else that had to be piled up.

EXCHEQUER Anglo-French *Escheker* Chessboard.
The Norman kings of England did their accounting using counters and a roll of chequered cloth. The letter X was added to the word due to the false assumption that it had a Latin root.

EXORBITANT Latin *Ex* From and *Orbita* An orbit or track.
Hence to be exorbitant is to be so far from the normal track as to be beyond all bounds of reasonableness.

EXOTIC Greek *Exo* From outside.
Exotic was used to describe any items that originated outside the country, not just those that were elaborate and ornate. But since imports were invariably such things as exotic silks and ornate ceramics the two meanings were easily interchangeable.

EXTERMINATE Latin *Ex* From and *Terminus* Boundary.
To exterminate meant to eliminate by banishing over the boundary into another country.

EXTRAVAGANT Latin *Ex* Outside of and *Vagare* Wander, roam (as in Vagrant).
To be extravagant is to be different or exotic. *See also Vagabond.*

F

FACSIMILE Latin *Facere* To make, to do and *Similis* Similar.
If you make a similar one you have created a facsimile.

FACTORY Latin *Facere* To make, to do.
The first factories were created in China in 750 BC.

FAMILY Latin *Famulus* A slave. *Familia*, the collective noun, referred to all the slaves of a household.

FAMINE Latin *Fames* Hunger.

FAN Latin *Vannus* A basket in which corn was tossed into the air to winnow it in order to separate the wheat from the chaff.

FARCE Latin *Farcire* To stuff.
Miracle plays were often extended by the addition of light-hearted interludes of humour that were stuffed into the traditional script. The derivation also explains how a Tomato Farci is one that is stuffed with something.

FAREWELL Anglo-Saxon *Fare* A passage.
We retain the original meaning in thoroughfare. Farewell means 'may all be well on your passage'.

FARM Anglo-Saxon *Feorm* Supper, food or hospitality.

One of the conditions of land tenancy was that the tenant would supply their lords with specified quantities of food, known as *ferme*, from their tenanted land. The land on which this food was produced also became known as the *ferme* and this later became the farm. *See also Tithe.*

FARRIER Latin *Ferrum* Iron.

Farriers use iron to make horse shoes.

FASCISM Latin *Fascis* Bundle.

In ancient Rome the symbol of power of the civic magistrates was the *fascis*, a bundle of white birch rods tied around an axe and carried by their lictors, or bodyguards. The bundle of sticks represented strength through unity since one stick is easily broken whereas a bundle is not. Both the axe and the sticks could also be used to carry out sentences imposed by the magistrates. Italian dictator Benito Mussolini (1883–1945) adopted the symbol for his National Fascist Party as part of his attempt to emulate the earlier Roman Empire.

FEBRUARY *See Months of the Year.*

FELON Gaelic *Faell* To deceive or betray.

FENDER An abbreviation of defender. A piece of furniture that defends the house against sparks from the fire.

FERN Scandinavian *Fer* A feather.

The fronds of some ferns resemble feathers. The Greek word for fern is *Pterin*, which also means feather.

FERRET Latin *Fur* A thief. The name seems to have originated because of the furtive or stealthy, thief-like habits of the ferret.

FIASCO Italian *Fiasco* A flask.

>If Venetian glass blowers created a flaw in their delicate work they turned the article into a flask, hence any failure became known as a fiasco.

FILLET Old French *Fil* Thread.

>The term was applied to cuts of meat on account of their being tied up with thread for storage.

FIRKIN Anglo-Saxon *Feowr* Four, *Kin* A diminutive.

>A firkin is a small cask holding a fourth part of a barrel equal to nine gallons or forty-one litres.

FLAMBOYANT French *Flamboyer* To flame.

>If something is flamboyant it is spectacular and showy like a fire. *See also Flamingo.*

FLAMINGO Provencal *Flamenc* Relating to a flame, specifically in reference to its colour. *See also Flamboyant.*

FLANNEL Welsh *Gwlanen* Wool.

>This became *flannen* before it became flannel.

FLATTERY Norman *Fladra* To pat or to stroke, as well as the wagging of a dog's tail. Many North European languages use the same word for flattery as they do for wagging a tail. If you flatter someone you heap praise on them, albeit falsely. Patting and stroking conveys the same message to a dog which will inevitably wag its tail as you do so.

FLIRT French *Fleureter* To talk sweet nothings.

FOB Old French *Forbe* Cheat.

>To fob someone off is to tell them a lie in order to divert their attention thus they are cheated of the truth.

FOLIO Latin *Folium* A sheet of paper.

FONDUE French *Fondre* To melt.
Small pieces of meat and bread are dipped into melted cheese.

FORNICATE Latin *Fornix* A brothel where fornication, sexual intercourse between unmarried people, invariably takes place.

FORTNIGHT Old English *Feorwertyne* Fourteen and *Niht* Nights. Few other languages have a word to describe a period of two weeks and it is little used in America.

FOSSIL Latin *Fossilis* Dug up.

FRANC French *Francorum Rex* The King of the Franks.
The French currency now replaced by the Euro derived its name from this early inscription on the coins. The Franks were a German tribe who invaded Roman Gaul in AD 200–400.

FREELANCE The term, now applied to a self-employed person available to work for any employer, was originally given to a mercenary soldier in the middle ages who was free to be employed as a lancer in any army that needed his services.

FREEMASON French *Frère-maçon* Brother mason.
With the corruption of the phrase came a corruption of its meaning and even the most high-ranking officials of the fraternity still erroneously refer to themselves as Freemasons rather than Brother Masons.

FRESCO Italian *Fresco* Fresh.
Frescoes are paintings applied to fresh plaster that is still wet enabling the paint to sink into the surface.

FRIAR Latin *Frater* A brother.

FRIDAY *See Days of the Week.*

FRIEND Old English *Froend* To love.

FUEL French *Fowaille* A fireplace.

FÜHRER German *Führen* To lead.
>   Hitler modelled his title on that chosen by Mussolini, Italian *Duce* Leader. *See also Nazism and Fascism.*

FUMBLE Norwegian *Falma* To grope.

FUNNEL Welsh *Ffynel* Air hole.

FUNNY BONE The name given to that part of the elbow that produces an intense tingling when struck is a pun on the bone's Latin name *humerus* and consequently has nothing to do with humour at all. The tingling is actually caused by a blow to the Ulnar Nerve.

FURLONG Old English *Furh* Furrow and *Lang* Long.
>   A furlong was the length of a furrow in one acre of land when an acre was defined as having fixed dimensions of one chain (66 feet) wide by ten chains or one furlong long. This was considered to be the maximum area that an oxen could plough in one day. The long thin shape was important because it is difficult to turn a plough being pulled by oxen so they went in a straight line for a furlong before that was necessary. So an acre was one furrow long, which became corrupted to a furlong. There are eight furlongs in a mile. *See also Acre, Delirious and Mile.*

FUSELAGE French *Fuselé* Spindle-shaped.
>   The body of an aeroplane resembles the spindle around which newly spun wool was wound. The spindle is thought to be the oldest piece of technology known to man.

G

GAB Anglo-Saxon *Gabben* To prate, to talk excessively.

Hence the gift of the gab. The slang word 'gob' to refer to the mouth probably derives from the same root.

GALAXY Greek *Galaxias* Milky circle.

Our sun is a star at the centre of the solar system which is part of a galaxy known as the Milky Way containing in excess of 300 million stars. It is so called because the light from the millions of stars resembles a spilt glass of milk. Astronomers have estimated that there are more than 100 billion galaxies.

GALLOP Anglo-Saxon *Gehlopen* To leap or jump.

GAMMON Old French *Gambon* A leg.

Gammon is cured meat taken from the hind legs of a pig.

GARGLE Old French *Gargouiller* Throat.

A gargoyle is a carved stone figure, usually grotesque in appearance, that projects from the side of a roof to convey rain water which flows through its throat and out of its mouth.

GAS Greek *Khaos* Atmosphere.

The word was coined by Jan Baptist van Helmont (d. 1644), a Flemish chemist and physician who was the first person to realise that the atmosphere was composed of different gases.

GASTRIC Greek *Gaster* Belly.

Referring to the stomach. Hence gastroenteritis is an inflammation of the intestine.

GAUZE French *Gaze*.

This material is believed to have originated from Gaza in Palestine.

GAWKY Middle English *Awk* Back-handed, left-handed.

Left-handed people were once thought to be clumsy because they were unable to use their right hands as effectively as right-handed people. Many tools such as scythes for cutting hay and corn were made specifically for right-handed people and left-handers using a scythe made specially for them would not be able to join a team of harvesters working their way across a field as they would be mowing in a different direction. *See also Ambidextrous, Awkward, Dexterity and Southpaw.*

GAZE Swedish *Gasa* To stare.

A gazebo is a summerhouse positioned to gaze at a splendid view.

GAZETTE Italian *Gazza* A magpie and *Gazetta* Idle chattering, reminiscent of the sound of magpies.

The word originated in Venice where the newspapers or gazettes were full of chattering tittle-tattle. The word has also been attributed to the *gazatta*, a small coin supposedly used to buy the newspaper, although doubt may be cast on that attribution as the value of the Venetian *gazatta* never exceeded that of an English farthing, too small a sum to purchase a printed sheet.

GAZUMP Yiddish *Gezumph* To swindle.

Gazumping is the dishonest disregard of a spoken agreement before a contract can be signed. Gazundering is when a buyer lowers his verbal offer before signing a contract.

GECKOS Javanese *Gekok* The shrill cry of the lizard that has adhesive pads on its feet that enable it to run up walls.

GENE Greek *Genes* Born.

A gene is the basic unit of heredity that defines the character of a living organism as soon as it is born.

GENITAL Latin *Genitum* To beget.

GENOCIDE Greek *Genos* Race and Latin *Caedere* To kill.
The word was first used by Raphael Lemkin in 1933 to describe the Iraqi extermination of Assyrians and again after World War II when Nazi leaders were charged with the crime.

GENUFLECT Latin *Genu* The knee and *Flectere* To bend.
The act of bending the knee in prayer. *See also Knee.*

GEOGRAPHY Greek *Ge* Earth and *Graphein* To write.
A geography was originally a book that described the natural features of the earth.

GEOLOGY Greek *Ge* Earth and *Logos* Speech.
Geology is therefore talking about the earth.

GEOMETRY Greek *Ge* Earth and *Metron* A measure.
Geometry is the division of mathematics relevant to the measurement of shape, size and volume and was originally primarily concerned with the dimensions of the earth and the universe.

GEORDIE Natives of Tyneside are called Geordies either because they supported the royalist cause of King George II in the Jacobite rebellion of 1745 or because the miners of that area preferred to use a safety lamp devised by George Stephenson rather than the better known one invented by Humphrey Davy.

GEOSTATIONARY Greek *Ge* Earth and *Statikos* To stand still.
A satellite in a geostationary orbit circles the earth at the same speed as the earth's rotation and therefore appears to stand still, remaining above the same point on the earth's surface. To achieve this the satellite must be 22,000 miles above the equator.

GERANIUM Greek *Geranos* A crane.

The common name of the geranium is cranesbill, named after the crane, a long-legged and long-necked wading bird, due to the resemblance of parts of the flower to the shape of the bird's head. *See also Pedigree.*

GERIATRIC Greek *Geras* Old age and *Iatros* Physician.

Geriatrics is the study by doctors of the conditions of old age.

GERRYMANDER American Elbridge Gerry (1744–1814), Governor of Massachusetts, manipulated the borders of constituencies in his state to favour his own party. The ruse was noticed when a map of the new boundaries was seen to resemble the shape of a salamander, but a wag observed that it was instead a gerrymander. Nonetheless he went on to become the fifth vice-president of the United States.

GEYSER Icelandic *Geysir* A famous erupting spring, from *Gjósa* To gush.

The first geyser to be known to Europeans is the Great Geyser in western Iceland, which sends boiling water 60 metres into the air.

GHERKIN German *Gurcke* Cucumber and Anglo Saxon *Kin* Small. A gherkin is a small member of the cucumber family

GHETTO Italian *Ghetto* A foundry.

Jewish quarters of cities became known as ghettos after the main Jewish district of Venice, where there was an iron foundry.

GHILLIE Gaelic *Gille* A lad.

A young man who assists a fisherman.

GIBRALTAR Arabic *Gibel el Tariq ibn Ziyad* The mountain of Tariq ibn Ziyad.

Tariq was the leader of the Saracens when they invaded Spain in AD 711 and he fortified the rock as a base for his operations. *See also Morris Dancing and Tariff.*

GIN Dutch *Ginivra* and French *Genievere* Juniper.

The flavour of gin is obtained from the juniper berry. At one time gin was known as Geneva, not because it has any specific connection with the city of Geneva in Switzerland but because the place also derives its name from the plant.

GINGERLY Latin *Gentius* Well-born.

To act gingerly is to act cautiously, daintily, as though born of the gentry.

GINGHAM Malay *Ginggang* Striped.

Gingham is a cloth woven in two colours arranged in stripes.

GIRL Middle English *Gyrle* A child of either sex.
See also Boy.

GLADIATOR Latin *Gladiolus* A sword.

The favoured weapon of the professional fighters who fought against each other and wild animals for the amusement of Romans. *See also Gladiola and Sedge.*

GLADIOLA Latin *Gladiolus* A sword.

The plant has sword-shaped leaves. *See also Blade, Gladiator and Sedge*

GLASS Celtic *Glâs* Green.

The colour of glass when seen edgeways. Alternatively, the word may be derived from the Latin *Glacies* Ice.

GLIB Low German *Glibberig* Smooth, slippery.
A person or speech described as glib is figuratively smooth or slick.

GLIDE Old English *Glidan* To slip.
To slip suggests movement with a lack of control quite different from gliding that now tends to describe a more graceful and managed action.

GLOAT Norse *Glotta* To grin.
Someone who displays a gloating expression of self-satisfaction invariably grins as he does so. *See also Grin.*

GLUCOSE Greek *Glykys* Sweet.
Glucose is sugar that occurs naturally and was therefore the only sweetness that was available in ancient Greece.

GLUTTON Latin *Glutire* To devour.
A glutton is someone who devours more food than is necessary.

GOB Old French *Gober* To gulp down.
Goblet derives from the same root.

GONG Malay. Clearly onomatopoeic since it resembles the sound of the instrument, this word was first coined in Malaya where gongs play an important part in religious festivals.

GOOLIE Hindustani *Goli* A ball. Enough said!

GOOSEBERRY FOOL French *Foulé* Milled, mashed or pressed.
The derivation of this dessert has no association with stupidity.

GORSE Welsh *Gores* Waste land.

Gorse, the highly invasive prickly shrub that is a member of the pea family, is usually one of the first plants to become established on waste land.

GOSSIP Old English *Godsibb* Godparent, relative.
The word was extended in Middle English to mean any close friend with whom one is likely to gossip.

GOULASH Hungarian *Gulyas* A herder of cattle.
Goulash, a stew of beef, vegetables and spices was the staple dish of the herdsmen on the plains of Central Europe.

GRADUAL Latin *Gradus* Step.
A gradual progress may be taken one step at a time.

GRAFFITI Greek *Graphein* To write.
Writing is a somewhat grand description for some of the mindless daubs that adorn modern city walls.

GRAMMAR Greek *Grammatik* A letter of the alphabet.
Grammar is the use of letters of the alphabet correctly and efficiently to create words and sentences.

GRANGE Anglo-Saxon *Grainage* A place where rent was paid in grain.
The word has come to describe a large country house such as the one where a landlord may have lived.

GRAVITY Latin *Gravis* Weight.
When Isaac Newton studied gravity and the movement of the planets he described the forces that defined their orbits as universal gravitation having established that it was a similar force that famously caused his apple to fall to the floor. *See also Aggravate.*

GREGARIOUS Latin *Gregis* A flock.

Animals or people that gather in a flock are said to be gregarious. *See also Congregate and Segregate.*

GRENADE French *Grenade* Pomegranate.

A grenade is an iron shell, filled with gunpowder and pieces of iron, that resemble the seeds of a pomegranate. Grenadiers were soldiers who, because of their height and therefore long arms, were able to throw grenades the furthest distance.

GRIMACE Anglo-Saxon *Grima* Mask.

Ancient comic masks were so distorted that hideous or distorted expressions of the human face were known as a *grima*, or grimace.

GRIN Old English *Grennian* Show the teeth, To Snarl.

To grin was originally a gesture of anger rather than mirth. *See also Gloat.*

GRIZZLY French *Gris* Grey.

Grizzly bears (Latin *Ursus Horribilis*) take their name from their colour and not from the alternative meaning of the word – to grumble and whine.

GROCER French *Grosse* Unbroken packages.

Grocers were originally wholesalers, that is people who deal in bulk or unbroken packages supplying retailers who break open the packs to sell in smaller quantities.

GROCKLE Used to describe non-Devonians by the people native to the county, *Grockle* was originally the name of a magical dragon in a Dandy comic strip called *Danny and his Grockle*. A Torquay man apparently applied it in the 1960s to a pensioner on holiday and the word was popularised by the 1962 film *The System* while it was being filmed in the town. *See also Emmet.*

GROG Admiral Edward Vernon (1684–1757) ordered in 1745 that men under his command should no longer be allowed to drink undiluted rum. Henceforth his dissatisfied sailors contemptuously referred to the new diluted tipple as 'grog', after the admiral's nickname Old Grog which in turn was derived from his custom of wearing a coat and breeches made of the coarse, stiffened fabric, grogram.

GROTTY An abbreviation of grotesque, meaning dirty or disgusting. It was first used by Beatle George Harrison, who, in the 1964 comedy *A Hard Day's Night*, described a range of shirts as being grotty, slang for grotesque.

GRUDGE Old French *Grouchier* To mumble, to grumble.
When a person holds a grudge against somebody, they are likely to grumble about him or her behind their backs.

GRUEL French *Gruau* Oatmeal.
Cereals such as oatmeal are boiled in either water or milk to make gruel.

GUILLOTINE Joseph Ignace Guillotin was a Parisian physician who, when elected to the National Assembly, proposed that decapitation should be used not just for noblemen but as the sole method of execution. However, he neither invented the machine nor, as is commonly asserted, did he perish by it. After a short period in prison during the Reign of Terror he founded the Academy of Medicine in Paris and died in 1814 aged seventy-six.

GYMKHANA Hindi *Gend* Ball and *Khana* House.
A gymkhana was a venue for any sporting event – particularly those involving ball games. However, the favourite sporting pursuits of Englishmen in India involved horses and they only used the word to describe equestrian events. When the word

travelled back to Britain it was this meaning that came with it. In India and elsewhere in the Far East the term gymkhana still refers to a club where members take part in a variety of social and sporting activities both with and without horses.

GYMNASIUM Greek *Gymnos* Naked.
Greek athletes invariably competed without clothes.

GYNAECOLOGY Greek *Gynaikeios* Womanly and *Logia* Study.

H

HABEAS CORPUS Latin *Habeas Corpus* You should have the body.
The Latin has been retained in English usage and refers to the writ ordering that a jailer either gives freedom to prisoners or else produces them before a judge. Considered a cornerstone of legal systems around the world, the writ has nevertheless been suspended at various times throughout history, in Britain during the World Wars and the Northern Irish Troubles, and more recently in the United States when indefinite unlawful detention was legitimized as part of their War on Terror.

HALLUCINATE Latin *Hallucinari* Wander about in the mind. To let your thoughts stray.

HAMMOCK Taino (Bahamas) *Hamacas* Sleeping net.
This type of bed, suspended between two trees, kept the sleeper away from dampness and dirt as well as snakes, spiders and other harmful creatures on the ground. They were made of bark from the *Hamacas* tree. They were known in ancient Greece but the word hammock was introduced to Europe by Christopher Columbus who brought a great many back from his first voyage to what is now the Bahamas.

HANDKERCHIEF French *Couvre* Cover and *Chef* Head.

In certain orthodox or devout religious groups a kerchief is a small piece of cloth for covering the heads of women. A handkerchief is similar but is held in the hand.

HARSH Scandinavian *Harske* Of a coarse texture.

The meaning of the word has now broadened to refer to a figurative coarseness of character as well as a physical coarseness of texture.

HAVOC Celtic *Hafoc* Hawk.

Havoc describes the devastation caused by a hawk if it lands in a poultry yard. To play havoc was also a military command to plunder captured territory.

HAZELNUT In most northern languages *hase* or similar means the husk, beard or shell of a fruit. Dutch *Hase*, Norwegian *Hasl*, Danish *Hase*. A hazelnut is therefore a bearded nut.

HEAD Anglo-Saxon *Heved* Heaved up.

The head is raised above the rest of the body.

HEATHEN German *Heidin* Dweller upon heaths.

When Christianity was introduced to Germany, the wild dwellers on the heaths resisted conversion to the new religion. The term also applies to people who are not Muslim or Jewish. *See also Pagan.*

HEAVEN Anglo-Saxon *Haefen* Raised or elevated.

HEIRLOOM Latin *Heres* Beneficiary and Anglo-Saxon *Loma* Household items.

In the days when all the family's clothes were spun and woven at home the loom was the most important article of furniture in the house. Later the word was used to describe all household furniture that would be passed down from generation to generation.

HERMIT Greek *Eremites* Desert. A hermit lives a life of seclusion in a deserted place.

HEROIN Coined as a trademark in the nineteenth century, the word heroin derived from 'hero' on account of the effects of the drug which was purported to bestow feelings of courage and strength upon those who took it. *See also Morphine.*

HERRING Anglo-Saxon *Hær* Army.
So numerous were the fish that an army best described their numbers.

HIBERNATE Latin *Hibernus* Wintry.
To hibernate is to pass the winter months in a dormant state.

HIMALAYA Sanskrit *Hima* Snow and *Alaya* Abode.

HINGE Old English *Hing* To hang.
A hinge is the hook on which a door is hung.

HIPPOPOTAMUS Greek *Hippos* Horse and *Potamos* A river.
Quite how this clumsy aquatic beast could have been named after a horse is not explained but possibly because they can run at 25 mph (40 kph), not a lot slower than a galloping horse. Their closest living relations are, surprisingly, whales and porpoises. *See also Walrus.*

HISTRIONIC Greek *Histrio* An actor.
Theatrical and melodramatic actions are most often performed by actors.

HOCKEY Old French *Hoquet* A shepherd's crook, on account of the similarity in appearance of the hockey stick to the crook.

HOCUS POCUS Latin *Hoc est corpus* This is my body.

The expression that now refers to anything magical or miraculous is derived from words spoken by Christ that now form part of the communion service.

HOLIDAY A corruption of holy day. At one time, religious festivals were the only times at which people did not work.

HOLLYHOCK Anglo-Saxon *Hoc* Mallow.

Hollyhocks are garden mallows indigenous to the holy land. Hence holy or holly hock.

HOLOCAUST Greek *Holo* Whole and *Kaustus* Burnt.

A holocaust is an event when everything from people to property is burnt.

HONCHO Japanese *Han Cho* Squad leader.

The term, often now prefixed with 'head', refers to any leader.

HONEYMOON Romans considered honey to be the food of the gods and thus it featured prominently in their wedding ceremonies. The word 'honeymoon' is derived from the ancient practice of the bride and groom drinking mead, which contains fermented honey, for a period of one moon (one month) after their wedding. When a groom carries his bride over the threshold he is perpetuating another Roman custom – that of keeping the bride's gown from the doorstep, which would have been smeared with honey as a blessing.

HOOCH Inupiaq (North and West Alaska) *Hoochino* The name of a tribe who made strong liquor from a distillation of fermented corn.

HOOLIGAN Derived from Houlihan's gang, an unruly Irish family.

HORDE Turkish *Ordu* A camp.

Hordes were nomadic tribes that seldom remained in permanent settlements, preferring to live in temporary camps instead.

HORIZON Greek *Horos* Limit.

A horizon marks the limit of your vision.

HORMONE Greek *Hormon* To stir up.

Hormones are bodily secretions transported to parts of the body where they stir up activity.

HOROSCOPE Greek *Hora* Hour and *Skopos* To observe.

A horoscope makes observations based upon the precise hour at which a person was born.

HORSERADISH The word horse was often used synonymously with large or powerful. Hence the meaning has remained in particular reference to the horseradish which has a very strong flavour. Radish is from Latin *Radix* A root.

HUMBLE Latin *Humus* The ground.

A humble person is someone who lives a lowly, unpretentious existence, so low in fact that they might appear close to the ground.

HUMBLE PIE Saxon *Umble* The entrails of a deer.

The best cuts of the venison were reserved for the lord of the manor, whereas those who sat below the salt, i.e. the Saxons following the Norman conquest, had to make do with the inferior portions, or umble. Hence, those whose pie was made with umble were accepting their humiliation as one does when humbly making an apology – a situation now termed 'eating humble pie'. The connection between umble and humble is therefore rather more than just a pun, since it was the humble people who ate the umble pie. *See also Animals and Venison.*

HUSBAND Anglo-Saxon *Hus* A house and *Bonda* Master.

HYDRAULIC Greek *Hydor* Water and *Aulos* A pipe.

HYPOTENUSE Greek *Hypoteinousa* Stretching under.
The hypotenuse is the line opposite the right angle of a right-angled triangle, thus looking as though it has been stretched between the ends of the two shorter sides.

HYSTERIA Greek *Hystera* The uterus.
The Greeks believed that only women suffered from hysteria. This was due to an assertion made by Hippocrates, often considered to be the father of medicine, that it was caused by the uterus rising up in the body and compressing the heart, lungs and diaphragm.

I

ICEBERG German *Eis* Ice and *Berg* A hill.

IDIOT Greek *Idiotes* A private citizen, as opposed to a public official.
The English word idiot originally had the same meaning, but in time it came to refer only to rude or ignorant rustics. Today it tends to describe someone who is born without understanding, a natural fool, as opposed to someone who chooses to behave stupidly.

IGLOO Inuit *Iglu* House.
Igloos were rarely used as permanent dwellings but were constructed by hunters needing a temporary shelter when away from home. *See also TeePee.*

ILLUSION Latin *Illudere* To mock.
Illusions were once the preserve of conjurors who mocked their audiences with tricks and hoaxes.

IMPALE Latin *In* In and *Palus* A stake.

Vlad the Impaler (d. 1476), otherwise known as Dracula and the inspiration for Bram Stoker's novel, was a sadistic torturer who impaled his enemies on stakes and is reputed to have murdered up to 100,000 people in this way.

IMPEACH Latin *Impedicare* To fetter.

A leader who is impeached is prevented from continuing in office in the same way that fetters or leg irons would prevent them from walking.

IMPLORE Latin *In* In and *Plorare* To weep.

A person imploring is making a request so earnestly that they may be reduced to tears.

INCARCERATE Latin *In* In and *Carcer* A prison.

INCH Latin *Uncia* A twelfth part.

An inch is a twelfth part of a foot.

INCOGNITO Latin *In* Not and *Cognitus* Known.

The term was originally applied only to sovereigns or princes who assumed fictitious names and dispensed with their retinues when they did not wish to be recognised.

INERT Latin *Inertis* Idle, lazy.

Alert is wide-awake, active and lively; inert on the other hand is sleepy, sluggish and indolent.

INFANT Latin *Infans* Speechless.

An infant is a child who has not yet learned to speak.

INFANTRY Latin *Infante* Youth.

The infantry were originally the youngest soldiers and those of low rank who did not merit inclusion in the smarter cavalry regiments.

INGENIOUS Latin *Ingenium* Mother-wit.

Ingenuity was considered to be an inborn quality and therefore bestowed by mothers.

INGOT Anglo-Saxon *In* In and *Geotan* To pour.

Ingots are made by pouring liquid metal into moulds.

INN Old English *Inne* Student lodging.

The Inns of Court, by which a barrister must be accredited, also provided accommodation for their members.

INOCULATE Latin *In* In and *Oculus* An eye (or, more relevant here, a bud).

The original meaning was the insertion by grafting of a bud into the stem of another plant by a gardener so that it will grow there. Medical inoculation is the insertion of a mild strain of a disease so that it will grow sufficiently to induce immunity. *See also Vaccine.*

INSECT Latin *In* In and *Seco* To cut as in secateurs.

An insect is a creature that has an apparent separation, or cut, between the head and the thorax.

INSULAR Latin *Insula* Island.

If something is insular, it is like an island in that it is isolated or separate.

INSULT Latin *In* In and *Salto* To leap.

Originally it meant to leap onto the land of an enemy. What could be more insulting than to find that someone had leapt on to your land?

INSULIN Latin *Insula* Islet.

The hormone that regulates glucose in the blood is produced in a part of the pancreas called the Islets of Langerhans.

INTERLOPER Dutch *Interlooper* A smuggler and *Loopen* To enter running.
Captured smugglers were made to run into court between two customs officers.

INTERNET From *Inter*national and *Net*work.

INTESTINE Latin *Intus* Inside.

INTREPID Latin *Intrepidus* Without trembling.
An intrepid person is one who shows no sign of fear and therefore does not tremble.

INUIT Inuit *Inuit* People.
The Eskimos of Northern Canada and Greenland call themselves Inuits, which in their language means people, the plural of *Inuk* (Person).

INVENTION Latin *Inventionem* A finding or discovery.
To invent something, therefore, means to find something that already exists rather than create something new.

INVINCIBLE Latin *Invincibilis*, from *In* Not, and *Vincibilis* Conquerable.

INVOICE Middle French *Invoyer* To send.
An invoice is a document sent to request payment. An envoy from the same source is someone who is sent to perform a task.

IODINE Greek *Iodes* Violet-like.
Iodine was first discovered by a saltpetre maker in Paris in 1812.

IRRIGATE Latin *In* Upon and *Rigare* To wet.

ISOBAR Greek *Isos* Equal and *Baros* Weight.
>An isobar is a line on a map joining places of equal pressure. The pressure is caused by the weight of the air above.

ISOTHERM Greek *Isos* Equal and *Therme* Heat.
>An isotherm is a line on a map joining places of equal temperature.

ISTHMUS Greek *Isthmos* Neck.
>An isthmus, such as the famous one at Corinth by which the Peloponnese are joined to the Greek mainland, has the appearance of a neck.

IVORY Sanskrit *Ibha* Elephant.
>Ivory was also obtained from the tusks of the walrus and narwhal.

IVY Gaelic *Eid* The plant that clothes.
>Ivy covers trees as if clothing them, but rather than providing warmth and protection it will eventually kill the host. The word ivy has also come to us via other languages, such as Welsh *Eiddew* and Anglo-Saxon *Ifig*.

J

JACKASS Arabic *Jackhsh* One who extends his ears.

JACK RUSSELL This small terrier took its name from a West Country parson, the Revd Jack Russell (1795–1883), who started the breed with Trump, a female he bought from a milkman for the purpose of ferret-hunting.

JANITOR Latin *Janua* Door.
>Janitors are now caretakers but originally they were doormen. From the same root as January, the door of the year. *See also Months of the year.*

JANUARY *See Months of the Year.*

JAUNDICE French *Jaune* Yellow.
The skin of Jaundice sufferers becomes yellow due to an excess of bile.

JAVELIN Spanish *Jabalína* Wild boar.
A boar-hunting spear.

JELLY Latin *Gelo* To congeal.

JERUSALEM Hebrew *Yaráh* A foundation and *Shalom* Peace.
Jerusalem is therefore translated into English as 'foundation of peace'.

JERUSALEM ARTICHOKE Italian *Girasole* Sunflower and *Articiocco* Artichoke.
The name is derived from the fact that the plant's flowers and leaves resemble those of the *Girasole* sunflower. The English term is therefore an absurd corruption of the Italian and has nothing whatsoever to do with Jerusalem. *Girasole* is derived from Italian *Gira* 'It turns to', and *Sole* 'The sun' because every morning the flower heads face the sunrise and, during the day, turn to follow the path of the sun across the sky. At night they turn back to await the next dawn. *See also Artichoke.*

JOB Old English *Gobbe* A lump.
The word job refers to a piece, or lump, of work needing to be done.

JODHPUR The tight-fitting riding breeches originated in the city of Jodhpur in Rajasthan, India.

JOURNEYMAN French *Journée* A day's work.
The word does not refer to a journey, it describes someone who works for a daily wage.

JOVIAL Latin *Jove* Jupiter.

The Romans thought that each person was born under the particular influence of one of the planets. Hence a *jovial* person, one who was born under Jupiter, the planet of happiness, was joyful. Likewise, *martial* people were influenced by Mars, *mercurial* people by Mercury.

JUDGE Latin *Jus* Law and *Dicere* To declare.

JUDO Japanese *Jiu* Gentleness and *Do* Way.

Judo is a competitive sport that enables martial arts to be performed without injury.

JUGGERNAUT Sanskrit *Jagannatha* Lord of the universe, a name for the Hindu god Krishna.

Each year at the Jagannath Temple in Orissa, India, Krishna devotees hold a procession of chariots containing statues, among them an enormous one of Jagganatha. So large is it that it has been known to slide out of control, crushing or injuring people in the crowd. British Christian missionaries in the colonial era spread the lie that Hindus were dangerous fanatics who threw themselves in front of the chariots in acts of misguided self-sacrifice. Henceforth, the word in English became synonymous with large unstoppable, destructive forces.

JUKE Bambara (a West African language) and Gullah (a Creole language developed in the southern United States by combining words from many languages brought over the Atlantic by slaves and English) *Juke* Bawdy.

In America the term can refer to a jukebox as well as a juke house, otherwise known as a brothel.

JULY *See Months of the Year.*

JUMBO Swahili *Jumbe* Chief.

Now applied not so much to some person or thing of importance but to anything of a great size, such as a jumbo jet. Use of the word to describe anything with an unusually large bulk derives from it being the name of a particularly large African elephant on display at London Zoo in 1865. Jumbo was bought by P. T. Barnum's Circus and shipped to America in 1882 where he was accidentally hit and killed by a railway train in 1885.

JUNE *See Months of the Year.*

JUNGLE Sanskrit *Jangala* Uncultivated wilderness.

JULY *See Months of the Year.*

JURY Latin *Jurare* To swear.

Members of a jury swear that they will reach a just verdict.

JUTE Sanskrit *Juta* Matted hair.

In fact jute is a vegetable fibre, not hair, but presumably the material, also known as hessian and used for making sacks, takes its names from its resemblance to hair.

K

KAGOOL French *Cagoule* A monk's hood, or cowl.

These lightweight waterproof coats have hoods that are similar to those of monks' habits.

KALE Middle English *Cawul* Cabbage.

Evidently in the Middle Ages a cabbage was a cabbage, and there was little, if any, differentiation made between different types. Coleslaw came to English from Dutch and is derived from *Kool* (Cabbage), of similar derivation to *Cawul*, and *Sla* (Salad).

KALEIDOSCOPE Greek *Kalos* Beautiful, *Eidos* Form and *Skopeein* To look.

A kaleidoscope consists of a tube containing mirrors set at fixed angles so that they reflect numerous images of coloured beads which create a beautiful form to look at.

KAMIKAZE Japanese *Kami* Divine and *Kaze* Wind.

During the Second World War *kamikaze* pilots were those who flew suicide missions, nose-diving their planes into Allied ships. They would be dispatched from their base with the farewell cry *kamikaze*, which is very similar in meaning to our God speed.

KANGAROO Guugu Yimithirr (Queensland, Australia) *Gangurru* The Grey kangaroo.

This little-known language is spoken by few Aborigines today but it does seem to be the source of the word kangaroo, albeit with a slight variation due to a mishearing by an early explorer. Sadly this dispels the myth that kangaroo is Aborigine for 'I don't understand you', allegedly the reply given to Captain Cook when he asked a native the name of the animal.

KARAOKE Japanese *Kara* Empty and *Okesutora* Orchestra.

Karaoke is a form of entertainment for which words are removed from recordings of songs, leaving just the orchestra on its own.

KARATE Japanese *Kara* Empty and *Te* Hand.

The martial art teaches unarmed self-defence.

KEDGEREE Hindi *Kitchri* A dish of smoked haddock, rice and eggs.

The recipe was taken to India by Scottish soldiers serving there in the nineteenth century where the dish was adapted and returned to the British Isles with a Hindi name.

KERFUFFLE Gaelic *Car* To turn and *Fuffle* To disarrange.
A kerfuffle is a state of confusion brought about by a lack of arrangement.

KETCHUP Malay *Kechap*, Chinese *Ketsiap*, Japanese *Kitjap* Any type of sauce, not necessarily tomato.

KHAKI Persian *Khak* Dust, ashes.
Until the end of the nineteenth century British soldiers wore red uniforms and were universally known as redcoats. But the development of sniper's rifles meant that a bright red garment was an easier target than one that blended in with the surroundings. The khaki battledress was adopted before the Boer War. Many regiments retain red uniforms for ceremonial occasions.

KIBBUTZ Hebrew *Qibbus* Gathering of people.
A kibbutz is an agriculturally based socialist commune consisting of a gathering of like-minded people.

KIDNAP Gypsy slang *Kid* A child and *Nab* To steal.
The word was originally *kidnabber* and so means to steal a child rather than an adult. We still use the word nab as in 'He nabbed my sweets'.

KIOSK Turkish *Kosk*, from Persian *Kushk* Summer House.
Most European languages have a similar word for small detached structures that give shade to street vendors, but in Turkey the word also refers to a garden shelter such as a gazebo.

KIP Danish *Kippe* Lodging or alehouse.
Going for a kip meant looking for a lodging when you needed somewhere to sleep.

KNEE Anglo-Saxon *Nicken* To bend.
Knuckles are from the same root. *See also Genuflect.*

KNIT Old English *Cnyttaan* Knot.

KNOT Latin *Nodus* Knot.
As in a measure of speed. One knot is defined as being one nautical mile per hour. The speed of a ship is measured in knots and this was achieved using a rope knotted every 51 feet so that 120 measured a nautical mile, there being 6,120 feet in a nautical mile. At one end was fixed a large flat piece of wood or a log. A floating log meets little resistance in the water and therefore remains stationary, so when thrown overboard from a moving boat the rope tied to it passes freely over the stern at the same speed at which the ship moves forward. The 120 knots in the rope represent the number of half-minutes in an hour, so it follows that the number of knots that pass over the stern in half a minute represent the number of nautical miles travelled in one hour. *See also Mile.*

KOSHER Hebrew *Kasher* Right in the sense of being correct or as it should be.
This word refers to the procedures laid down in the Torah for the right way to prepare food.

KOWTOW Mandarin *K'o* Touch and *T'o* Head.
Subjects coming before the Chinese Emperor had to kneel and bow so low that their heads touched the ground.

KRAFT German *Kraft* Strength.
Kraft wrapping paper is strengthened to help it withstand damage in transit.

L

LABORATORY Latin *Labore* To work.
A laboratory is therefore any place of work not necessarily only those associated with scientific endeavours.

LACE Latin *Laqueus* A noose.

This derivation is relevant to all three of the word's primary meanings, a shoe lace, the delicate stitched fabric and the verb, each of which involve threading. Curiously, though, our word 'noose' derives from Latin *Nodus* Knot.

LACONIC The Spartans were parsimonious with words. On one occasion they were approached by a herald from the Athenian army who told the Spartan commander: "If we come to your city, we will raze it to the ground." The Spartan answer was one word: "If." From the name of the land of which Sparta was capital, Laconia, comes laconic, meaning using few words. The leaders of Sparta imposed a strict militaristic lifestyle on their people, discouraging all forms of culture, and from this we have the word spartan, meaning an austere existence.

LACROSSE French *Crosse* A bishop's crook which bears a resemblance to the stick used by lacrosse players.

The sport of lacrosse, short for *le jeu de la crosse*, or 'the game of the Bishop's crook', was adapted from an ancient Native American practice known as *baggataway*. Unlike the modern version, it involved hundreds of players and a pitch up to one square mile in size. Its role in Native American culture was to train young men to be warriors, to settle inter-tribal disputes and, religiously, as entertainment for the Creator. When in 1763 French colonists, impressed with the game but appalled by its violent nature, attempted to organize it by establishing a set of rules and reducing the number of players, the natives did not approve and massacred every one of them with their tomahawks.

LAGER German *Lager* Storehouse.

Lager beer is stored for a minimum of three weeks before it is served.

LARD Greek *Larinos* Fat and *Laros* Pleasant to taste.

LARVA Latin *Larva* Masked.
>An insect in the grub stage of its life remains hidden or masked.

LASER An acronym standing for *L*ight *A*mplification by *S*timulated *E*mission of *R*adiation.

LAVATORY Latin *Lavare* To wash.
>Originally a vessel for washing in, the *lavitorium* later became a room in which the vessels were kept. Since these washrooms invariably had lavatories as well, they adopted the same name.

LAVENDER Latin *Lavare* To wash.
>Romans placed the dried flowers of the lavender plant in their wash tubs to add a pleasant aroma to their clean laundry.

LAW Old English *Lagu* Something laid down or fixed.
>The law is laid down by the government and enforced by their police.

LEGUME Latin *Legere* To gather.
>Once fully grown the plants are gathered together for use. The word has the same root as legion, which refers to a group of soldiers that have been gathered together to form a unit.

LEMUR Latin *Lemure* Ghost.
>Lemurs are long-tailed animals that live wild only in Madagascar. They are grey, mainly nocturnal and have large, staring eyes that give them a ghostlike appearance.

LENIENT Latin *Lenis* Soft.
>To be lenient is to be mild, tolerant or soft.

LENT Anglo-Saxon *Lenet* Length.

The Anglo-Saxon name for March was *lenet-monat*, or length-month, due to the lengthening days. Lent, which falls mainly in March, is therefore a contraction of the Anglo-Saxon word for length.

LEOPARD Latin *Leo* Lion and *Pard* Panther.

The leopard was anciently thought to be a cross between a lioness and a male panther. Its name was therefore a combination of the two.

LESBIANISM The earliest written references to same-sex love between women are in poems written by Sappho. She lived on the Greek island of Lesbos in 600 BC.

LETTUCE Latin *Lactuca* Milk. The lettuce plant, introduced to England from the Netherlands in 1520, is so named because of the milky sap that exudes from the stem when it is cut.

LEVANT Italian *Levant* Rising. The eastern end of the Mediterranean is where the sun was seen rising by Europeans.

LIBRARY Latin *Liber* The thin coating found on the inner bark of the Egyptian papyrus plant. This was the material used by the ancient Greeks and Romans for making paper, the word for which was also derived from *papyrus*.

LIEBFRAUMILCH German *Liebfrau* The Virgin Mary and *Milch* Milk.

This Rhineland wine was first made in a convent dedicated to the Virgin Mary.

LIMOUSINE Shepherds in the Limousin region of southern France wore distinctive hooded cloaks, a style of clothing that was popular with chauffeurs in the early days of motoring – that is, when the driver sat outside while the passengers had a separate enclosed compartment behind. The cloaks, which became known as Limousins, gave their name to the type of motor car they were used in. *See also Chauffeur.*

LINOLEUM Latin *Linum* Flax and *Oleum* Oil.
This floor covering was invented in 1869 by an Englishman who devised the name from the materials he used.

LITTER Anglo-French *Litere* A portable bed.
In order to make a comfortable bed travellers would scatter straw or some other soft material. Over time the term came to describe the scattered material alone and lost all association with bedding.

LOO French *Garde de l'eau* Watch out for the water.
In medieval times chamber pots were emptied from upstairs windows, often to the misfortune of unsuspecting pedestrians in the street below. This cry, often abbreviated to *L'Eau*, was the only warning of what was about to befall them.

LOOT Hindi *Lut* A stolen thing.

LOVE Latin *Lubere* To please.

LUKEWARM Celtic *Liegh* Half, partly. Hence lukewarm is half-warm.

LULLABY Middle English *Lullen* To lull, and *By*, as in goodbye.
Children are sung lullabies in order to lull them to sleep.

LYRICS Greek *Lyrikos* A lyre, the ancient stringed instrument originally using a tortoise shell as a sound box that was the precursor of the harp and which generally provided the musical accompaniment when the lyrics of a song were being sung.

M

MACARONI Latin *Macarare* To crush.

During production the wheat is crushed to make flour for the dough. Macerate is from the same origin.

MACHINE Latin *Machina* and Greek *Makhos* A contrivance.

MACKEREL Old English *Mackled* Spotted or speckled.

The fish has a speckled colouring.

MAD Old English *Gemaedde* To be out of one's mind.

Insane is from the Latin *Sane* (healthy), of which the negative is formed by the addition of the prefix *in-*. Insane originally meant to be unhealthy in body as well as in mind but the former was gradually dropped.

MADONNA Latin *Mea Domina* My lady.

MAGAZINE Middle French *Magasin* A storehouse, especially of military munitions.

Magazines, being storehouses of information rather than weapons, were first published in the eighteenth century.

MAGENTA Magenta, a fuchsia red colour, is one of the three primary colours, the others being yellow and cyan, an aquamarine shade of blue.

A perfect shade of magenta dye was developed in 1859, the same year as the battle of Magenta near Milan when a French and Sardinian army commanded by Napoleon III defeated an Austrian army.

MAGIC Avestan (An extinct language of the Zoroastrians of ancient Persia) *Magi* Sorcerer via Greek *Magike* Magus.

The Magi were astrologers and followers of the prophet Zoroaster who lived in present-day Iran in approximately 600 BC. This would tie in with the origins of the three wise men visiting Jesus shortly after his birth but in no way explains how they came from the east after seeing a star in the east as that would have been behind them.

MAGNET The word magnet is derived from the city of Magnesia on the eastern coast of the Greek mainland where the magnetic quality of lodestone is said to have first been noticed.

MALARIA Latin *Malus* Bad and *Aeris* Air.

It was believed that malaria was caused by unhealthy air rising from swamps and marshes. In fact it is caused by a parasite in the blood of the *Anopheles* mosquito that thrives in undrained land.

MALLEABLE Latin *Malleus* Hammer.

A malleable material such as copper can be beaten or hammered into a different shape without breaking.

MAMMOTH Yakut (the language of the Sakha Republic, Eastern Siberia) *Mama* Earth and Old Vogul (the language of the Mansi, Western Siberia) *Memont* Earth-horn.

This great prehistoric elephant, with 10-foot-long tusks (or horns as the Mansi people called them), became extinct 10,000 years ago and now lends its name to anything of great size. It was erroneously thought to have burrowed in the earth, undoubtedly due to the only evidence of these animals having existed being the occasional discovery of fossilized remains under the ground.

MANGER Latin *Manducare*, via French *Manger* To eat or to chew.

A manger is a trough to hold animal food such as the one that the baby Jesus was laid in when there was no room at the inn.

MANIFESTO Latin *Manifestare* To make public.

A manifesto makes public the policies of a political party seeking support prior to an election.

MANTELPIECE Latin *Mantellum* Cloak.

The mantel or mantle of a fireplace is the shelf from which wet coats or mantels were hung to be dried. In terms of a covering the word mantel is also used for a gas mantel that covers the flame and the earth's mantel that covers the inner core.

MAP Latin *Mappa* Napkin.

The first maps were drawn onto sheets of cloth such as were used for napkins. *See also Napkin.*

MARATHON A marathon is a race of 26 miles 385 yards. It commemorates the legend of Pheidippides, a Greek who ran from Marathon to Athens in 490 BC with news that the Greeks had defeated the Persian navy. He is reputed to have cried 'We have won' before dropping dead. The precise length of the run is not, however, the same that Pheidippides ran but the distance between Windsor Castle and the White City stadium which was the route of the race in the 1908 Olympic Games held in London.

MARBLE Latin *Marmor* Sparkling.

The Latin later came to describe gleaming or shiny stone and marble in particular.

MARCH *See Months of the Year.*

MARCH HARE The phrase 'as mad as a March hare' should actually be 'as mad as a *marsh* hare', since hares in wetland areas tend to rush about more as there is an absence of cover in marshland.

MARMALADE Portuguese *Marmelo* Quince.

A popular derivation for this word holds that Mary Queen of Scots, who spent much of her life in France, ordered orange jam whenever she was ill. The words '*Marie est malade*', or 'Mary is ill', are therefore supposed to have become synonymous with the preserve, the phrase being corrupted to 'marmalade'. However, since marmalade was originally made from the quince berry (Portuguese *Marmelo*), it is very likely that the word has a Portuguese derivation.

MARSH Gaelic *Mar* Pool.

MATRIX Latin *Matrix* Womb, from *Mater* Mother (as in Maternal).

The sense of a matrix containing something has been retained and the word now more commonly refers to mathematical data tables, or in geology to a mass of rock containing gems and fossils.

MATTRESS Arabic *Al Matrah* To throw.

A place where anything is thrown. Mattresses were thrown on the floor to provide sleeping quarters for travellers who carried their bedding with them.

MAUSOLEUM Derived from the tomb of Mausolus, King of Caria erected in AD 353 in present-day Turkey. It was destroyed by an earthquake and its stones were then used by crusaders to build Bodram Castle. It was one of the Seven Wonders of the Ancient World, the others being the Hanging Gardens of Babylon, the Temple of Artemis at Ephesus, the Colossus of Rhodes, the Statue of Zeus at Olympia, the Lighthouse of Alexandria and the Great Pyramid of Giza.

MAY *See Months of the Year.*

MAYONNAISE Mahon, after which the sauce of egg yolks, vinegar and oil is named, is the capital of Minorca in the Balearic Islands. Mayonnaise's popularity in Britain dates from the British occupation of Minorca between 1707 and 1713.

MEANDER The River Meander in Phrygia, in modern-day Turkey, wanders in a serpentine manner.

MEASLES French *Meseau* Leprosy.
Chaucer used this word to describe leprosy but since then it has been applied to measles, the highly contagious disease caused by a virus. German measles, a quite unrelated disease, acquired its name from the same inaccurate source and was first identified by German physicians. Its proper name, *Rubella*, is derived from the Latin for little red, a reference to the colour of the rash that covers much of the body.

MEDIEVAL Latin *Medius* Middle and *Aevum* Age.
Medieval therefore means Middle Ages and is generally used to describe the 1,000 years between the fall of the Western Roman Empire and the Renaissance.

MEDITERRANEAN Latin *Medius* Middle and *Terra* Land.
The name of the sea dates from the time when it was the centre of the known world. The Romans called it *Mare Nostrum* Our Sea.

MELANCHOLY Greek *Melas* Black and *Chole* Bile.
Hippocrates believed that the body was filled with four substances: black bile, yellow bile, phlegm and blood. These were represented by the four cardinal humours: melancholic, choleric, phlegmatic and sanguine. Their balance was supposed to dictate a person's temperament. Prolonged chronic depression was thought to be caused by an excess of black bile, hence the condition is known as melancholia.

MELODRAMA Greek *Melos* Song and *Drama* Action.

A melodrama was therefore a musical performance rather than an expression of overdramatic behaviour.

MENOPAUSE Greek *Men* Month and *Pausis* Cessation.

The cessation of a monthly event.

MEWS French *Muer* To change.

Mews are small streets behind grand town houses with stabling for horses and cages for hunting falcons. The birds were kept there while they were moulting and unable to hunt. Moulting is a natural process when birds change their feathers.

MICROBE Greek *Mikros* Little and *Bios* Life.

Microbes are very small living organisms. The word was coined in the nineteenth century when scientists first became aware of them.

MICROFICHE Greek *Mikros* Little and French *Fiche* A small piece of paper or card such as a page.

The word was coined when the miniaturisation of pages, usually to about one twenty-fifth the size of the original, was devised in the twentieth century for storage purposes. This is usually a photographic process but the word can also apply to a printed page composed of miniature type.

MILE Latin *Mille* A thousand.

The Roman mile was equal to 1,000 paces of a soldier with a pace being two steps. Each pace was 5 Roman feet, which was equivalent to 58 Roman inches. The Roman mile was 1,618 modern yards in length and the modern English mile is 8 furlongs or 1,760 yards. A nautical mile is defined by the Admiralty as 6,080 feet, 15 per cent more than a land mile, this distance being one minute of latitude in the south of England. A minute is one-sixtieth of a degree, there being 360 degrees in a circle, or around the world. A nautical mile is therefore 1/21600th of a line drawn around the world through London. *See also Furlong and Knot.*

MILLENNIUM Latin *Mille* One thousand and *Annus* A year. AD 2000, or 2001 if you are a perfectionist, was described as 'the Millennium', but the term is more accurately applied to a whole period of 1,000 years and not simply the dawn of a new one.

MILLINER A Milaner is a native of Milan where the fancy goods market has always thrived. In particular they produced fashionable women's hats.

MINIATURE Latin *Minium* Red lead.
The word miniature, when applied to small paintings, has nothing to do with their size. It is derived from the practice of ornamenting the margins of books with pictures highly coloured with *minium*.

MINISTER Latin *Minister* Servant.
Whether in the church or government, ministers are appointed to serve the community.

MINUTE A minute (as in time) is a minute (as in small) portion of an hour. So the two words, spelled the same but pronounced differently, are connected in this way. The Romans called minutes *Minuta Prima* the first small division of the hour. Then we divide it again, a second time, and they called these yet smaller periods of time *Minuta Secundum*, the second small division of the hour – seconds.
The Sumerians, who lived in Mesopotamia (present-day Iraq), are usually credited with devising the sexagesimal counting system with a base of 60. The measurements of sixty seconds in a minute and sixty minutes in an hour were therefore devised in 4000 BC and remain the oldest unchanged method of measuring.

Minutes can also be notes taken at a meeting that are usually written in shorthand or in an abbreviated small way before being written up in more detail later.

MIRROR Latin *Mirare* To wonder at.

MISSILE Latin *Missilis* To throw.
The derivation is therefore from the act of launching the item rather than the object itself.

MODEM Derived from the first syllables of *Mod*ulator and *Dem*odulator. A modem is a device for connecting a computer and a telephone line, a process that requires modulation of the signal suitable for transmission by an audio device and then demodulation when it arrives at the destination computer.

MODERN Latin *Modo* Just now, lately.

MONARCH Greek *Monos* Single and *Archein* To rule.
Rule by a single person.

MONDAY *See Days of the Week.*

MONEY Juno was the Roman goddess of many things including all matters relating to the state and was, when acting in her capacity as guardian of the state finances, additionally known as Juno Moneta. The Roman mint was located in her temple.

MONOCLE Greek *Monos* Single and Latin *Oculus* Eye.
A monocle is a single lens to improve the sight of just one eye. A binocular Greek *Bi* Two and Latin *Oculus* Eye is the same thing for two eyes.

MONOPOLY Greek *Monos* Single and *Poleein* To sell.

A monopoly exists when a single person or company has exclusive rights to sell an item.

MONTHS OF THE YEAR The names of the months are all of Greek or Latin derivation whereas the days of the week, with the exception of Saturday, are all northern European and Scandinavian. *See also Days of the Week.*

JANUARY: The first month of the year is dedicated to Janus the Roman god whose two heads enabled him to look both ways at once as he guarded doorways. Since a doorway often marks the beginning of a journey he also keeps watch over the beginning of the year.

FEBRUARY: Latin *Februum* Purification. The Februa purification ritual was held on 15 February just before the end of the year, since February was, until 450 BC, the final month of the year.

MARCH: Named after Mars, the Roman god of war. He started as a protector of cattle and farmland but as the Roman Empire expanded so too did his brief which eventually extended to include protecting the legions whose business was war. Originally the first month of the year.

APRIL: Latin *Aprilis* To open. This derivation is uncertain but likely to be from the spring when flowers open.

MAY: Named after the Greek goddess of fertility, Maia, whose festival takes place at the time of year when many fertile animals produce their offspring.

JUNE: Juno was the Roman goddess of marriage and it was considered particularly lucky to be married in her month. *See also Money.*

JULY: Formerly called *Quintilis* since it was the fifth month of the year when March was the first. It is commonly believed to have been renamed in honour of Julius Caesar, who was born on 13 July 100 BC, however there is also evidence to suggest that this summer month was called *Jule* before the emperor was born and that the word was derived from *Huil* (wheel), the symbol of the summer solstice.

AUGUST: Renamed after Emperor Augustus in 8 BC, having previously been called *Sextilis* as it was the sixth month of the old calendar, which had twenty-nine days. Not happy to be outdone by Julius Caesar, whose month had thirty-one days, legend has it that Augustus took two from February and added them to August, thus breaking the simple rule that alternate months had thirty and thirty-one days.

SEPTEMBER: Latin *Septem* Seven. The seventh month of the old calendar.

OCTOBER: Greek *Octo* Eight. The eighth month of the old calendar.

NOVEMBER: Latin *Novem* Nine. The ninth month of the old calendar.

DECEMBER: Latin *Decem* Ten. The tenth month of the old calendar.

MOPED A *Mo*tor assisted *Pe*dal Cycle.
The first mopeds were powered by a combination of motor and pedal power.

MORGANATIC German *Morgengabe* Morning gift.
A morganatic marriage is one between people of unequal social rank who are required to accept that their children have no rights

of succession to the higher-ranking parent's titles, hereditary position and property, etc. The 'morning gift' was a token gift given to a bride by a husband on the morning following their wedding and, in the case of a morganatic marriage, represented his only obligations to her and any children.

MORPHINE Greek *Morpheus* The god of dreams.

Morpheus was the brother of Hypnos, the god of sleep (from whom we derive hypnosis) and Nyx, the goddess of night. Morphine, the pain-relieving drug that induces relaxation and possibly dreams, is named after Morpheus. *See also Heroin.*

MORRIS DANCING Latin *Mauri* The tribe that inhabited the Roman province of Mauretania.

When the Moors, as they became known, were expelled from Spain in 1492, celebrations known as *Morescas* were held throughout the country and in some areas they still are. The folk dances we call Morris dancing, characterised by the hitting of sticks, waving handkerchiefs and bells sewn on to clothing, were performed at these events before spreading throughout Europe. *See also Gibraltar and Tariff.*

MORSEL Latin *Morsus* A bite.

A small, bite-sized piece of anything.

MORTAR Latin *Mortarium* The vessel in which Roman builders mixed sand and cement.

Mortar became the word for the mixture itself and has also been retained as the word for a vessel in which substances are ground with a pestle. *See also Pestle.*

MORTGAGE Old French *Mort* Death and *Gage* Pledge.

A mortgage is a loan agreement that remains in place until the loan is dead, in other words repaid.

MOSAIC Named after Moses who dictated that the breastplates of high priests be divided into twelve squares, each of a different colour. Hence inlaid work of different-coloured stones is called mosaic work.

MUFFIN Old French *Moufflet* Soft.

MUGGY Welsh *Mwygl* Tepid, sultry.

MULLED Old Norman *Molda* To bury.
Ale given at funerals was always warmed and was called *molde* ale or funeral ale. Later any warmed ale or wine became known as mulled.

MULLIGATAWNY Tamil *Milagu* Pepper and *Tannir* Water.
The soup originated in Tamil-speaking Sri Lanka and southern India and consists of ingredients produced there such as rice, noodles and turmeric.

MUMMY Persian *Mum* Wax.
Wax plays an important part in the process of embalming Egyptian mummies.

MUM'S THE WORD The word 'mum' is produced with closed lips, and therefore indicates a necessity for silence. Thus the phrase *Mum's the word* is often said after a secret has been shared, or when something needn't be said. It has nothing to do with mothers.

MUMBO JUMBO Mandingo (Central West Africa) *Mama Dyumbo* An idol worshipped by certain African tribes.
Christian colonists, obviously considering the idol to be false, considered the practice nonsensical, thus the term *Mumbo Jumbo* has become synonymous with any kind of nonsense.

MUSEUM Greek *Mousa* Muse. The muses were a group of Greek goddesses who inspired all branches of the arts. Hence museums, the modern-day custodians of the arts, are named after them. *See also Music.*

MUSHROOM French *Mousseron* A plant that grows in the forest among the moss or *mousse.*
The French call the mushroom *champignon* a plant that grows in the fields or *champs.*

MUSLIN Muslim dress was often composed of muslin, a light cotton fabric well-suited to the hot climates of the near- and middle-east. When it was first imported to England in 1670 it was given the name, albeit the phonetic name, of the people who had created it.

MUSIC Greek *Mousa* Muse.
The Muses most associated with music were Polyhymnia and Terpsichore. Given that they all have a Greek origin, it is very likely that the music-related words polyphonic, hymn, chord, chorus and harpsichord are all derived from the names of these two Muses. *See also Museum.*

N

NAPKIN Old French *Nappe* Tablecloth and Middle English *Kin* Small. A napkin is a miniature tablecloth for personal use. *See also Map.*

NARCISSUS The Flower. Greek *Narke* Numbness.
The plant has a sedative effect and thus derives from the same Greek root as Narcotic. In Greek mythology Narcissus was a beautiful young man who fell in love with his own reflection on the surface of a pond and killed himself when his approaches were not reciprocated.

NARK Romany *Nak* Nose.

A nark is someone who sticks his nose into other people's business, such as police informers, otherwise known as copper's narks.

NASTY Finnish *Naski* Pig.

The word is an allusion to the supposedly filthy habits of pigs. In Danish *Smaské* is to eat like a pig and in Swedish *Snaskig* means filthy. But as any farmer will tell you the pig's attention to matters of personal hygiene in their sties shows that, at the very least, this is inappropriate.

NAVVY Labourers who undertook the immense task of building Britain's navigation canals were nicknamed navvies and the name is still used for any manual worker.

NAZI An abbreviation of *Nationalsozialist*, in turn abbreviated from *Nationalsozialistische Deutsche Arbeiterpartei* (National Socialist German Workers' Party) the political party led by Hitler. *See also Fascist.*

NEANDERTHAL German *Neander* and *Thal* Valley.

The first evidence of Neanderthals was discovered in the Neander Valley, east of Dusseldorf. *See also Dollar.*

NECTARINE Persian *Nectarine* Perfect.

A nectarine was considered to be the perfect peach. The word does not share an origin with Nectar as that is Greek *Nec* Death and *Tar* Overcoming. Being the food of the Gods, it is the fare of those who have overcome death. *See also Peach.*

NEIGHBOUR Old English *Neah* Near and *Gebur* A farmer.

A reference to the days when pretty well everyone worked on the land and so all neighbours were farmers.

NEOLITHIC Greek *Neo* New and *Lithos* Stone.
The Neolithic people lived in the New Stone Age, commencing 10,000 BC.

NEPOTISM Latin *Nepos* Grandson and Italian *Nepotismo* Nephew. Nepotism originally referred to the habit of popes granting undue favouritism to young members of their own families but now applies to the same practice regardless of the position of the person who grants the favour.

NEUTER Latin *Ne* Not and *Uter* Either.
A neutered animal is not either gender.

NICKEL German *Nickel* Deceitful.
In German the malleable silvery metal is called *Kupfernicke* from *Kuper* Copper and *Nickel* Deceitful. The derivation is on account of the similarity in appearance of nickel and copper ore which deceived miners into believing they had found the latter when in fact they had not.

NICOTINE Named after John Nicot (1530–1600) who introduced tobacco to France in 1560.

NIGHTINGALE Anglo-Saxon *Niht* Night and *Galan* To sing.
Though the nightingale sings throughout the day, its song can be better heard at night when other birds are silent.

NISI Latin *Nisi* If not.
A 'decree nisi' is a court ruling that has no force if specified conditions are not met. Only when they are met does it become a 'decree absolute'.

NITWIT Variations of no and none appear in most European languages – No, Non, Nix, Niet, Nein – so *Nit* No and English *Wit* Intelligence. A nitwit is therefore a person devoid of intelligence.

NOB This slang word for nobles originated with the habit of their sons writing *fil. nob.*, meaning 'son of a noble', after their names in college registers. *See also Snob.*

NOOK Gaelic *Nuic* A corner.
The word that is so often coupled with nook, a cranny comes from an old French word, *Cran* (fissure). The expression nooks and crannies must therefore have been devised in English after the two words arrived here from different origins.

NOON Latin *Nona hora*. The ninth hour of the day.
Noon was originally two hours later, the ninth hour being 2.00 p.m. or nine hours after 5.00 a.m., at which hour monastic life commenced. Noon was the hour at which monks took a break for a meal but later, when it became common practice to eat the midday meal earlier, the term noon moved as well. With this new definition came the unsubstantiated folk etymology that after the clock strikes the number twelve there are no more numbers – none or *noon* – to count until the number one, after which the sequence begins again. So noon or midday was the hour thought to have no number, but the former derivation is perhaps more plausible.

NORTH Indo-European *Ner* Left.
North is to the left when facing the rising sun. *See also East, South, and West.*

NOSE Anglo-Saxon *Ness* A prominence.
We still use the word unchanged from the original in the names of geographical promontories such as Sheerness and Shoeburyness. The word nostril is also Saxon, from *Ness Thyrell*. *Ness* referring to the prominence on your face and *Thyrell* meaning holes.

NOSH Yiddish *Nāsh* Snack and German *Naschen* To nibble.

NOVEMBER *See Months of the Year.*

NUCLEUS Latin *Nucis* A nut.

A nucleus lies at the centre of something just as a kernel of a nut lies at the centre of its woody shell.

NUMBERS The English names for numbers 1 to 999,999 are all of Anglo-Saxon origin, but the word million comes through French, from Latin. Similarly, all ordinals, those words that describe a position or order such as first, second, third, etc., are Anglo-Saxon with the sole exception of second, which is of French origin. This is because the Anglo-Saxons counted first, other, third, fourth, etc. Since other had an alternative meaning, the word second was introduced to clarify the situation. Second originally comes from the Latin *Sequor* to follow, the number that follows one, and is derived from the same root as 'sequential'.

NURSE Latin *Nutrix* To nourish.

To nurse a child is to suckle it for nourishment. Later a nurse was anyone who cared for or nourished a person in need of help.

NUTMEG French *Noix muscade* Scented nut.

The nutmeg is the fruit of the *Myristaca moschata* tree, a native of the Molucca Islands, and has a distinctive aroma.

O

OAF Norwegian *Alfr* A silly person.

OBAMA Dholuo (Luo tribe of Kenya) *O* He and *Bama* Slightly bent – but, we hasten to add, as in angular rather than corrupt. *See also Barack.*

OBELISK Greek *Obelos* A spit.

An obelisk, as in a tall pillar, resembles the shape of a spit used in cooking.

OBITUARY Latin *Obituarius* On the way to meet one's ancestors.

Death was as taboo a subject for the Romans as it is for many people today, hence expressions that avoid use of the word death such as 'passed away' or 'fallen asleep'. In a similar way, the Romans said that the dead had gone to meet their ancestors.

OBLIVION Latin *Oblivisci* To forget.

Oblivion refers to the total eradication of something from memory.

OBNOXIOUS Latin *Noxa* Injury.

Obnoxious behaviour used to refer to an action that exposed people to injury but now it tends only to refer to behaviour so dreadful that it might lead to injured feelings.

OBSCURE Greek *Skeue* Covering.

A covering renders an item obscure.

OBSEQUIOUS Latin *Sequi* To follow.

Obsequiousness is an over willingness to follow someone in a servile manner.

OBSTREPEROUS Latin *Strepere* To shout.

To be obstreperous is to shout and make a lot of noise, particularly in resistance of authority.

OBSTRUCT Latin *Ob* Against and *Structum* To build.

To construct is to build. Something which is counterproductive to, or against progress, is to obstruct.

OCTOBER *See Months of the Year.*

OCTOPUS Greek *Octo* Eight and *Pous* Foot.
An octopus has eight legs which are quite different to the tentacles found in other marine species.

ODD Old Norse *Oddi* The third number.
In Norse Oddi also means the point of a spear or sword.

OIL Greek *Elaion* An olive tree.
The olive was the principal source of oil.

OK American slang. An abbreviation of 'oll korrect'.
It was a common fad in the mid-nineteenth century, especially in New York and Boston, for people to spell words based on the way they sounded and abbreviate them accordingly. OK was originally OW, standing for 'oll wright'. Several other acronyms arose around the same time, including NS ('nuff said'), but none of these have survived as well or spread so widely as OK, which has now infiltrated virtually every language in the world.

OMBUDSMAN Old Scandinavian *Umbodsmann* Representative.
An ombudsman represents the interests of the people against those who govern.

OMELETTE Latin *Lamella* A thin layer.
An omelette is prepared by frying a thin layer of egg in a thin layer of oil. The word laminate derives from the same root.

OPAL Polish *Opalać* To burn on all sides, from *Palać* To glow.
The opal, when exposed to light, could be said to glow from all sides.

OPEN SESAME Arabic *Simsim* Sesame.

The seedpods of the sesame burst open when they reach maturity; hence Ali Baba famously spoke the words so that the mouth of the treasure cave would burst open and admit him. The sesame seed also has mythological associations with immortality and witchcraft.

OPIUM Greek *Opos* Sap.

Opium is obtained from the sap of a poppy.

ORANGE Sanskrit *Naranj* Orange.

The fruit entered English vernacular as 'a Naranj'. Hearing this aloud, it is understandable how it was gradually corrupted to 'an orange'.

ORANGUTAN Malay, Indonesian *Orang* Person and *Hutan* Forest.

The highly intelligent orangutan, the largest animal to live in the trees, was considered a person from the forest.

ORCHID Greek *Orchis* Testicle.

The plant is named because of the similarity of shape between its tubers and a testicle. There are in excess of 20,000 species of orchid one of which is vanilla. *See also Avocado and Vanilla.*

OREGANO Greek *Oros* Mountain and *Ganos* Brightness.

The name refers to the bright purple flowers of the oregano plant and its mountainous natural habitat.

ORIGAMI Japanese *Ori* Folding and *Kami* Paper.

The art of folding paper to resemble birds and flowers originated in Japan.

OUIJA French *Oui* Yes and German *Ja* Yes.

The board with a letter and a pointing device used in a séance is therefore a Yes Yes board, that being the usual answer to the question 'Is there anyone there?'

P

PACIFIC Latin *Pax* Peace and *Facere* To make.

In 1520, after passing through the straits at the southernmost part of South America that would later bear his name, Ferdinand Magellan (1480–1521), the Portuguese explorer, headed north-west into the Pacific Ocean, sailing for three months and twenty days before coming across land. He found the weather so fair and the winds so favourable that he named the body of water the *pacifique*, the peaceful ocean. *See also Patagonia.*

PAGAN Latin *Paganus* Villager.

The spread of Christianity in the Roman Empire was slower in the country than in the cities. Hence those outside the cities, the *paganii*, were likely to be unbelievers and followers of more primitive, folk traditions. *See also Heathen.*

PAIN Latin *Poena* Penalty.

It was believed that suffering pain was the penalty for having committed a sin.

PAL Romany *Pal* Brother.

PALACE Latin *Collis Palatinus* Palatine Hill.

The most central of the seven hills on which the city of Rome is built, the Palatine Hill is the site of the cave where the she-wolf suckled the abandoned Romulus and Remus and where the former created the first Roman settlement which was named after him. From about 500 BC emperors built their palaces on the hill, which overlooked the Circus Maximus on one side and the Forum on the other. The word palace is derived from that original location, the Palatine Hill, as is the adjective palatial. *See also Suburb.*

PALL MALL Italian *Pallamaglio* Mallet ball.

A game in which a wooden ball was struck through one of two iron hoops set up at either end of an alley; the player who achieved this with the least strokes was the winner. When the game was introduced to London in the early seventeenth century, it was first played in an alley near St James's Street, later to be known as Pall Mall, a corrupted name of the game. Later still the game ceased to be popular and the streets became shopping centres and the expression shopping mall was born.

PAMPHLET French *Par un filet* By a thread.

A pamphlet is a booklet with the pages stitched together with a piece of thread.

PANAMA HAT These wide-brimmed straw hats are made in Ecuador, not Panama. During the construction of the Panama Canal, which opened in 1914, so many of the workers suffered from sunburn that they were issued with hats brought in from Ecuador. After they returned home, when asked where their hats came from, they replied 'Panama'.

PANE A pane as in a pane of glass is a shortening of the word panel.

PANIC Pan was a general who, being surrounded by an opposing army while camped one night in a valley, ordered his men to shout. The sound echoed around the hills, increasing in volume so much that the enemy fled, fearing a much greater opposing force than there actually was. Hence groundless fear is known as panic.

PANNIER Latin *Panis* Bread.

Panniers are baskets for carrying bread. While originally they would be suspended from either side of a pack animal's back, they are now more frequently seen on bikes and motorcycles.

PANSY Greek *Panacea* All healing.

It was believed that the pansy plant was a cure for all known diseases. The English also believed that the plant's medicinal qualities provided a cure for sorrow and called it Heart's Ease.

PANTRY Latin *Panis* Bread.

A pantry was originally the room where bread was kept.

PAPER Greek *Papyros.*

The Egyptian reed of that name grows in the marshes of the Nile delta and, when pulped, produces a soft pith from which early paper was made. *See also Library.*

PAPIER MÂCHÉ *Paper* and Latin *Masticatus* Chewed.

Papier mâché is a paper that has been pulped, or chewed, before being pasted together.

PAPOOSE Algonquin (central North America around the Great Lakes and eastern Canada) *Papoos* Child.

It refers to a native American child of any tribal origin.

PARACHUTE Italian *Parare* To defend and French *Chute* To fall.

Parachutes are described in Chinese texts from AD 500 and a thousand years later in Europe, most famously by Leonardo da Vinci. In the absence of airplanes they were mostly used to escape from burning buildings.

PARAFFIN Latin *Para* Little and *Affinis* Affinity.

Paraffin, or paraffin wax, is unusual in having little similarity or affinity with other chemicals. In America it is called kerosene, which is derived from Greek *Keros* Wax.

PARANOIA Greek *Para* Beyond and *Noos* The mind.

Paranoia is a mental disorder exhibiting characteristics beyond the normal processes of the mind.

PARAPHERNALIA Greek *Para* Beyond and *Pherne* Dowry.

The word originally described any possessions brought by a woman into a marriage that were not classed as dowry and thus remained her property as opposed to becoming her husband's. Perhaps it was the latter who turned the word into a derogatory term for unwanted and miscellaneous articles. *See also Trousseau.*

PARASITE Sanskrit *Paraasritahah* and Greek *Parasitos* One who is dependent on another, or who lives at another's expense.

PARENT Latin *Parere* To bring forth.

PARKA Aleut *Parqua* Skin.

A Parka is a hooded jacket similar to an anorak and made originally from skins. Aleut is the language of the inhabitants of the Aleutian Islands which stretch in a long line from the south of Alaska across the north Pacific towards the Kamchatka Peninsula. Also in the Nenets vocabulary, a language spoken in eastern Siberia. *See also Anorak.*

PARLIAMENT French *Parler* To speak.

The French described meetings of their state assembly as a *parlement* in the mid-twelfth century. The first English parliament met on 22 January 1265. The shortest lasted for one day in 1399 in order to depose Richard II and the longest from 1640 until dissolved by Cromwell in 1653.

PARSNIP Latin *Pastinum* Forked and Anglo-Saxon *Næpe* A tap root.

A parsnip frequently forks to end in two points. *See also Turnip.*

PARVENU French *Pervenir* To attain.

A parvenu is someone who has attained a social standing through the acquisition of wealth and position but is still considered an upstart.

PASTA Latin *Pasta* Dough.

PASS Latin *Passus* A step.
To pass by anything you need to move one step at a time.

PASTOR Latin *Pascere* To feed.
A pastor cares for his congregation as a mother cares for and feeds her child.

PASTURE Latin *Pascere* To feed.
A pasture is where animals feed.

PATAGONIA Spanish *Patagon* Big feet.
When the explorer Ferdinand Magellan visited the southern tip of South America before rounding the cape and becoming the first European to sail across the Pacific, he noticed that the natives were, on average, 10 inches taller than his crew and therefore had very large feet. *See also Pacific.*

PATHETIC Greek *Pathetikos* Sensitive, capable of emotion.

PAWN Spanish *Peone* A foot soldier.
A pawn is the smallest piece on the chess board, one of a row of foot soldiers that protect the important pieces behind them. It can also be used in the sense of someone who plays a mere supporting role in some aspect of life.

PEACH Latin *Pesca* Peach, from *Malum Persica* Persian apple.
The peach, though native to China, came to Europe via ancient Persia. *See also Nectarine.*

PEARL BARLEY A corruption of peeled barley, that is barley without its outer shell or husk.

PEDIGREE Old French *Pe de gru* Crane's foot.

The connecting lines on a family tree resemble the widely splayed claws of the bird's foot. *See also Geranium.*

PEN Latin *Penna* A feather.

The first writing implements were made from reeds in Egypt 5,000 years ago. In the Middle Ages they were replaced by quill pens, which were made from the large feathers of geese or, better still, swans. Pen knives are so named because they were used to shape the feathers for quill pens. Somewhat confusingly, an adult female swan is also called a pen, but this is derived from the Welsh *pynne* (loud).

PENINSULA Latin *Pene* Almost and *Insula* Island.

A peninsula, a strip of land barely attached to the mainland, was thought of as being almost an island.

PENTHOUSE French *Appentis*, from Latin *Appendicum* Appendage.

A penthouse is a separate part of a building, usually a luxury flat, that was often added as a later appendage.

PERFUME Latin *Per* and *Fumus* Smoke.

Perfumes were originally scents derived from burning flowers, spices and essential oils.

PERISCOPE Greek *Periskopeein* To look around.

PERIWINKLE Anglo-Saxon *Petty* Small and *Wincle* Shell-fish.

PESTLE Old English *Pestle* The leg of an animal, usually a pig.

The grinder used in a mortar was originally made from a leg bone. *See also Mortar.*

PETRIFY Latin *Petra* Rock and *Facere* To make.

To petrify is to make something into stone. This can be either literal, via the long geological process, or figuratively, as in the temporary, rock-steady paralysis induced by fear.

PETROLEUM Latin *Petra* Rock and *Oleum* Oil.

The crude oil from which petrol is made occurs naturally in rock formations, however the name is misleading since it is not, as the name suggests, distilled from the rock itself. Equally inaccurate is the American term for the same substance, gasoline, since it is a liquid and not a gas.

PHARMACY Greek *Pharmakon* A drug.

PHEASANT Greek *Phasianos* Phasian.

These ornate birds, though nowadays found throughout the world, are named after the Phasis River in the kingdom of Colchis, where they were first encountered. Colchis was in present-day Georgia and the river, which flows into the Black Sea, is now called the Rioni.

PHILOSOPHER Greek *Phile* Lover of and *Sophia* Wisdom.

PHONEY Gaelic *Fainne* Ring.

In the nineteenth century, swindlers sold gilt brass rings to recently arrived Irish immigrants, telling them they were real gold.

PHOTOGRAPHY Greek *Photos* Light and *Graphein* To draw.

PISTOL Pistols were first shipped to England in 1526 from Pistoia, Tuscany, where the handheld gun was invented for use on horseback.

PLACEBO Latin *Placebo* I shall please.

A placebo is a type of treatment that will do nothing for the patient other than give him peace of mind. It is made to look like the real thing but in reality is often no more than a sugar pill. A doctor prescribing it for psychological benefit, as opposed to its other use as a control in testing drugs, might therefore say, 'This will not provide any cure but it will please him.'

PLANET Greek *Planetes* To wander.

Before the discoveries by early astronomers such as Galileo (1564–1642), who proved that the planets circled the sun, and Kepler (1571–1630), who showed that their orbits were elliptical, it was thought that planets wandered aimlessly through space rather than taking clearly defined routes.

PLANTAGENET The name of the royal house that provided England with monarchs from 1154 to 1485 was first adopted by the counts of Anjou after the first count caused himself to be scourged as penance for some crime he had committed by being beaten with branches of broom plant *Planta Genista*. Geoffrey, Count of Anjou was father of the first Plantagenet king, Henry II (1154–1189).

PLASTER OF PARIS Greek *Plassein* To mould.

This material was first imported to England from a gypsum mine at Montmartre in Paris.

PLASTIC Greek *Plassein* To mould.

Plastic originally referred to an object's pliability, or plasticity, but the word is now much more widely used to describe things that have already been moulded into a shape.

PLUMMET Latin *Plumbum* Lead.

Early builders used lumps of lead on strings called plumb lines or plumb bobs to check that constructions were vertical. Any weight on a string will plummet downwards.

PLUNDER Dutch *Plunderen* To steal household goods.

POACHER French *Poche* Pocket, bag.
A poacher is one who unlawfully kills and pockets another man's game.

POETRY Greek *Poieo* To create and *Poiesis* Imaginative.
Creative and imaginative use of language. The word originally had no connection with rhyme or metre.

POLICE Latin *Politia* Civil administration, from Greek *Polis* City.

POLO Tibetan *Pulu* Ball.
Polo is a ball game played on horseback, in the water and occasionally on elephants or bicycles.

POM Australian slang *POME* Prisoner of Mother England.
It is believed that deported prisoners arriving in Australia had these initials printed on their shirts.

PONG Romany *Pan* To stink.

PORCELAIN Italian *Porcellana* A cowrie shell.
The delicate shell-like surface of porcelain resembles the smooth surface of a cowrie. Porcelain is also known as china, because that country was its only producer before 1600 and, like so many other early imports, it took its name from its place of origin.

PORCUPINE Latin *Porcus* A pig and *Spina* A spine.
A porcupine was considered to be a pig with spines. In fact they are in the rodent family. *See also Rodent.*

PORPOISE French *Pore* Hog and *Poisson* Fish.

It is curious that while the English call the animal by a French name, the French have adopted an Anglo-Saxon one: *mere-swine*, or sea-pig.

PORTCULLIS French *Porte* Gate, door and *Coleice* Sliding.

Entrances to large castles invariably had two portcullises. The enemy would be enticed into the castle through the open outer one before being stopped by the locked inner one, trapped there when the outer portcullis slammed down behind them.

POST Latin *Positus* Placed.

The word 'post' is used in a variety of senses – post office, a post in the ground, a military posting, posting to a ledger – but an understanding of the root explains each one as a placement of something – a letter, a wooden pole, a person or some figures – in its appointed place.

POTATO Taino (West Indies) *Batata* Sweet potato and Quechua (Andean) *Papa* Potato.

Many European explorers, notably Sir Walter Raleigh (1552–1618), have been credited with introducing the potato to Europe from Haiti and the Bahamas, the islands they first came to having sailed across the Atlantic.

POULTICE Greek *Poltos* Porridge.

A poultice is a warm coating applied to a wound originally made with foods such as porridge or bread. In the eighteenth century, poultices were infused with lead. Such a mixture was administered to Beethoven in order to cure his distended abdomen; however, it probably hastened his death.

POSTSCRIPT Latin *Post Scriptum* Written afterwards. A PS.

PRAIRIE French *Prairie* Meadow, pasture land.

French settlers in America used the word to describe the endless plains they found there.

PRECOCIOUS Latin *Prae* Early and *Coquere* To cook or ripen.

A precocious child is one that is an early developer. A precocious fruit or vegetable is one that has ripened early. *See also Apricot.*

PREFACE Latin *Prae* Before and *Fatus* To speak.

A preface can therefore be a spoken introduction as well as the more accepted written form at the beginning of a book.

PREGNANT Latin *Prae* Before and *Gnasci* To be born.

PREJUDICE Latin *Prae* Before and *Judicium* Judgement.

Prejudice is a judgement made before the matter is judged upon in a court of law.

PREPOSTEROUS Latin *Præ* Before and *Posterus* After.

It is preposterous to place before that which should be after. The word therefore has the same meaning as the saying 'to put the cart before the horse'.

PROFIT Latin *Profectus* To make progress.

PROGNOSIS Greek *Pro* and *Gignoskein* To know.

PROGRAMME Greek *Programma.*

Before being presented to the Athenian senate for debate, proposed laws were published on tablets for inspection. At this stage it was therefore a plan or programme and not yet the final draft. A *programma* was similar to a present-day white paper, issued to familiarise members of parliament with proposed legislation.

PROLETARIAT Latin *Proles* Offspring.

In ancient Rome the proletariat were the lowest of the six classes and comprised people who owned no property and whose only contribution to the state was to provide children.

PRONOUNCE *Pro* Forth and *Nuntius* A messenger.

PUFFIN Cornish. The puffin used to be found on most Cornish cliffs where for centuries they provided food and oil, but now the colonies have tended to move further north to more productive feeding grounds. The Norse for Puffin is *Lund*, hence Lundy off the coast of Devon is Puffin Island but now the birds are seldom seen there either.

PUKKA Hindi *Pukka* Cooked or perfectly done.

Adapted throughout the British Empire to describe not just food but anything that is perfect. It is most frequently used to describe good people, as with the phrase *pukka sahib* meaning 'excellent fellow'.

PUNT Latin *Pons* Bridge.

From *pons* is derived the French *pontoon*, which in most European languages now signifies a flat-bottomed vessel used as a temporary floating bridge. The word punt, referring to a flat-bottomed boat, is a contraction of *pontoon*.

PUSS Ancient Gaelic *Puss* A cat.

PYGMY Greek *Pygmaeus* Dwarf.

As well as being applied to certain tribes in sub-Saharan Africa whose average height was appreciably less than that of the European explorers who discovered them, a pygmy was also a measure of length said to be the distance from the elbow to the knuckle. *See also Elbow.*

PYJAMAS Persian *Payjama* Leg garment.

PYRRHIC A pyrrhic victory is one achieved with great loss to the victor. King Pyrrhus of Epirus defeated the Romans twice, at Heraclea in 280 BC and at Asculum in the following year, but his losses were so great that he commented, 'One more battle like these and we will be totally undone.'

Q

Q Latin *Cauda* A tail. The letter Q is simply the letter O, but with a tail.

QUAFF Low German *Quassen* To overindulge, especially in food or drink.

QUAKER The Religious Society of Friends was founded in the mid-seventeenth century by George Fox, the son of a Leicestershire weaver, who was disillusioned with the existing Christian denominations. His supporters became known as Quakers after Fox exhorted a Derby magistrate to quake at the word of the Lord.

QUALM Old English *Cwealm* Disaster usually associated with the pain of the plague.
The word's current meaning, a state of unease, is moderate by comparison.

QUANDARY French *Qu'en dirai-je?* What shall I say of it?
The word is a corruption of this query, which seeks explanation for a puzzle or perplexity.

QUANGO *QU*asi *A*utonomous *N*on-*G*overnmental *O*rganisation. An acronym to describe government-appointed bodies that operate away from mainstream government and are often ridiculed for lack of accountability and excessive expenditure.

QUARANTINE Latin *Quadraginta* Forty, the number of days of isolation necessary to prevent the spread of contagious diseases. Ships entering harbour were required to fly a yellow flag to show if they were 'in quarantine', or a yellow and black one to indicate that a contagious disease was on board. The first astronauts returning from the moon also underwent a period of quarantine however no similar precautions were made to prevent diseases from earth reaching space.

QUARREL Latin *Querula* To complain.
A quarrel was therefore the complaint of one party against another that led to a quarrelsome disagreement rather than the resulting altercation itself.

QUART Latin *Quartus* Fourth.
A quart is one fourth of a gallon.

QUICHE German *Kuchen* Cake.
The quiche originated in Lorraine, a region in the north-east of France where dialects of German are still spoken.

QUIZ Latin *Quaestio* Ask.
Probably from the same root as question. There is sadly no truth in the oft-quoted suggestion that this strange word originates from a bet accepted by a Dublin theatre proprietor in 1790 that he could not introduce a new word into the language overnight. He persuaded friends to write 'quiz' on walls all over the city so that in the morning everyone was seeking an explanation for this puzzling word. But sadly it cannot be true as the word was in use a century before.

R

RABBI Hebrew *Rabbi* My great one, or teacher.

RACE As in nationality. Mœso-Gothic *Raz* House.
We use this in the sense of the House of Israel or the House of Windsor, both of which have a strong connection to nationality.

RACKET Arabic *Rahat* The palm of the hand.
Many games now played with a racket or racquet once used the bare or gloved hand to strike the ball. In fives, however, a game similar to squash, the ball is still struck with a gloved hand.

RACKETEER In the seventeenth century English pickpockets would cause a racket, or a loud noise, by throwing devices such as squibs and rockets in order to otherwise engage their victims' attention and allow them to steal undetected. *See also Whippersnapper.*

RADAR American acronym for *RA*dio *D*etecting *A*nd *R*angefinding, first used during the Second World War.
The device was perfected for military use by Sir Robert Watson-Watt, a descendant of James Watt, the inventor of the steam engine. It is considered to have played a major role in winning the war.

RAMBLE Latin *Perambulo* To wander about.

RASCAL French *Racaille* Scum or rabble, from Norman-French *Rasque* Mud.

RATHER Old English *Hrathor* More quickly, sooner.
To say that one would *rather* do one thing over another is to say that one would *sooner* do that one thing over the other.

RAVIOLI Italian *Rava* Turnip.

A popular filling was originally puréed turnip.

RAVISH Latin *Rapere* and French *Ravir* To seize and carry off.

RECTOR Latin *Rectum* To rule.

A rector is someone appointed to a position of leadership, be it of a parish or university, or, in some cases, as headmaster of a school.

REFRIGERATE Latin *Re* From and *Frigus* Cold.

To refrigerate something is to change its temperature from one level to a colder one.

REGATTA Venetian *Regatta* An annual race between gondoliers.

REJUVENATE Latin *Juvenescere* To become young again.

To rejuvenate means to return to a state of youthfulness, to reinvigorate. No cure for advancing years has yet been devised and so there is no word for literally becoming younger!

REPTILE Latin *Repere* To creep.

Most members of the class *Reptilia* – snakes, lizards, crocodiles and alligators – creep along with their bodies close to the ground.

RETICENT Latin *Re* and *Tacere* To be silent.

Reticence, a reluctance to express oneself, is usually demonstrated as silence.

RETORT Latin *Torquere* To twist.

To retort is to turn an argument back on its originator, as if twisting its direction.

RHINOCEROS Greek *Rhinos* Nose and *Keras* Horn.

The distinctive horn on the noses of these ancient creatures gave rise to their name. The largest of the five species remaining, the

African white rhinoceros, second in size only to elephants as land animals, is not white at all but grey. The use of the word white in its name derives from Afrikaans *Wyd* Wide. The white rhinoceros has a wide lip, whereas the smaller black rhinoceros has a pointed lip. The black rhinoceros is grey as well, but was termed black to distinguish it from the inappropriately named white rhinoceros.

RHODODENDRON Greek *Rhodos* Rose and *Dendron* Tree.
This Himalayan tree has rose-like flowers. The popularly held belief that the tree has a connection with the island of Rhodes is erroneous.

RIBALDRY *Rabod*, the seventh-century heathen king of Friesland, is thought to be the derivation of this word. While standing in a pool awaiting baptism, he is said to have asked his Christian mentor, Bishop Wipan, where his forefathers had gone. As they had not been baptised, the response was that they had been sent to Hell, to which the king replied that he would rather spend eternity with his ancestors in Hell than with a few Christian strangers in Heaven. This rejection of God was thought to be so vulgar and hateful that the king's name gradually came to be applied to anything deemed coarse or obscene.

RIDICULE Latin *Ridere* To laugh.
An expression of derision about an object or situation is often expressed with mocking laughter.

RIDING As in a division of a county. Norwegian *Trethingr* A third. The county of Yorkshire is divided into three ridings – North, East and West – and the derivation explains why there is no South Riding.

RIFLE German *Reifeln* To form small grooves.
The firearm takes its name from spiral flutes in the barrel that cause the bullet to spin, thus ensuring a straighter flight.

RIP Latin *Requiescat in pace* May he or she rest in peace.

RIVAL Latin *Rivalis* One who shares a brook, from *Rivus* Brook as in river.
The word originally referred to two people owning property on opposite sides of a brook and both claiming exclusive ownership of the stream.

ROAM Italian *Romeo* A pilgrim going to Rome.
The word later became associated with vagrants who, despite their actual destination, would always say they were going to Rome. From this we also get the saying, 'All roads lead to Rome.'

ROBOT Czech *Robota* Work, labour.
This word was first used by Czech writer Karel Čapek in his 1921 play *Rossum's Universal Robots*. It was about artificial men who were manufactured to perform hard labour and explored the idea, as they could think and feel just as humans did, that they were being exploited.

RODENT Latin *Rodere* To gnaw.
Rodents, which vary in size from the tiny Pygmy Jerboa with a body under 2 inches long to the Capybara that measures over 4 feet, have sharp incisor teeth that continue to grow throughout their lives and are kept short by constant gnawing. *See also Rostrum.*

ROMANCE When, in the ninth century, the French language began to replace that of the Romans as France's main vernacular, early tales of chivalry and romance such as *Beowulf* and *King Arthur* were still recounted in Latin or, more accurately, in a Latin dialect which became known as known as *Romance*. The term therefore became interchangeable with the genre, one of knights, princesses, magic and fantasy.

ROSEMARY Latin *Ros* Dew and *Marinus* Sea.

The rosemary plant is native to the rocky coasts of southern France and Italy where the early morning dew clings to its silvery grey leaves.

ROSTRUM Latin *Rostrum* Ship's prow, from *Rodere* To gnaw.

The Romans applied the term to the bow of a boat, which was fitted with sharp irons for attacking, or gnawing into, an enemy ship. It was also applied to the orator's stage in their *forum* because of its resemblance to the prow of a ship. *See also Rodent.*

ROUNDHEAD This term of contempt applied to the Puritans at the time of the civil war was derived from their custom of cutting their hair close to the head, which was in total contrast to the Royalists, who wore their hair in elaborate ringlets.

ROUTINE French *Route* A road.

A routine is the metaphorical practice of travelling down a well-defined road.

ROVER Dutch *Roover* Robber and Danish *Röverskip* Pirate ship.

RUBICON The Rubicon is a small river that once marked the border between Italy and Gaul. Due to a treaty, Roman generals were forbidden to cross it. When Julius Cæsar did so in 49 BC, it caused a violent civil war. Hence to 'cross the Rubicon' is to embark on a rash and irrevocable act.

RUM DEAL There was a practice among booksellers in the eighteenth century of sending books to the plantations of the West Indies in exchange for barrels of rum. However, due to their customers' isolation from British culture they often seized on this arrangement as an opportunity to get rid of titles that did not sell well in England. Hence the phrase rum deal refers to a deal in which one party does not receive a fair deal.

RUGBY William Webb Ellis (1806–1872) was credited with the invention of this game when, during a football match at Rugby School, he picked up the ball and ran with it. A plaque at the school records the event thus: 'This stone commemorates the exploit of William Webb Ellis who, with a fine disregard for the rules of football as played in his time, first took the ball in his arms and ran with it thus originating the distinctive feature of the rugby game AD 1823.' The William Webb Ellis Trophy is now awarded to the winner of the Rugby World Cup. *See also Cricket and Soccer.*

RUSTIC Latin *Rusticus* The country.
A rustic is someone from the countryside. To be rusticated is to be banished to the countryside from a university.

S

SABOTAGE Turkish *Shabata* Galosh via French *Sabot* Wooden shoe.
French peasants fearful that their livelihoods were threatened by the introduction of machinery used to throw their wooden shoes into the mechanisms to cause damage. Later, striking railway workers removed the 'shoes' that held railway lines in place and thus became known as saboteurs. The flat Italian *ciabatta* bread, named after the Italian for slipper, also derives from *Shabata*.

SADDLE Anglo-Saxon *Sadle* Seat.
Settles, the long, high-backed wooden seats found in farmhouses and pubs, are derived from the same root.

SAFARI Arabic *Safara* Travel.

SAGO Malay *Sagu* A species of palm, the pith of which is processed to extract the starch that is used as a thickening agent in puddings.

SALAD Latin *Sal* Salt.

In ancient Rome it was customary to eat vegetable leaves with a lot of salt. Hence the dish that is nowadays associated with healthy eating has a name that derives from a substance now associated with quite the opposite when used to excess. Salami is similarly derived from the Latin for salt. *See also Sausage.*

SALARY Latin *Salarium* Salt money.

Roman soldiers were originally paid in salt as it was considered to be a vital yet scarce food. Payment with salt was later replaced by money with which to buy it, and this was called salt money or *salarium. See also Soldier and Wage.*

SALUTE Latin *Salus* Health.

Originally a salute as a greeting was an enquiry after someone's health. It was much the same as our semi-automatic greeting 'How are you?' The military salute originated at jousting tournaments when the winner shielded his eyes from the bright light that was supposedly radiating from the lady or senior person who presented the prize. Military salutes are always carried out with outstretched fingers, showing that the hand holds no weapon. Finally, a military salute with guns firing blanks or purposely aimed in some safe direction shows that there is no hostile intent and therefore indicates respect for the person in whose honour the salute is fired.

SAMBA Portuguese *Zamparse* To bump and crash.

This type of dance is always set to lively music and drums. Although introduced into Europe from Brazil when it was a Portuguese colony, the dance originated in Africa and was carried across the Atlantic by slaves.

SAMBUCA Arabic *Sambuq* A type of ship used to import the aniseed-flavoured alcoholic drink.

SAMPAN Mandarin *Sam* Three and *Pan* Plank.

A sampan has the simplest of constructions – a flat board for the bottom and another to form either side of the boat.

SANDWICH John Montagu, 4th Earl of Sandwich (1718–1792), asked that his meals to be brought to him between two slices of bread, so that he could eat without having to either leave or make a mess of his gaming table. A more generous explanation is that he worked so hard after his appointment as First Lord of the Admiralty that he seldom left his desk and asked that his food be brought to him as sandwiches in his office so that he could continue directing the British navy without a pause.

SANGRIA Spanish *Sangria* Bleeding.

Made with red wine, orange juice and brandy, this traditional Spanish drink is so called because of its deep red colour.

SANITATION Latin *Sanitus* Health.

The Romans recognised that there was a strong connection between sanitation systems and good health. The Cloaca Maxima sewage system, a large drain flowing through Rome, was constructed in about 600 BC and continued to drain marshland and convey sewage to the River Tiber for 1,000 years and may still be seen today.

SAPPER Latin *Sappa* A pick.

A sapper is a military engineer whose duties were originally to gain access to the enemy's position by digging trenches and tunnels with picks and shovels. Here they would undermine and destroy the fortifications to help their colleagues advance. To sap, from the same source, means to weaken.

SATIN Chinese *Zaytun* A seaport on the south-east coast of China, also known as Quanzhou, which was the world's largest during the Yuan Dynasty (1279–1368). Satin, a closely woven, glossy fabric was first made in China and then exported by Arab traders through the port of *Zaytun*, from which it derived its name.

SATURDAY *See Days of the Week.*

SAUCER Latin *Salsa* Sauce.
Saucers were originally used alone as table dishes for sauces and salt. Their association with teacups is a more recent innovation.

SAUNA Finnish *Savna* Bath.
The practice of pouring water on to hot stones to create very hot steam takes its name from Sami *Suovdnji* a depression in the snow created to give warmth and protection to a person or an animal. The Samis, frequently known as Lapps, a term they consider uncomplimentary, occupy the northern coastal regions of Scandinavia and western Russia.

SAUSAGE Latin *Salsus* Salted.
The sausage was invented 5,000 years ago by the Sumerians in present-day Iraq. However, the name derives from the Roman practice of stuffing salted meat into animal intestines as a means of preserving it. *See also Salad.*

SAVAGE French *Sauvage* from Latin *Silva* Forest, grove.
To be savage is to act as though one is from the wild.

SAVVY Latin *Sapere* To be wise or knowing.
To be tech-savvy is to be knowledgeable about and competent with technology.

SCALLYWAG Gaelic *Sgaileog* Farm labourer.
The term is now most frequently used in English towns that have a high proportion of people of Irish descent.

SCAMP Latin *Ex* From and *Campus* Field.

A scamp originally described a soldier who absented himself from the battlefield. More recently it has been used to describe mischievous little boys.

SCAMPI Italian *Scampo* A shrimp.

The species of shrimp that is supposedly used to prepare scampi is also known as the Norway Lobster or the Dublin Bay Prawn. So it is a puzzle why we use the Mediterranean name when others from our own waters are available. Perhaps it sounds more exotic.

SCANDAL Greek *Scandalon* A stumbling block.

Scandals can certainly prove to be a stumbling block to both the private and professional lives of those whose secrets are exposed.

SCARLET Latin *Carnis* Flesh, through Italian *Scarlatino* Flesh-coloured.

SCENT French *Sentir* To smell.

It is not known why the silent 'c' was added.

SCHEDULE Latin *Schedula* A strip of paper.

Originally any piece of paper on which a schedule might be written.

SCIENCE Latin *Sciens* Knowing.

SCISSORS Latin *Scindere* To split.

Scissors is one of the few nouns in English that has no singular.

SCORE Old Norse *Skor* Notch.

An early way of recording a score of points in a game or kills in battle was to carve a notch in a tally stick.

SCOUNDREL Anglo-French *Escoundre* To hide oneself.
A scoundrel is someone who lurks in the shadows and operates among the criminal underclass of a society.

SCRUTINY Latin *Scruta* Rags.
This term referred to rag-and-bone men, whose work demanded that they scrutinise even old rags thoroughly because by doing so they were able to find materials that would otherwise be rejected as being valueless.

SCUFFLE Swedish *Skuffa* To push.
Scuffles invariably result in people pushing each other.

SCULPTOR Latin *Sculptum* To carve.

SCUPPER Old French *Escopir* To spit out.
The word was originally used to refer to the drainage holes in the side of ships intended to let out water. A scupper therefore saves a ship from sinking. But curiously as a verb it means to deliberately destroy a plan or an item. Therefore it would be acceptable to report the sinking of a ship by saying, 'The ship was scuppered because someone blocked the scuppers.'

SECOND Latin *Secundus* To follow.
Second is the number that follows the first. *See also Minute and Numbers*

SEDGE Anglo Saxon *Sæcg* Sword.
The plant has little sword-like leaves. *See also Gladiator and Gladiola.*

SEDUCE Latin *Seducere* To lead.
Seduction involves leading someone in a particular direction and invariably leading them astray.

SEGREGATE Latin *Se* Apart and *Gregis* A flock.
Segregation is the setting apart of a person or an item from a larger group or flock. *See also Congregate and Gregarious.*

SEPIA Greek *Sepia* A cuttlefish.
These marine creatures are cephalopods in the same class as squid and octopuses and, as a defence mechanism, they eject clouds of opaque ink which can also be used as a sepia dye.

SEPTEMBER *See Months of the Year.*

SERENADE Spanish, Italian *Serenata*, from Latin *Serenus* Calm and Italian *Sera* Evening. Originally a serenade was music played out of doors on a serene evening.

SERIOUS Old English *Swaere* from Latin *Serius* Gloomy.
A serious matter can often be a gloomy one.

SERPENT Latin *Serpere* To creep.

SHAMPOO Hindi *Chāmpo* Massage and Hindi *Champā* The flowers of the plant *Michelia champaca*, which were once used to make scented hair oil.
The word 'shampoo' entered the English language in 1759 when the Indian Vapour Baths were established in Brighton by the Bengali entrepreneur Sake Dean Mahomed. His *champi* or 'shampooing' service, a therapeutic head massage, was so popular that a new title was created for him and he was appointed 'Shampooing Surgeon' to both George IV and William IV. To make the early formulations of what would later come to be known as *shampoo*, manufacturers would boil soap in water and add to it such plants as henna, aloe, jasmine, rose and musk, all of which were traditional Indian ingredients.

SHANGHAI Mandarin *Shang* On and *Hai* The sea.

China's largest city owes its prosperity to being a port, but the other meaning of the word – to be shanghaied – meant to be pressganged into joining the navy for a life on the sea.

SHANK'S PONY Frisian S*chanke* Leg.

To ride on Shank's pony is to walk so there is no pony and instead you must use your legs. The word shank is used for anything relating to a leg, such as lamb shank or anything that is long and thin such as the shank of a nail or an anchor. The tall Plantagenet King Edward I was nicknamed Longshanks.

SHARK Mayan (Central American) *Shoc* Fish.

The word is thought to have been brought to England by the explorer Sir John Hawkins (1532–1595) who exhibited a shark in London after returning from the Caribbean.

SHAWL Persian *Shal* A strip of cloth.

SHERIFF Old English *Scir* Shire, county and *Reeve* An official appointed to keep the peace.

A reeve is one of the oldest democratically elected positions as he was a serf appointed by other serfs to keep order for the lord who owned both the land and those who worked it during feudal times. An early example of self-regulation. Later the title was applied to law-keepers responsible for whole counties or shires, so they became shire reeves, which was corrupted to sheriffs. *See also Alderman.*

SHERPA Tibetan *Shar* East and *Pa* Inhabitant.

Men from the mountains of Nepal (the women are called *sherpinis*) have immense natural strength at high altitudes and are therefore frequently called upon to assist in mountaineering expeditions, notably up Mount Everest. The most famous sherpa was Tenzing Norgay (1914–1986) who, with Edmund Hillary (1919–2008), reached the summit on 29 May 1953.

SHERRY A corruption of Jerez, in the Cádiz region of Spain, where sherry is produced. Any sherry produced outside of Cádiz must not be called sherry, nor jerez or *Xérès*, unless it is clearly stated that it was produced elsewhere.

SHODDY Scraps of wool surplus to requirements in the weaving process were called shoddy, as were recycled fabrics. Since this material invariably had shorter strands, the clothing made from it soon became dishevelled and the wearer was said to be shoddily dressed.

SHOULDER Anglo-Saxon *Scylan* To divide.
The shoulders are the point at which the arms divide from the body.

SHOULDER-BLADE German *Blatt* A leaf.
The derivation is an allusion to the bone's broad, flat surface.

SIERRA Spanish *Sierra* Saw.
The word is applied to mountain ranges such as the Sierra Nevada, on account of their jagged peaks' resemblance to the teeth of a saw.

SIESTA Spanish *Sesta* Sixth hour.
The midday nap takes place during the sixth hour of daylight.

SIN Latin *Sons* Guilty.

SINISTER Latin *Sinister* On the left side.
The Romans always entered the houses of friends with their right foot first, because the left side of the body was associated with evil and was therefore sinister.

SIRLOIN French *Sur* Upon or above and *Longe* Loin.
This cut of meat is taken from below the ribs and above the loins. Samuel Johnson was the first to spell the word sirloin,

probably having been taken in by claims of King James I knighting a piece of meat. According to this folk etymology, while being entertained at Hoghton Tower near Blackburn, the king exclaimed, 'Bring hither the sirloin, for it is worthy of a more honourable post, being, as I may say, not sirloin, but Sir Loin – the noblest joint of all!' In actuality, the word *surlonge* had entered the language during the reign of James's predecessor, Queen Elizabeth I.

SKEDADDLE Greek *Skedannumi* To retire tumultuously.
The word skedaddle originated in America, in the nineteenth century, describing a hasty retreat.

SKI Old Norse *Skith* Snowshoe, length of wood.
Skiing is Scandinavian in origin, only being introduced elsewhere for recreational purposes in the early twentieth century.

SKILL Old Norse *Skil* Discernment.
A person said to be skilful was one who could accurately distinguish between different things of a given class.

SKINFLINT In Old England, having walls made of flint blocks was a sign of affluence. In order to imitate it, poor people who were unable to afford whole blocks would 'skin the flint', that is face walls made of ordinary bricks with thinner pieces of flint. Hence people who were loath or unable to spend money were referred to as skinflints.

SKIP Norse *Skopa* To run.
History does not relate why the usually ferocious Norsemen were inclined to run in this way.

SKIRT Norse *Skyrta* A shirt.

SKY Swedish *Sky* Cloud.

Originally sky referred not to the upper atmosphere but to the cloud formations lower down.

SLAVE Old French *Esclave* Slav.

The people of Slovenia were so frequently captured and enslaved by other Europeans that their name became synonymous with slavery.

SLEAZY Latvian *Silesian* From Silesia.

The large area of central Europe known as Silesia was once noted for fine-quality fabrics that were often shipped out of the Baltic ports of Latvia. When poor-quality imitations began arriving the Latvians coined the derogatory term sleazy.

SMITH Saxon *Schmeid* Smite.

A smith or blacksmith smites hot metal on an anvil with a hammer. The word was later used to describe any type of craftsman such as goldsmith, silversmith, tinsmith, locksmith and even wordsmith, but smith on its own, or smithy, always refers to the original blacksmith or metalworker. After the Norman Conquest, the French *Carpentier* Carpenter was introduced for woodworkers, who had previously been known as woodsmiths.

SNAIL Old English *Snaca* Snake, creeping thing.

The term was also once used to describe slugs.

SNIP Anglo-Saxon *Snippe* or *Snibbe* The bill of a bird.

To snip something is to cut it with scissors, similar to the action of a bird's beak.

SNOB Latin *Sine Nobilitate* Without nobility.

Those who were not of noble birth were listed in college registers as *s.nob*, an abbreviation of *Sine nobilitate*. Thus it has become a label for anyone who strives to associate with those of a higher social class. *See also Nob.*

SNOOKER Derives from the military slang for a newly joined cadet. The game was invented by British officers stationed in India as an alternative to billiards.

SOCCER Abbreviation of *Association*, from Football Association (FA), in much the same way as rugger is the slang term for rugby. *See also Cricket and Rugby.*

SOCIAL Latin *Socius* A companion.

SOFA Arabic *Suffa* A bench.

SOLDIER There are two possible derivations suggested for this word. One is that it comes from Latin *Sal dare* To give salt, since early Roman soldiers were certainly paid in salt as it was considered a scarce but essential part of their diet without which their health would be threatened. A more likely possibility, however, is that it comes from the *solidus*, a solid gold coin first introduced by Emperor Diocletian in AD 301 with which soldiers were paid. *See also Salary.*

SOMBRERO Spanish *Sombra* Shade.
A hat with a particularly wide rim, much used to provide shade in sunny climates such as Mexico.

SOMERSAULT Old French *Sobresault* from Latin *Supra* Above and Latin *Saltus* Leap.

SOPRANO Latin *Supra* Above.
The Soprano sings with a voice above all others.

SOUFFLÉ Latin *Sufflare* To blow.
Food with air blown into it by being whisked into a froth.

SOUTH Germanic *Sunnon* Sun and the region of the sun.
  To northern European observers, the sun is always in the south of the sky. *See also North, East, and West.*

SOUTHPAW American. This term for a lefthander originated in baseball. Most pitches are arranged so that the batter faces east, thus avoiding the sun in his eyes during the afternoon, when most games are played. The pitcher or bowler therefore faces west, and if he is a lefthander, with the ball in his left hand or left paw, he holds it on the south side of his body. *See also Awkward and Gawky.*

SOVEREIGN Italian *Sovrano* Above and Latin *Regno* To govern.
  A sovereign is above the government. The term was first used to describe a gold coin by King Henry VII (reigned 1485–1509), due to its great size and importance.

SPAGHETTI Italian *Spago* Cord.
  Spago means a cord of any size, so spaghetti are tiny cords.

SPANIEL Spanish *Hispaniola* The West Indies, where this breed of dog originated.

SPHINX Greek *Sphingein* Bind.
  The mythological sphinx is a creature that is formed by joining, or binding together, the body of a lion, the wings of a bird and usually the head of a woman.

SPIDER German *Spinne* To spin.
  Spiders spin webs. A cobweb is derived from Old English *Coppe* Spider. *See also Spinster.*

SPINACH Arabic *Hispanach* The Spanish plant.
  The first known mention of spinach is in *Turner's Herbal* of 1568, where it is described as 'a herb lately found and not much in use'.

SPINNEY Latin *Spina* Thorn.

A spinney is a small woodland, very often with thorny shrubs and bushes.

SPINSTER German *Spinne* To spin.

It was once said that a young woman should never be married until she had spun herself a complete set of linens, for herself, for her table and for her bed. As a result, it was fairly common to see unmarried women spinning away. Hence they were known as spinners or spinsters. *See also Spider.*

SPLENDID Latin *Splendeo* To shine.

SPRITZER German *Spritzen* To squirt.

A spritzer is a measure of wine and a squirt of soda water.

SPUTNIK Russian *Sputnik* Travelling companion.

The Russian satellite *Sputnik 1*, launched in 1957, was the first man-made object to orbit the earth.

SQUASH Narragansett (Rhode Island) *Ascutaquash* Pumpkin.

A North American plant with a particularly difficult name, the early settlers renamed it the squash. It is unclear why they did not call it a pumpkin as that word is European, being derived from the Greek *Peopon* Large melon.

SQUIRREL Greek *Skiouros* Shadow tailed.

Squirrels have large tails which they can use to shade the rest of their bodies when it gets hot.

STADIUM A Greek racecourse of 607 feet. The first to be built was at Olympia, where the original Olympic Games were held.

STAGNANT Latin *Stagnum* A pond or pool.
Stagnation rarely occurs in bodies of water larger than ponds as there is more opportunity for movement.

STAIR Anglo-Saxon *Astigha* Mounting, climbing up.

STALACTITE Greek *Stalaktos* Dropping.
Stalactites are rock formations that 'drop down' from the ceilings of caverns. They are created by particles of rock held in the water that remain behind when the water drops from the ceiling. A stalagmite is the opposite formation, created by particles of rock still held in the water after it has dropped off the end of the stalactite down on to the floor where it slowly accumulates to form a pillar.

STAMPEDE Spanish *Estampida* A crush.
A stampede is a panic-stricken rush of animals or people that may well result in participants being crushed.

STARBOARD Old English *Styri* Rudder.
Before ships had fixed rudders they were steered with very large oars held over the stern of the ship. These tended to be on the right side of the ship as that was most convenient for the majority of sailors, who were right-handed. Port, the left side of the ship, is derived from the usual practice of docking in a port with that side of the ship alongside the quay, thereby ensuring that the steering oar on the starboard side was not crushed against the harbour wall. *See also Stern.*

STARCH Old English *Sterchan* To stiffen.
Starch is a thickening agent used in cooking, paper manufacturing and to stiffen formal clothes.

STARVE Anglo-Saxon *Steorfan* To die, not necessarily from starvation.

Thus when Chaucer wrote in *Troilus and Criseyde* about people starving he meant that they died but not from lack of food.

STEAK Norse *Steik* To roast.

STEEPLECHASE Horse races used to take place on unmarked courses between towns and with prominent church steeples very often marking the finishing point.

STEGOSAURUS Greek *Stego* Roof and *Saurus* Lizard.
This dinosaur is so named because of the bone plates that lined its spine and which might be described as a 'roof' in the same way that a snail's shell might be viewed as its 'house'. *See also Dinosaur.*

STEPFATHER Anglo-Saxon *Stoep* Bereaved.
The prefix *step-*, when applied to father, mother, son, etc., reflects the lack of blood relation.

STERLING A corruption of German *Easterling*.
A name given to money from the Hanseatic towns, which was highly regarded for the purity of the metal used in the coins. Indeed, so poor was the quality of English money during the reign of Richard I that it was often stipulated that payments be made in *easterling*.

STERN As in severe. Old English *Austern* Austere.

STERN As in the back of a ship. Norse *Stjorn* Steering.
Ships are steered from the stern. *See also Starboard.*

STET Latin *Stet* Let it stand.
The word is used when a correction is made that should not have been. Stet is an instruction to the printer to ignore the correction and let the typesetting stand as it once was.

STETHOSCOPE Greek *Stethos* Chest and *Skopeein* To examine.
Stethoscopes were invented in France in the nineteenth century to investigate conditions in the chest.

STEWARD Anglo-Saxon *Stiward*, from *Sti* A house and *Ward* A guardian as in a ward of court.

STIMULATE Latin *Stimulus* A goad or spur.
There was nothing like a spur to stimulate a horse into action.

STINK Anglo-Saxon *Stenc* Fragrance.
The word originally described pleasant aromas. Stench is from the same source.

STINGY Anglo-Saxon *Skinch* To give short measure or to squeeze out in driblets.

STIRRUP Old English *Stig* To mount and *Rap* A rope.
Stirrups, the means by which a rider mounts up into the saddle, were originally fixed to either end of a rope across the horse's back. The earliest horsemen did not use stirrups but the invention proved crucial when horses were first used in warfare as they enabled the rider to turn in his saddle and fight without falling off. The derivation shows that to start with they were an aid to climbing into the saddle rather than a means of providing stability to the rider.

STOMACH Greek *Stomakhos* Gullet.
Tummy is a child's way of simplifying the word stomach.

STRANGLE Greek *Strangos* Twisted.
A twisted ligature is the most effective method of strangulation, whether a scarf as used by the thugees or a mechanical garotte as used in executions. *See also Thug*.

STRATEGY Greek *Strategos* A general, from *Statos* Army and *Aegin* To lead.

STRING Latin *Stringo* To draw tight.
Stringent, meaning adhering tightly to rules, is from the same root.

STYLE Latin *Stylus* A pencil.
The word style was originally applied only to the appearance and design of the written word such as would be created by a pencil.

SUBURB Latin *Sub* Under and *Urbs* City.
Rome was built on seven hills, and the outskirts of the city, mainly outside the city wall, were therefore below the level or 'under' the central urban part of the city. *See also Palace.*

SUCCUMB Latin *Cumbere* To lie down.
Physically giving way to overwhelming pressure results in lying down, sometimes even to die.

SUEDE French *Suède* Sweden.
The earliest trade route for the soft leather was from Sweden to France, where it was used in the manufacture of gloves.

SUFFRAGE Latin *Suffragium* Voting tablet.
In Rome votes were recorded on tablets of stone or wood. The process of voting is therefore closely connected to the tablet or *suffragium* so much so that the right to vote became known as suffrage. The term suffragette was coined in a disapproving English newspaper by feminising suffrage, the right to vote, with the feminine suffix 'ette'. But instead of the word remaining a derogatory expression as intended, it was adopted by the campaigners who achieved female suffrage in Britain in 1928.

SUGAR Entering the English language from Sanskrit *Sharkara*, through Persian and Arabic *Shakar*, through Italian *Zucchero* and French *Sucre*, the etymology of this word follows the proliferation of the commodity it describes and is a perfect example of a word's migratory habits through many languages before reaching English.

SUNDAY *See Days of the Week.*

SURLY Anglo-Saxon *Sur* Sour and *Lic* Like.
From this we get sour-like, which was later contracted to surly.

SURRENDER French *Se rendre* To yield oneself.

SWAN Old English *Geswin* Singing bird, an illusion to the song, the swansong, that the birds are supposed to sing before death, an expression that now describes any final performance.

SWASTIKA Sanskrit *Svasti* Well-being.
The cross with arms turning at right angles to each other is one of the most ancient good-luck symbols known to man, evidence of its use dating back to Neanderthal times. It features heavily in Hindu and Buddhist cultures and was in use throughout Europe in flags, coats of arms and mosaic decoration until its adoption by the Nazi Party, at which point its popularity and usage understandably decreased. The title pages of books about India by Rudyard Kipling (1865–1936) were decorated with swastikas, not something that would have been done after 1939. *See also Nazi.*

SYNAGOGUE Greek *Syn* Together and *Agoge* Gathering.
Originally called *Beth Keneseth* House of Assembly by the Hebrews, but was changed with the translation of the Old Testament into Greek.

SYNTAX Greek *Syn* Together and *Tassein* To arrange in order. Syntax is the structuring of words and language into correct sequences.

T

TABBY Arabic *Attabiya* A district of old Baghdad where a patterned silk with stripes resembling those of a tabby cat was made.

TABOO Tongan (Polynesian) *Tapu* Forbidden.
Captain Cook brought the word back to Britain after being impressed by the constraint that the inhabitants of Tonga, or the Friendly Islands as he named them, had shown when faced with various practices and customs which they had declared taboo.

TACKY Archaic slang *Tackey* A small and therefore inferior horse. It now refers to any cheap and corny goods.

TANDEM Latin *Tandem* At length.
Originally referring to a carriage pulled by two horses going in single file, tied one behind the other, and now mainly used to describe a bicycle made for two where the riders sit one behind the other. *See also Bicycle.*

TANTALISE From the Greek mythological tale of Tantalus, who, afflicted with constant thirst, was submerged up to his chin in water and rendered unable to drink it. A tantalus is a case or stand for a collection of decanters, glass containers for wine or spirits.

TARAMASALATA Greek *Taramas* Salted roe of cod and *Salata* Salad.

TARANTULA This poisonous spider takes its name from *Taranto*, a port in southern Italy. Although they have now worked their way further north, at one time tarantulas were relatively unknown in Europe, being present only in the southernmost parts of the continent, where they probably arrived on ships from Africa. It was believed in Doctor Johnson's time, and for a significant period afterwards, that the tarantula's bite could 'only be cured by music'. This cure is most likely to be related to the relaxation of the heart rate that can be achieved by listening to soothing music which in turn limits the flow of poison in the bloodstream.

TARIFF Berber Tariq ibn Ziyad was a general in the Muslim army that conquered North Africa in AD 710 and was then sent across the Strait of Gibraltar to reconnoitre possibilities of invading Europe as well. He created a settlement in the southernmost point of Spain which was named Tarifa in his honour. Later, in command of the Moorish army (Latin *Mauri* The tribe that inhabited the Roman province of Mauretania), he conquered most of Iberia. Tariffs were charges imposed at Tarifa on shipping passing through the Strait of Gibraltar. *See also Gibraltar.*

TARPAULIN A corruption of 'tarred palling'.
A pall is a cloth covering for something, such as a funeral pall over a coffin. A tarpaulin is a cloth covering which has been waterproofed with tar.

TATTOO Interestingly, both senses of this word have a similar, onomatopoeic derivation. In the military sense the word is derived from Dutch *Tap-too*, the drumbeat that called soldiers back to their barracks after the gin shops had closed. Later the word came to mean a gathering of troops for more sober activities such as marching to military bands. In its other sense, the marking the skin with ink, the word comes from Polynesian *Ta-ta-u* Hand colour, mimicking the repetitive tapping action of the hand in the application of ink. Tattoos in this latter sense were an indication of rank, as well as tokens of bravery and religious or personal devotion. The practice became popular in Europe after early explorers arrived home with tattoos they had acquired while visiting Pacific Islands.

TAVERN Latin *Taberna* A hut.
This word shares the same root as Latin *Tabernaculum* Tabernacle, the portable temple in which the Israelites carried the Ark of the Covenant.

TAWDRY The word derives from St Audrey, or to give her proper name Etheldreda, who was Abbess of Ely in the seventh century. Lace sold at a fair in Ely on St Audrey's day fell out of fashion and was eventually considered tasteless, particularly by the Puritans, who rejected all forms of adornment and gave it the derogatory name tawdry.

TAXIDERMY Greek *Taxis* An arrangement and *Derma* Skin.
Taxidermy is the skilful arranging and preservation of the skin of a dead animal.

TAXI Latin *Taxa* Charge and Greek *Metron* Measure.
A taximeter cab is a vehicle in which the charge is recorded by a measuring device. *See also Cab.*

TEEPEE Lakota (Sioux) *Tipi* Dwelling.
A teepee is a conical tent constructed with poles and either hide or canvas that could easily be moved as the nomadic North American tribes moved across the plains. A wigwam is a more solid construction with a thatched, domed roof giving the appearance of an igloo and was erected for use over a longer period. *See also Igloo.*

TEETOTAL Total, with the initial letter doubled for emphasis. One who abstains absolutely from alcohol, although its derivation suggests that it could also be used to describe any totality.

TELEPHONE Greek *Tele* Far and *Phone* Voice. *See also Cacophony.*

TEMPERANCE Latin *Temperantia* Moderation.
Temperance is one of the four cardinal virtues, the others being prudence, justice and courage. The Temperance movement, however, campaigned not for moderation in the consumption of alcohol but for its outright prohibition.

TERRIER Old French *Chien Terrier* Earth Dog.
A terrier is a small dog trained to flush foxes and badgers from their holes underground.

TEXT Latin *Textum* To weave, as in to create.
A text is a group of words that have been woven into sentences.

THEATRE Greek *Theasthai* To view.
The theatre is now usually a place to see dramatic performances, but at one time it was a place to see anything. For example, an operating theatre is a room where surgery takes place and medical students gather to view and to learn. *See also Audience.*

THIGH Anglo-Saxon *Theo* To swell.
The thighs are the thickest or most swollen part of the leg.

THIMBLE A corruption of thumb bell, since the thumb was where sail makers wore them.

THRASHING When a father threatened to give his naughty son a good thrashing he was unconsciously alluding to threshing, the ancient practice of using a flail consisting of a hinged piece of wood to strike corn and remove the grain. *See also Threshold.*

THRESHOLD Old English *Therscold* To thresh.

Threshing is the task of trampling cut corn to detach the grain from the straw. A threshold, the doorway of a building, is likely to be trampled more than any other part of the house. The second meaning, a significant moment, a new opening that ushers in a new start in a series of events (as in 'he was on the threshold of a great discovery'), stems from the first.

THROMBOSIS Greek *Thrombosis* Curdling.

Curdling is the process of thickening milk, the start of cheese making and other processes. A thrombosis is likewise a thickening of the blood that causes a clot.

THUG Hindi *Thag* Thief.

The thuggees were a network of thieves and bandits who preyed on travellers in India from the seventeenth to the nineteenth century. Hence the word *thug* entered the English language during the colonial era. *See also Strangle.*

THURSDAY *See Days of the Week.*

THYME Greek *Thyein* To burn a sacrifice.

Thyme had great religious significance as well as being used for embalming, incense and a variety of medicinal purposes.

TIDDLY Slang for slightly drunk.

TIDDLYWINK Slang for an unlicensed public house, where the game was often played.

TINNITUS Latin *Tinnire* To ring.

Tinnitus is a condition of the ear that artificially generates a constant ringing sensation.

TIP Originally written on tip boxes as TIP, an acronym meaning To Insure Promptness.

TIPSTAFF The attendant officer to a judge is so called because of his staff, which is tipped with a gold or silver crown.

TITHE Old English *Teotha* A tenth part.
A tithe is a tax that requires one-tenth of the produce grown by a tenant to be paid to the landlord, who would then store it in a tithe barn. *See also Farm.*

TOAST The practice of proposing a toast to someone's good health was originally restricted to that of beautiful or popular women. Bread that had been toasted and flavoured with spices was added to the wine, so that after raising a glass to the woman in question, it would seem as though her mere presence had improved its taste when sipped. The practice of clinking glasses together that often accompanies a toast derives from a much earlier, more discourteous time when, in order to put everyone at ease, Viking feasts would begin with the slamming together of goblets. The contents of one would splash and mingle with everyone else's, thus sharing around any poison that had been added to a particular drink, so it worked as a deterrent to prevent one man poisoning another.

TOBACCO Arawak (Northern South American and Caribbean) *Tobago* Smoking pipe, rolled tobacco leaves.
Though credited with introducing tobacco from the New World, Sir Walter Raleigh was not the first to discover it. Almost a century earlier, Columbus named the island of Tobago after the plant, having been astonished to find people smoking there.

TOBOGGAN Algonquin (central North America around the Great Lakes and eastern Canada) *Toboggan*. This was the language of tribes such as the Cree in modern-day Canada.

A toboggan has a flat base with a curved front so that it rides with its full width over the snow. A sleigh or sledge, Norse *Sled* To slide, differs in that it has two runners.

TOIL Anglo-Saxon *Tilian* To till.
Tilling the ground with the primitive implements of the Anglo-Saxons must have been exceedingly hard work. Hence the adapted term is now applied to any arduous task.

TOMATO Nahuatl (Aztec) *Xitomatl* Plump thing with a bellybutton.
The Spanish brought tomatoes to Europe and the first Englishman to cultivate the plant was John Gerard, author of *Gerard's Herbal* in 1597.

TOMB Greek *Tumbos* A burial mound under which were buried the ashes of a cremated corpse. The Latin *tumulus* is from the same root.

TORNADO Latin *Tonare* To turn.
A tornado is a rotating storm. From the same derivation we get tourniquet, a ligature that is tightened by turning to stem the flow of blood.

TORPEDO Latin *Torpere* To stun.
Electric eels belong to the order *Torpediniformes*, and the naval weapons took their name from the species. In his dictionary, Dr Johnson noted that the 'fish, while alive, if touched even with a long stick, benumbs the hand that so touches it, but when dead is eaten safely'.

TORTURE Latin *Tortum* To twist.
Twisting of body parts often played a part in the torture chamber. The same root explains the word tortuous, meaning twisted but without being connected to torture.

TORY Gaelic *Tar a Ri* 'Come O King'.

The first Tories were the Irish supporters of the exiled King Charles II during the Cromwellian era. The cry was so frequently on their lips that it was adopted as the name for their movement.

TOWEL French *Touaille* Linen cloth.

TOWN Anglo-Saxon *Tune* A hedge or fence.

All early settlements were surrounded by defensive fortifications, meaning that the first thing visitors came across was a hedge or fence. Hence the word was given to the group of dwellings within. *See also Wall.*

TOXIC Greek *Toxikon* Poison used on arrows, from *Toxon* Arrow. *See also Arrowoot.*

TRASH Norwegian *Trask* Fine brushwood, such as the clippings of trees and hedges, too fine to be used for firewood.

Unscrupulous firewood traders would swell the size of their bundles by padding the middle with this worthless *trash*. Hence the word is used nowadays to describe anything deemed worthless, while in some parts of Britain the original meaning is preserved through *brash*, a combination of branch and trash, which is specifically applied to useless brushwood.

TRAUMA Greek *Trauma* A wound.

TREACHERY Norman English *Treacher* A traitor.

TREACLE Latin *Theriaca* Antidote to poison.

Treacle was originally a thick, syrupy medicine prepared as a treatment for snake bites. The word was also applied to the curative ingredients of water in what became known as spa towns. Springs or wells from which this water was obtained were called treacle wells, made famous by Lewis Carroll's

Alice's Adventures in Wonderland in which Dormouse claimed he had friends who lived in a treacle well, but by that time the medicinal origins had largely been forgotten, making it an absurd idea well suited to the story. *See also Dormouse.*

TREASURE Latin *Thesaurus* Storehouse.
A treasury is a storehouse for money and a thesaurus was a storehouse for any treasure. The popularity of *Roget's Thesaurus* has largely caused the word's meaning to be used exclusively for a storehouse of definitions, synonyms and antonyms.

TREK Africaans *Trekken* To haul.
This word was used by Dutch settlers in South Africa who undertook long, arduous journeys from the coast inland to find farmland suitable for settlement. The terrain over which they travelled invariably meant they had to haul their carts manually.

TREMBLE Latin *Tremulus* To shake.

TRENCHER Old French *Trenchier* To cut.
In the Middle Ages, slabs of old bread that were thick and stale enough to cut something on were often used as meat plates and were called trenchers. After a meal, the used bread would then be given to peasants or dogs. Later the word described wooden platters on which whole meals were served without being changed between courses. A trencherman is one who is a heavy feeder and is probably not too concerned about how the food is served. A trench, a cut in the ground, derives from the same root – an example of one root providing two unconnected English words.

TRESS Greek *Trikhia* Rope.
A tress is a lock of hair that has been divided into three and braided so that it resembles rope. *See also Twine.*

TRIGGER Dutch *Trekken* To pull.

TRIM Old English *Trymman* Strengthen.

To trim a lamp or candle wick is to cut away unwanted and burnt sections in order to strengthen that which remains.

TROUSSEAU Old French *Truss* Bundle.

A trousseau is the small bundle in which a bride carries her possessions to her new home after marriage. *See also Paraphernalia.*

TROUT Greek *Trogein* To nibble.

Though a perceptive glimpse of every fisherman's dream, the derivation actually comes from the grazing habits of the fish.

TRIVIAL Latin *Trivialis*, from *Tri* Three and *Via* Road.

Trivialis referred to a place where three or more roads met and where people were likely to gather to discuss matters of little consequence.

TRUNK As in an Elephant's trunk. Old English *Trump* as in trumpet since an elephant uses his trunk to trumpet. The French retain *la trompe* but in English this has evolved into the less suitable trunk.

TRUTH Anglo-Saxon *Triewth* Faithfulness.

TSUNAMI Japanese *Tsu* Harbour and *Nami* Wave.

Enormous and destructive waves used to be called tidal waves, but since it is now realised that they are not caused by tidal movements that name has lapsed. Tsunamis are caused by the displacement of sea water by earthquake or volcanic eruptions.

TUESDAY *See Days of the Week.*

TUMBLER A tumbler was originally a glass or other drinking vessel that had a rounded bottom which prevented the drinker from laying it down until they had drained the last drop. In other words, they are glasses that tumble as they cannot stand upright.

TUNDRA Lapp *Tundar* Elevated wasteland.

The word refers to the permanently frozen subsoil of the Arctic regions.

TURKEY Early settlers in America wrongly identified the native bird as a guineafowl, believing it to be the same as the European turkey, a type of guineafowl so called because it was originally imported from Africa via Turkey. The popularity of the American bird has resulted in it becoming the sole possessor of the name.

TURNCOAT This label for traitors originated from Savoy, where the armies of the first duke considered it prudent to alternate their support between the French and the Spanish, both of whom had designs on his dukedom and could easily have overwhelmed him with superior forces. To successfully maintain this flux of allegiance, it was sometimes necessary for his troops to wear the blue uniforms of the Spanish and on other occasions the white ones of the French. The duke therefore designed a coat with a different colour on either side that could be reversed, or turned, as it became politically prudent to do so.

TURNIP Anglo-Saxon *Næpe* Neep.

The turnip looks as though it is a neep that has been turned on a lathe. *See also Parsnip.*

TURNPIKE The barriers on main roads where tolls were levied invariably consisted of a series of pikes on a pivot that could be swivelled, or turned, to open the road to a traveller who had paid his dues. Something similar is still seen at football stadiums and railway stations.

TURQUOISE French *Turquois* Turkish.

Though actually mined in the Middle East, Iran and Sinai, this blue-green stone was named by Europeans after the Turkish bazaars at which it was purchased.

TUTTI FRUTTI Italian *Tutti* All and *Frutti* Fruits.

TWENTY, THIRTY, ETC. The *-ty* suffix in these words is from the Anglo-Saxon *tig*, ten. Twenty is *twaintig*, two tens; thirty is *thritig*, three tens, etc.

TWILIGHT Anglo-Saxon *Tweon* Between and *Leoht* Light. Originally the word was *tween-light*.

TWINE Old English *Twin* Twin.
    Twine is composed of two cords twisted together. Thread, Old English *Thre* Three, on the other hand, signifies three cords twisted together. *See also Tress.*

TYCOON Japanese *Tai* Great and *Kun* Lord or Prince, referring to the shogun or commander-in-chief of the army.
    More recently the military connection has been lost and it now refers to captains of industry.

TYMPANUM Greek *Typtein* To strike.
    Tympani are kettle drums in an orchestra and the tympanic membrane is the eardrum.

TYPHOON Mandarin *Tai* Great and *Fung* Wind.
    Typhoons are tropical cyclones in the north-western Pacific. Variations of the word appear in Cantonese, Arabic and Greek. It arrived in western Europe with early explorers such as Vasco da Gama (1469–1524).

U

UMBRELLA Latin *Umbella*, from *Umbra* Shade.
    In the sunnier Mediterranean area, umbrellas would have been used rather more to provide shade from the sun than for protection against the rain.

UMPIRE Old French *Non* Not and *Per* Pair.

An umpire is someone who is not paired with either party in a contest and is therefore able to provide an impartial verdict.

UNION JACK French *Jaque* A jacket.

The national flag of England, the cross of St George, was embroidered on to the coats of English infantrymen so that they could be identified in battle. This embroidered coat came to be known as the 'jack'. When Scotland and Wales united with England to form the British Isles, the jack was amended to include the colours of their flags and henceforth became known as the Union Jack.

URANUS Greek *Ouranos* Heaven and the God of Heaven.

The planet was discovered by British astronomer Sir William Herschel (1738–1822), and was named after him by the French, despite the fact that he himself had suggested naming it Georgius Sidus (George's Star) after his patron, King George III, in whose 'auspicious reign the star began to shine'.

URCHIN Old English *Yrichon* Hedgehog.

Hence the spiny globular sea creatures that resemble hedgehogs are called sea urchins. Young people who are unkempt, dishevelled and very likely with uncombed hair resemble hedgehogs and are also known as urchins.

URL An acronym for *U*niform *R*esource *L*ocator, the term used to refer to a web address in general.

UTOPIA Greek *Ou* not and *Topos* a place.

A word thought to have been coined by Sir Thomas More (1478–1535) for use as the title of his book in which he described a perfect society in order to draw attention to shortcomings in the current style of government. Of course, this was not a place that could ever exist.

V

VACATION Latin *Vacare* Empty, at leisure.
Days that are empty of responsibility. *See also Vacuum.*

VACCINE Latin *Vacca* Cow.
A vaccine is a means of introducing a mild dose of a disease sufficient to induce immunity. Edward Jenner (1749–1823) noticed that milkmaids, who were constantly touching cows, did not suffer from smallpox but did catch the far less virulent disease cowpox and from this he deduced that the latter was producing immunity to the former. *See also Inoculation.*

VACUUM Latin *Vacare* Empty.
A vacuum is created when a vessel is emptied, even to the exclusion of air. *See also Vacation.*

VAGABOND Latin *Vagari* To wander.
Vagabonds and vagrants are impoverished people who wander for lack of homes. *See also Extravagant.*

VANDAL The Vandals were a tribe from Germany who invaded the Roman Empire and, most famously, sacked Rome in AD 455, showing their revulsion for the clean living and cultured inhabitants by wantonly destroying buildings and works of art. Since then the word has described anyone who deliberately destroys someone else's property.

VANILLA Spanish *Vainilla* Little pod.
Vanilla is a member of the orchid family. *See also Orchid.*

VALENTINE Little is known about St Valentine, but one theory claims that he secretly married young men to their lovers having been forbidden from doing so by Roman Emperor Claudius II, who believed that single young men made better soldiers. When his dissension was discovered, St Valentine was thrown in jail and on the night before his execution is reputed to have sent a note to his own beloved, signing off with that immortal cliché, 'From your Valentine.'

VALOUR Latin *Valere* To be strong.

VAMPIRE Magyar (Hungarian) *Vampir* Witch.

VARNISH Middle Latin *Vernix* Odorous resin, from Greek *Verenike*, from *Berenike*, the name of an ancient Egyptian queen, and the Libyan city named in her honour credited with the use of the first varnishes (modern-day Benghazi).

VASECTOMY Latin *Vas* Tube or vessel and *Ectomy* Excision, removal by cutting.
An appendectomy, for another example, is the removal by cutting of the appendix.

VELLUM Old French and Norman *Veel*, *veau* Calf.
Vellum refers to a type of fine parchment that was made from the skin of a calf. It has the same root as veal.

VENISON Latin *Venare* To hunt. Latin *Ventionem* A hunt.
Venison was the meat obtained by hunting and originally referred to any meat of large game, such as deer or boar. *See also Humble Pie.*

VENTRILOQUISM Latin *Venter* Stomach and *Loqui* To speak.
A ventriloquist entertains his audience by deceiving them into believing that his voice is coming from his dummy and not from his own mouth. To achieve this he must not move his lips and instead must speak from further down inside his body.

VERGER A verge is a staff carried as a mark of authority. The verger of a cathedral carries the mace or verge of the dean.

VERMICELLI Latin *Vermiculus* Little worm.

An allusion to the worm-like appearance of this delicate pasta.

VERMIN Latin *Vermis* Worm.

The first creatures to be described as vermin were worm-like larvae that infested food. Now it describes any animal that becomes a nuisance, whether a worm or something far larger like a mouse or a rat.

VERMOUTH German *Wermuth* Wormwood.

Antonio Bendetto Carpano, the Italian inventor of vermouth, was inspired by a German wine containing wormwood. Hence he honoured the herb by naming his new concoction after it.

VERTEBRA Latin *Vertere* To turn. The vertebral column is able to bend, twist and turn.

VEST Latin *Vestis* A gown.

Samuel Pepys wrote that King Charles II popularised the simple sleeveless garment to teach the nobility to be thrifty. *See also Vestry.*

VESTRY Latin *Vestarium* A room attached to a church used by the priest for storing his vestments. *See also Vest.*

VIGNETTE Latin *Vinea* Vine. Small decorative paintings.

The first capital letters of ancient manuscripts were so called on account of them being ornamented with flourishes reminiscent of vine branches.

VIKING Anglo-Saxon *Wicing* A pirate.

Vikings derived their name from *viks*, or coastal inlets, in which they hid. The element *vik* appears in many Icelandic coastal place names, such as Reykjavik, Húsavík and Keflavik, as well as one town simply called Vik.

VINEGAR French *Vin* Wine and *Aigre* Sour or rough.
See also Eager.

VISCOUNT The title of 'count' was given to a nobleman entrusted with the administration of a county. His deputy was therefore referred to as a 'vice count', which was reduced to viscount. In Britain counts are now called earls, from the Norse *Jarl* Chieftain, but their wives are still called countesses.

VISCOUS Latin *Viscum* Mistletoe.
A sticky viscous glue-like substance called birdlime was made from mistletoe to be spread on branches to catch birds. The word was later applied to any sticky substance.

VITAMIN Latin *Vita* Life and *Amine* Containing amino acids.
The word was coined as vitamine in 1912 by Polish biochemist Casimir Funk (1884–1967), but with the discovery that vitamins did not in fact contain amino acids, the 'e' was dropped and the term became vitamin.

VODKA Russian *Vodit* To dilute with water.
The spirit, often used in pharmaceuticals, was also known as the 'vodka of bread wine', a diluted version of a spirit made from grain.

VOLCANO Latin *Vulcan* The Roman god of fire, forges and volcanoes. The equivalent god in Greek mythology is Hephaestus.

VOLUME Latin *Volumen*, from *Volvo* To roll.
Before books were bound with pages, ancient volumes were simply long, narrow strips of parchment or papyrus that were rolled up when not in use. *See also Book and Vellum.*

VOYAGE Latin *Via* A way and *Ago* To pursue.
A voyage once described a journey by land as well as by sea. This meaning has been preserved in the French language, as in the

phrase '*Bon Voyage*', to bid farewell and good luck to someone embarking on a journey whether it be on land or sea.

VULGAR Latin *Vulgaris* Common.
The original meaning did not signify something objectionable, but something that was ordinary. Vulgar Latin, for instance, was simply the dialect that was most commonly spoken.

W

WAGE Middle English from Old Norman *Wage* Pledge.
An employer pledges to pay a wage when work is completed. *See also Salary.*

WAIFS AND STRAYS Anglo-Norman *Waif* Ownerless property and *Estrayer* Stray livestock.
This expression is now normally applied to abandoned children, or people with very slender, child-like bodies, but the origin of these words shows that this was not always so. A waif was a stolen object that had been abandoned by the thief, whereas a stray was a domesticated animal that had strayed from its owner's premises. Waifs and strays became the property of the Crown until rightful ownership had been satisfactorily proved.

WAIST Old English *Waest* Growth.
So called, perhaps, because this is where one's body is most likely to expand.

WAKE As in a funeral gathering. Old English *Wacu* Watch, as in guard.
The wake, originally the period before a funeral, is when the deceased is guarded or watched over in their home. Now invariably and inaccurately used to describe a gathering after the burial when it is no longer possible to watch over the deceased.

WALL Latin *Vallum* Rampart.

Cities were once surrounded by rampart fortifications for defence against invasion. The most usual form of rampart was a stone wall. *See also Town.*

WALNUT A corruption of Gall- or Wall-nut; the nut of Gaul, or France. *Gallia* and *Wallia* were interchangeable in reference to the country.

WALRUS Old Norse *Hrosshvalr* Horse-whale.

This entered into Old English as *Horschvael*, which has been reversed to *vael-Horsch* and corrupted to walrus. *See also Hippopotamus.*

WAR German *Werra* To quarrel.

WATERSHED German *Scheide* To divide.

A watershed is the divide between the catchment areas of two river systems.

WAVER Old Norse *Vafra* To flicker as a candle flame.

WEDNESDAY *See Days of the Week.*

WEED Old English *Woed* A herb.

What a turnaround, from a herb, the icing on the culinary cake, to the popular derogatory term for a plant in the wrong place.

WELCOME Anglo-Saxon *Wil* Well and *Coma* Someone who comes. *Wilcoma* was only used to welcome visitors who were gladly or well received. It was never applied to objects or concepts such as a welcome gift.

WELD A corruption of *Welled*, from *Well* To boil.

Welding involves heating metal until it 'boils' when it can be fixed to other pieces in a similar state.

WELLINGTONS The long waterproof boots were not invented by the Duke of Wellington but he did popularise them, rarely being seen without a pair. When mounted he wore a pair with the back removed at the top for comfort when his knees were bent.

WENCH Old English *Wenchel* Child and *Wancol* Fickle, weak.
Now applied only to young women whose weakness has led to loose morals.

WEST Latin *Vesper* Evening. The sun sets in the west.
Vespers is the evening service held as the sun sets. *See also North, East and South.*

WHORE Norse *Hore* Adulteress.

WHIPPERSNAPPER This term was applied in the seventeenth century to young loiterers on street corners, who were often to be seen idly passing the time by snapping whips. Whippersnappers were therefore lazy young men who lacked ambition. They may well have been distracting people to enable a robbery to go unnoticed. *See also Racketeer.*

WHISK Anglo-Saxon *Flederwisch* Feather broom made from a dried goose wing.

WHISKY Irish *Uisge-beatha* Water of life.
Latin *Aqua vitæ* and French *Eau de vie* both mean precisely the same thing.

WICKED Old English *Wicca* Wizard.
Wizards are now generally considered somewhat comical participants in Halloween festivities but at one time, when people were not quite sure if they really did have magical powers, they were undoubtedly feared and, in all probability, frequently also wicked.

WICKER Middle English *Wiker* Willow and Old Norse *Veikr* Weak.

On its own a branch of willow is spindly and weak but this makes it ideal for weaving into basketwork.

WIDOW Latin *Vidua* Bereft. A widow is bereft of a husband.

WILDEBEEST Dutch *Wilde* Wild and *Beest* Ox. Otherwise known as the gnu, a kind of antelope.

WILL Old English *Willa* Determination. A will is a declaration of a determination of what is to happen after death.

WINDFALL When the navy built ships of wood and at a time when timber was becoming scarce due to excessive felling, a law was passed to prevent people from chopping down trees that might be used for shipbuilding. The only exception was that they could make use of the timber if the tree fell due to storm damage and was therefore a windfall. Since these occurrences could not be planned, they, and later any unexpected piece of good fortune, have become known as windfalls.

WINDOW Old Norse *Vind* Wind *Auga* Eye.

The window allows us to see outside; it is our eye to the wind.

WINTER Norse *Wetr* Water.

Perhaps the climatic condition most noticeable in the English winter.

WITCH Old English *Wicce*, female form of *Wicca* A man who practices witchcraft. From German *Wicken* To conjure.

WOMAN Old English *Wamb* Womb.

An undeniable reference to femininity that shows that the 'man' part of the word woman has a quite different root to the word man.

WORLD Old English *Woruld* Human affairs, All humankind.

World means everything, the complete experience of humankind and not just the planet we inhabit. Hence we say that farmers are in the farming world, or that the world and his wife – everyone – did something.

WORM Norse *Waurms* Serpent.

It seems inconceivable that the humble earthworm could ever have been thought to be menacing yet it was. In Old English it was a *Wyrm* Dragon.

WREATH Old English *Writhan* To writhe.

The derivation is due to the method of construction of the wreath, as opposed to the tormented behaviour of mourners at a funeral where wreathes would have been found. Wreathes are made by twisting and turning branches and flowers in a writhing fashion.

WRECK Scandinavian *Wrek* To wreak.

There are few situations in which more havoc is wrought than when a ship is wrecked.

X

XENOPHOBIA Greek *Xenos* Foreigner and *Phobos* Fear.

Xenophobia is a fear of people from other countries.

XMAS Despite the traditionalist insistence on spelling Christmas in full, the substitution of X for Christ has been around since before AD 1100. It is the first letter of Christ's name when spelt in Greek.

XYLOPHONE Greek *Xylon* Wood and *Phone* Voice.

Y

YAHOO In *Gulliver's Travels* by Jonathan Swift, Lemuel Gulliver visits the Country of the Houyhnhnms, where horses are the rulers and 'yahoos' are described as brutes in human form. Hence it is also applied to a crude, brash, uncultured person. The founders of the internet services company were apparently aware of the origin.

YANKEE Janke, a common Dutch surname, was a term used to describe Dutch-speaking colonists in America, generally in the north-eastern states. Eventually it came to refer to English-speaking colonists as well and to residents of New England with English ancestry in particular. Hence the Confederates of the South applied it derisively during the American Civil War, presumably as an allusion to their enemies' un-American provenance.

YEAST Sanskrit *Yasyati* To boil or bubble.
The expanding froth created when yeast is activated in the baking and fermenting process resembles the movement of water when it boils. Yeast is the oldest domesticated organism, having been used in the preparation of food and drink for 5,000 years.

YELL German *Gellen* To sing.
Not a very complimentary transition to the shrieking and shouting that we mean when we use the word today.

YOKEL A Yokel was a rustic who yoked oxen or other working animals.

YOLK Anglo-Saxon *Gealow* Yellow and the yolk of an egg.
In Anglo-Saxon, the letters *G* and *Y* were frequently interchanged, resulting in the adaptation of *gealow* to our yellow, which in turn was contracted to *yelk* and eventually corrupted to yolk.

YO-YO Tagalog (Philippines) *Yo-Yo* Come-Come, which describes the actions of a yo-yo as it repeatedly climbs back up its string.

YNGLING Norwegian *Yngling* Youngster.

The *yngling* is a type of sailboat that is a cross between a dinghy and a small keel boat. It now has its own class in Olympic yachting. It is so called because the designer, Jan Linge, built one for his young son.

YUCK An expression of disgust that is onomatopoeic for the action of vomiting.

YULE Old Norman *Jol*

A twelve-day midwinter pagan feast, later adopted by Christianity. We still burn Yule logs as part of the season's festivities.

Z

ZIP CODE American *Zoning Improvement Plan* The USA postcode.

ZOMBIE Kongo (A Bantu language spoken in present-day Congo and Angola) *Zombi*, from *Jumbie* Ghost.

The word travelled across the Atlantic with the slave trade. In voodoo, a zombie is a dead person who has been resurrected and enslaved, or else a living person who has been given the 'zombie drug', which simulates death. The most famous case of the latter is that of the Haitian Clarvius Narcisse who in 1962 was poisoned by a *bokor*, or sorcerer, with naturally occurring neurotoxins, then 'resurrected' and regularly given doses of the hallucinogenic plant datura. Along with many others he was forced to labour in a trance on the bokor's sugar plantation until 1964 when his master died and the supply of the hallucinogen ran out.

ZOO Greek *Zoion* Animal.

An exhibition of animals.

ZULU Zulu *Amazulu* The People of Heaven.

PART TWO
Changes

Words and their meanings that time forgot

Imagine all these new words pouring in as the Renaissance, the British Empire and the Industrial Revolution changed every aspect of life. What did they all mean? How could people keep track of them and learn to use them? Samuel Johnson and six copyists spent nine years poring over every printed word that had appeared in any literature since the accession of Elizabeth I. His dictionary definitions are often witty, at times ridiculous and always historically illuminating. So admired was his dictionary that it is referred to in the writing of Jane Austen, William Wordsworth and Anthony Trollope.

But times have changed and now, 250 years after Johnson laid down his quill, many words have slipped away from everyday use. This section contains words that urgently need your help. *Fopdoodle*, *kissingcrust*, *runnion* and *stingo* are far too good to be forgotten, and whatever happened to *fizgig*, *jobbernowl* and *sponk*? Please bring them back to life.

A

ABACTOR *n.* Those who drive away or steal cattle in herds, or great numbers at once, in distinction from those that steal only a sheep or two.

ABANNITION *n.* A banishment for one or two years, among the ancients, for manslaughter.

ABBEY-LUBBER *n.* A slothful loiterer in a religious house, under pretence of retirement and austerity.

ABECEDARIAN *n.* From a, b, c. He that teaches or learns the alphabet, or first rudiments of literature.

ABLIGURITION *n.* A prodigal spending on meat and drink.

ABORIGINES *n.* The earliest inhabitants of a country; those of whom no original is to be traced; as the Welsh in Britain.

ABOVE-BOARD *adj.* In open sight; without artifice or trick. A figurative expression, borrowed from gamesters, who, when they put their hands under the table, are changing their cards.

ABOVE-GROUND *adj.* An expression used to signify that a man is alive, not in the grave.

ABRACADABRA *n.* Superstitious charm against agues.

ABSCESS *n.* A morbid cavity in the body; a tumour filled with matter; a term of surgery.

ABSENTEE *n.* He that is absent from his station or employment or country. A word used commonly with regard to Irishmen living out of their country.

ABSINTHIATED *adj.* Imbittered, impregnated with wormwood.

ACCOUNTANT *n.* A computer; a man skilled or employed in accounts.

ACCUMB *v.* To lie at the table, according to the ancient manner.

ACRE *n.* A quantity of land containing in length forty perches and four in breadth or four thousand eight hundred and forty square yards.

ADDER'S-GRASS *n.* A plant so named because serpents lurk about it.

ADDER'S-WORT *n.* A herb so named on account of its virtue, real or supposed, of curing the bite of serpents.

ADDLE *adj.* Originally applied to eggs and signifying such as produce nothing, but grow rotten under the hen; thence transferred to brains that produce nothing.

ADDLE-PATED *adj.* Having addled brains.

ADIPOUS *n.* Fat.

ADJUTANT *n.* A petty officer whose duty is to assist the major by distributing the pay and overseeing the punishment of the common man.

ADJUTRIX *n.* She who helps.

ADMURMURATION *n.* The act of murmuring or whispering to another.

ADREAD *adv.* In a state of fear, frightened, terrified.

ADULTERINE *n.* A child born of an adulteress.

ADULTERY *n.* The act of violating the bed of a married person.

ADVENTURER *n.* He that seeks occasions of hazard; he that puts himself in the hands of chance.

AFTERCLAP *n.* Unexpected events happening after an affair is supposed to be at an end.

AFTER-DINNER *n.* The hour passing just after dinner which is generally allowed to indulgence and amusement.

AFTERTOSSING *n.* The motion of the sea after a storm.

AGAZE *v.* To strike with amazement; to stupefy with sudden terror.

AGRAMMATIST *n.* An illiterate man.

AGUE *n.* An intermitting fever with cold fits succeeded by hot. The cold fit is more particularly called the ague, the hot a fever.

AIRLING *n.* A young light, thoughtless, gay person.

ALACKADAY *interj.* A word noting sorrow and melancholy.

ALCOHOL *n.* An Arabic term used by chemists for a high rectified dephlegmated spirit of wine, or for any thing reduced into an impalpable powder.

ALECONNER *n.* An officer of the city of London whose business is to inspect the measures of public houses. Four of them are chosen annually by the common-hall of the city and whatever might be their use formerly, their places are now regarded only as sinecures for decayed citizens.

ALEHOUSE *n.* A house where ale is publicly sold; a tippling-house. It is distinguished from a tavern where they sell wine.

ALGID *adj.* Cold; chill.

ALIFEROUS *adj.* Having wings.

ALTIOQUENCE *n.* High speech; pompous language.

AMARULENCE *n.* Bitterness.

AMATORCULIST *n.* A little insignificant lover; a pretender to affection.

AMAZON *n.* The Amazons were a race of women famous for valour who inhabited the Caucasus; they are so called from their cutting off their breasts, to use their weapons better. A warlike woman; a virago.

AMORIST *n.* An *inamorato*; a gallant; a man professing love.

AMPER *n.* A tumour with inflammation; bile. A word said to be much used in Essex but perhaps not found in books.

AMYGDALATE *adj.* Made of almonds.

ANARCH *n.* An author of confusion.

ANATIFEROUS *adj.* Producing ducks.

ANILENESS *n.* The state of being an old woman.

ANSWER-JOBBER *n.* He that makes a trade of writing answers.

ANTICK *adj.* Odd; ridiculously wild; buffoon in gesticulation.

ANTIDYSENTERICK *adj.* Good against the bloody flux.

APRICATE *v.* To bask in the sun.

ARIETATE *v.* To butt like a ram.

ARITHMANCY *n.* Foretelling future events by numbers.

ARMISONOUS *adj.* Rustling with armour.

ARTERIOTOMY *n.* The operation of letting blood from the artery; a practice much in use among the French.

ARTUATE *v.* To tear limb from limb.

ASCII *n.* Those people who, at certain times of year, have no shadow on them at noon; such are the inhabitants of the torrid zone, because they have the sun twice a year vertical to them.

ASKER *n.* A water newt.

ASPERSE *v.* To bespatter with censure or calumny.

ASS *n.* An animal of burden, remarkable for sluggishness, patience, hardiness, coarseness of food and long life.

ASSHEAD *n.* One slow of comprehension; a blockhead.

ASTROLOGY *n.* The practice of foretelling things by the knowledge of the stars; an art now generally exploded, as without reason.

ATOM *n.* Such a small particle as cannot be physically divided.

AULD *adj.* A word now obsolete, but still used in the Scotch dialect.

AURIFEROUS *adj.* That which produces gold.

AUSTRALISE *v.* To tend towards the south.

AWME *n.* A Dutch measure of capacity for liquids, containing eight steckans, or twenty verges or verteels; answering to what in England is called a tierce, or one sixth of a ton in France or one seventh of an English Ton.

AXILLAR *adj.* Belonging to the armpit.

B

BABBLEMENT *n.* Senseless prate.

BACCHANALIAN *n.* A riotous person; a drunkard.

BACKBITER *n.* A privy calumniator; a censurer of the absent.

BACK-FRIEND *n.* A friend backwards; that is an enemy in secret.

BADGER *n.* One that buys corn and victuals in one place and carries it unto another.

BADGER-LEGGED *adj.* Having legs of unequal length, as the badger is supposed to have.

BAGNIO *n.* A house for bathing, sweating and otherwise cleansing the body.

BALBUCINATE *v.* To stammer in speaking.

BALDERDASH *v.* To mix or adulterate any liquor.

BALDRICK *n.* A girdle.

BANSTICKLE *n.* A small fish also called a stickleback.

BARBECUE *n.* A hog dressed whole as in the West Indian manner.

BARBER-MONGER *n.* A word of reproach to signify a fop; a man decked out by his barber.

BARLEY CORN *n.* A grain of barley, the beginning of our measure of length; the third part of an inch.

BASTARDY *n.* An unlawful state of birth, which disables the bastard, both according to the laws of God and man, from succeeding to an inheritance.

BATTEN *v.* To grow fat; to live in indulgence.

BATTLEDOOR *n.* An instrument with a handle and a flat blade, used in play to strike a ball, or shuttlecock.

BAUBEE *n.* A word used in Scotland and the northern counties for a halfpenny.

BAWD *n.* A procurer or procuress; one that introduces men and women to each other, for the promotion of debauchery.

BAWDY-HOUSE *n.* A house where traffick is made by wickedness and debauchery.

BEADROLL *n.* A catalogue of those who are to be mentioned in prayers.

BEADSMAN *n.* A man employed in praying, generally in praying for another.

BEARD *v.* To take or pluck by the beard, in contempt or anger.

BEAR-GARDEN *adj.* A word used in familiar or low phrase for rude or turbulent; that is a man rude enough to be a proper frequenter of a bear-garden.

BEAVER *n.* A hat of the best kind; so called from being made of the fur of a beaver.

BEAVERED *adj.* Covered with a beaver.

BECHICKS *n.* Medicines proper for relieving coughs.

BEDABBLE *v.* To wet; to besprinkle. It is generally applied to persons in a sense including inconvenience.

BEDLAMITE *adj.* An inhabitant of Bedlam; a madman.

BEDPRESSER *n.* A heavy lazy fellow.

BEDRAGGLE *v.* To soil the clothes by suffering them, in walking, to reach the dirt.

BEDRITE *n.* The privilege of the married bed.

BEDSTRAW *n.* The straw laid under a bed to make it soft.

BEDSWERVER *n.* One that is false to the bed; one that ranges or swerves from one bed to another.

BEER *n.* Liquor made of malt and hops. It is distinguished from ale either by being older or smaller.

BEGETTER *n.* He that procreates; the father.

BELDAM *n.* An old woman; generally a term of contempt, marking the last degree of old age, with all its faults and miseries.

BELLIBONE *n.* A woman excelling both in beauty and goodness. A word now out of use.

BELLYGOD *n.* A glutton; one who makes a god of his belly.

BELLY-TIMBER *n.* Food; materials to support the belly.

BELSWAGGER *n.* A whoremaster.

BELWEATHER *n.* A sheep that leads the flock with a bell on his neck.

BEMONSTER *v.* To make monstrous.

BESMUT *v.* To blacken with smoke or soot.

BESPAWL *v.* To dawb with spittle.

BESPUTTER *v.* To sputter over something; to dawb anything by sputtering, or throwing out spittle upon it.

BETTY *n.* An instrument to break open doors.

BIBACIOUS *adj.* Much addicted to drinking.

BIBBER *n.* A tippler; a man that drinks often.

BICE *n.* The name of a colour used in printing. It is either green or blue.

BIDALE *n.* An invitation of friends to drink at a poor man's house and there to contribute charity.

BIESTINGS *n.* The first milk given by a cow after calving, which is very thick.

BIGSWOLN *adj.* Turgid; ready to burst.

BILBO *n.* A rapier; a sword.

BILBOES *n.* A sort of stocks, or wooden sheckles for the feet, used for punishing offenders at sea.

BILINGSGATE *n.* Ribaldry; foul language. A word borrowed from Billingsgate in London, a place where there is always a crowd of low people and frequent brawls and foul language.

BILK *v.* To cheat; to defraud, by running in debt, and avoiding payment.

BINARY *adj.* A method of computation in which, in lieu of the ten figures in common arithmetick, and the progression from ten to ten there are only two figures using the simple progression from two to two. This method appears to be the same with that used by Chinese four thousand years ago.

BIRDLIME *n.* A glutinous substance, which is spread on twigs by which the birds that light upon them are entangled.

BIRDER *n.* A birdcatcher.

BIRTHDOM *n.* Privilege of birth.

BISCUIT *n.* A kind of hard dry bread, made to be carried to sea; it is baked for long voyages four times.

BLACKBERRIED *n.* A little shrub that grows wild upon the mountains in Staffordshire, Devonshire and Yorkshire.

BLATANT *adj.* Bellowing as a calf.

BLEAKY *adj.* Bleak; cold; chill.

BLEB *n.* A blister.

BLENCH *v.* To hinder; to obstruct.

BLENDER *n.* The person who mingles.

BLINKARD *n.* One that has bad eyes.
    and n. Something twinkling.

BLISSOM *v.* To caterwaul; to be lustful.

BISHOP *n.* A mixture of wine, oranges and sugar.

BISSON *adj.* Blind.

BLAB *n.* A telltale; a thoughtless babbler; a treacherous betrayer of secrets.

BLATTERATION *n.* Noise; senseless roar.

BLOBBER *n.* A word used in some counties for a bubble.

BLOBBERLIP *n.* A thick lip.

BLOCKHEAD *n.* A stupid fellow; a dolt; a man without parts.

BLONKET *n.* A blanket.

BLOODGUILTINESS *n.* Murder; the crime of shedding blood.

BLOODY-FLUX *n.* Cold, by retarding the motion of the blood and suppressing perspiration, produces giddiness, pains in the bowels, looseness.

BLOWZE *n.* A ruddy fat-faced wench.

BLUNDERBUSS *n.* A gun that is charged with many bullets so that, without any exact aim, there is a chance of hitting the mark.

BLUNDERHEAD *n.* A stupid fellow.

BLUNTWITTED *adj.* Dull; stupid. Ignoble in demeanour.

BOGHOUSE *n.* A house of office.

BOG-TROTTER *n.* One that lives in a boggy country.

BOGGLER *n.* A doubter; a timorous man.

BONDMAID *n.* A woman slave.

BONNY-CLABBER *n.* A word used in some counties for sour buttermilk.

BOOBY *n.* A dull heavy, stupid fellow; a lubber.

BOOKISH *adj.* Given to books; acquainted only with books. It is generally used contemptuously.

BOOTCATCHER *n.* The person whose business at an inn is to pull off the boots of passengers.

BORREL *n.* A mean fellow.

BOTCHER *n.* A mender of old clothes; the same to a tailor as a cobbler to a shoemaker.

BOUNCER *n.* A boaster, a bully, an empty threatener.

BOUTISALE *n.* A sale at a cheap rate; as booty or plunder is commonly sold

BOUSY *adj.* Drunken.

BRAGGADOCIO *n.* A puffing, swelling, boastful fellow.

BRAINPAN *n.* The skull containing the brains.

BRAINSICK *adj.* Diseased in the understanding; addleheaded; giddy; thoughtless.

BRANGLE *v.* To wrangle; to squabble.

BRAVO *n.* A man who murders for hire.

BREAKPROMISE *n.* One that makes a practice of breaking his promise.

BREEDBATE *n.* One that breeds quarrels; an incendiary.

BRONTOLOGY *n.* A dissertation upon thunder.

BRUNION *n.* A sort of fruit between a plum and a peach.

BUB *n.* Strong malt liquor.

BUBBLER *n.* A cheat.

BUBBY *n.* A woman's breast.

BUDGET *n.* A bag, such as may be easily carried.

BUFFLEHEADED *adj.* A man with a large head like a buffalo; dull; stupid; foolish.

BUFFOON *n.* A man whose profession is to make sport, by low jests and antick postures; a jackpudding.
and n. A man that practices indecent raillery.

BULL-BEGGAR *n.* Something terrible; something to fright children with.

BUMBAILLIFF *n.* A bailiff of the meanest kind; one that is employed in arrests.

BUSH *v.* To grow thick.

BUSHY *adj.* Thick as a bush.

BUMPKINLY *adj.* Having the manners or appearance of a clown; clownish.

BUNGLE *n.* A botch; an awkwardness; an inaccuracy; a clumsy performance.

BURBOT *n.* A fish full of prickles.

BUTTERFLY *n.* A beautiful insect, so named because it first appears at the beginning of the season for butter.

BUXOM *adj.* Obedient; obsequious, gay, lively, brisk.

BUZZER *n.* A secret whisperer.

BY-COFFEEHOUSE *n.* A coffeehouse in an obscure place.

C

CABARET *n.* A tavern.

CABBAGE *v.* To steal cloth in cutting clothes.

CACHECTICAL *adj.* Having an ill habit of body; shewing an ill habit.

CACKEREL *n.* A fish, said to make those who eat it laxative.

CALCULUS *n.* The stone in the bladder.

CALKER *n.* A worker that stops the leaks of a ship.

CALLOW *adj.* Unfledged; naked; without feathers.

CAMELOPARD *n.* An Abyssinian animal, taller than an elephant, but not so thick. He is so named because he has a neck like a camel, he is spotted like a pard, but his spots are white upon a red ground. The Italians call him a giraffe.

CAMELOT *n.* A kind of stuff originally made by a mixture of silk and camel's hair; it is now made with wool and silk.

CAMISADO *n.* An attack made by soldiers in the dark; on which occasion they put their shirts outward to be seen by each other.

CANAL *n.* A bason of water in a garden.

CANDLEWASTER *n.* That which consumes candles; a spendthrift.

CANKERBIT *adj.* Bitten with an envenomed tooth.

CANNIBALLY *adv.* In the manner of a cannibal.

CANTER *n.* A term of reproach for hypocrites, who talk formally of religion, without obeying it.

CAR *n.* A small carriage of burden, usually drawn by one horse or two.

CARAVAN *n.* A troop or body of merchants or pilgrims, as they travel in the east.

CART-JADE *n.* A vile horse, fit only for the cart.

CARTOON *n.* A painting or drawing upon large paper.

CASEOUS *adj.* Resembling cheese; cheesy.

CASHEWNUT *n.* A tree.

CENSOR *n.* An officer of Rome who had the power of correcting manners.

CHIVALROUS *adj.* Relating to chivalry or errant knighthood; knightly, warlike; daring. A word now out of use.

CHOCOLATE-HOUSE *n.* A house where company is entertained with chocolate.

CHUET *n.* An old word, as it seems, for forced meat.

CHUFF *n.* A coarse, fat-headed, blunt clown.

CHUFFY *adj.* Blunt, surly; fat.

CHUM *n.* A chamber fellow; a term used in universities.

CIDERIST *n.* A maker of cider.

CINDER-WENCH *n.* A woman whose trade is to rake in heaps of ashes for cinders.

CIRCUMGYRATION *n.* The act of running round.

CIT *n.* An inhabitant of a city, in an ill sense. A pert low townsman. A pragmatical trader.

CLAPPERCLAW *v.* To tonguebeat, to scold.

CLICKER *n.* A low word for the servant of a salesman, who stands at the door to invite customers.

CLODPATE *n.* A stupid fellow; a dolt; a thickskull.

CLOGGINESS *n.* The state of being clogged.

CLOOM *v.* To close or shut with glutinous or viscous matter.

CLUSTER-GRAPE *n.* The small black grape is by some called the currant.

CLOWN *n.* A rustick; a country fellow; a churl. A coarse ill-bred man.

COCKATRICE *n.* A serpent supposed to rise from a cock's egg.

COCKNEY *n.* A native of London, by way of contempt.

COCKSHUT *n.* The close of the evening, at which time poultry go to roost.

COEMPTION *n.* The act of buying up the whole quantity of anything.

COETERNALLY *adv.* In a state of equal eternity with another.

COFFEE *n.* A drink prepared from berries very familiar in Europe for these eighty years, and among Turks for one hundred and fifty. Brought into England by a Turkey merchant, in 1652. Coffee is a drink made of a berry as black as soot which they take, beaten into powder, in water, as hot as they can drink it. The drink comforteth the brain and heart, and helpeth digestion.

COFFEE-HOUSE *n.* A house of entertainment where coffee is sold and the guests are supplied with newspapers.

COGGER *n.* A flatterer, a wheedler.

COGGLESTONE *n.* A little stone; a small pebble.

COGNOMINATION *n.* A surname, the name of the family.

COLBERTINE *n.* A kind of lace worn by women.

COLE *n.* A general name for all sorts of cabbage.

COLLIQUEFACTION *n.* The act of melting together; reduction to one mass by fluxion in the fire.

COLOQUINTEDA *n.* The fruit of a plant of the same name, brought from the Levant, about the bigness of a large orange, and often called a bitter apple. Its colour is a sort of golden brown: its inside is full of kernels, which are to be taken out before it is used. Both the seed and pulp are intolerably bitter. It is a violent purgative, of considerable use in medicine.

COMEDY *n.* A dramatic representation of the lighter faults of mankind.

COMING-IN *n.* Revenue, income.

COMMODE *n.* The head-dress of women.

COMMONER *n.* One of the common people; a man of low rank; of mean condition.

COMMONS *n.* The vulgar; the lower people; those who inherit no honours.

COMPOTATION *n.* The act of drinking or tippling together.

COMPRINT *v.* The word properly signifies to print together; but it is commonly taken, in law, for the deceitful printing of another's copy or book, to the prejudice of the rightful proprietor.

COMPUTER *n.* Reckoner; accountant.

CONCUBINAGE *n.* The act of living with a woman not married.

CONDERS *n.* Such as stand upon high places near the sea-coast, at the time of the herring fishing, to make signs to the fishers which way the shoal of herrings passeth, which may better appear to such as stand upon some high cliff, by a kind of blue colour that the fish causeth in the water.

CONFABULATE *v.* To talk easily or carelessly together; to chat; to prattle.

CONFARREATION *n.* The solemnization of marriage by eating bread together.

CONGE *v.* To take leave.

CONSOPIATION *n.* The act of laying to sleep.

CONTRAVALLATION *n.* The fortification thrown up by the besiegers, round a city, to hinder the sallies of the garrison.

CONVENTICLER *n.* On the supports or frequents private and unlawful assemblies.

CONY *n.* A rabbit. An animal that burrows in the ground.

COOM *n.* Soot that gathers over and oven's mouth.

COPPER-NOSE *n.* A red nose.

COQUET *v.* To entertain with compliments and amorous tattle; to treat with an appearance of amorous tenderness.

CORNUTE *v.* To bestow horns; to cuckold.

CORROBORANT *adj.* Having power to give strength.

CORRUGANT *adj.* Having the power of contracting into wrinkles.

COSCINOMANCY *n.* The art of divination by means of a sieve. A very ancient practice mentioned by Theocritus, and still used in some parts of England, to find out persons unknown.

COSIER *n.* A botcher.

COSTARD *n.* A head.

COTTAGE *n.* A hut, a mean habitation.

COTTAGER *n.* One that lives in a hut or cottage on the common without paying rent and without any land of his own.

COUPLE-BEGGAR *n.* One that makes it his business to marry beggars to each other.

COUNTERMARK *v.* A horse is said to be countermarked when his corner-teeth are artificially made hollow, a false mark being made in the hollow place, an imitation of the eye of a bean, to conceal the horse's age.

COVERT *adj.* The state of a woman sheltered by marriage under her husband.

COZENER *n.* A cheater; a defrauder.

CRACK-ROPE *n.* A fellow that deserves hanging.

CRICKET *n.* A sport, at which the contenders drive a ball with sticks in opposition to each other.

CRINIGEROUS *adj.* Hairy, overgrown with hair.

CROCITATION *n.* The croaking of frogs and ravens.

CROWDER *n.* A fiddler.

CUBATION *n.* The act of lying down.

CUCKINGSTOOL *n.* An engine invented for the punishment of scolds and unquiet women.

CUCKOLD *n.* One that is married to an adulteress; one whose wife is false to his bed.

CUCKOLDMAKER *n.* One that makes a practice of corrupting wives.

CUNNINGMAN *n.* A man who pretends to tell fortunes, or teach how to recover stolen goods.

CURFEW *n.* An evening-peal by which the conqueror willed, that everyman should rake up his fire and put out his light.

CURTAIN-LECTURE *n.* A reproof given by a wife to her husband in bed.

CUSTARD *n.* A kind of sweetmeat made by boiling eggs with milk and sugar 'till the whole thickens into a mass. It is a food much used in city feasts.

CUTPURSE *n.* One who steals by the method of cutting purses; a common place practice when men wore their purses at their girdles, as was once the custom.

CYNANTHROPY *n.* A species of madness in which men have the qualities of dogs

D

DALLIANCE *n.* Interchange of caresses; acts of fondness.

DAMNINGNESS *n.* Tendency to procure damnation.

DANDIPRAT *n.* A little fellow; an urchin: a word used sometimes in fondness, sometimes in contempt.

DANGLER *n.* A man that hangs about women only to waste time.

DAPATICAL *adj.* Sumptous in cheer.

DEAD-DOING *adj.* Destructive; killing; mischievous; having the power to make dead.

DEAMBULATION *n.* The act of walking abroad.

DEARBOUGHT *adj.* Purchased at a high price.

DEATHWATCH *n.* An insect that makes a tinkling noise like that of a watch, and is superstitiously imagined to prognosticate death.

DEBARB *v.* To deprive of his beard.

DEBULLITION *n.* A bubbling or seething over.

DECEMBER *n.* The tenth month when the year began in March.

DECIMATION *n.* A selection by lot of every tenth soldier, in a general mutiny, for punishment.

DECOLLATION *n.* The act of beheading.

DEEMSTER *n.* A judge; a word yet in use in Jersey and The Isle of Man.

DEEP-MUSING *adj.* Contemplative; lost in thought.

DEFERENTS *n.* Certain vessels in the human body appointed for the conveyance of humours from one place to another.

DEFLOURER *n.* A ravisher; one that takes away virginity.

DEGLUTITION *n.* The act or power of swallowing.

DEHORTER *n.* A dissuader; an adviser to the contrary.

DELICES *n.* Pleasures. This word is merely French.

DEMI-MAN *n.* Half a man. A term of reproach.

DEMONOCRACY *n.* The power of the devil.

DEOSCULATION *n.* The act of kissing.

DEPOPULATOR *n.* A dispeopler; a destroyer of mankind; a waster of inhabited countries.

DEPUCELATE *v.* To de-flower; to bereave of virginity.

DETERRATION *n.* Discovery of anything by the removal of the earth that hides it; the act of unburying.

DEUTEROGAMY *n.* A second marriage.

DEVILKIN *n.* A little devil.

DEWBESPRENT *adj.* Sprinkled with dew.

DIDDER *v.* To quake with cold; to shiver.

DISARD *n.* A prattler; a boasting talker.

DISCALCEATION *n.* The act of pulling off the shoes.

DISCASE *v.* To strip; to undress.

DISH-WASHER *n.* The name of a bird.

DISLIMB *v.* To dilaniate; to tear limb from limb.

DISPLODE *v.* To disperse with a loud noise. To vent with violence.

DISWITTED *adj.* Deprived of the wits; mad; distracted.

DITHYRAMBICK *n.* A song in honour of Bacchus; in which anciently and now among the Italians, the distraction of ebriety is imitated. Any poem written with wildness and enthusiasm.

DIZZARD *n.* A blockhead; a fool.

DOGHOLE *n.* A vile hole; a mean habitation

DOGSLEEP *n.* Pretended sleep.

DOGWEARY *adj.* As tired as a dog; excessively weary.

DOLLAR *n.* A Dutch and German coin of different value, from about two shillings and sixpence to four and sixpence.

DOLT *n.* A heavy stupid fellow; a blockhead; a thick skull; a loggerhead.

DOODLE *n.* A trifler; an idler.

DORR *n.* So named probably from the noise which he makes. A kind of flying insect, remarkable for flying with a loud noise.

DOSIFEROUS *n.* Having the property of bearing or bringing forth on the back. May be properly used of the American frog, which brings forth young from her back.

DOTARD *n.* A man whose age has impaired his intellects; a man in his second childhood; called in some provinces a twichild.

DOUBLE-DIE *v.* To die twice over.

DOWDY *n.* An awkward, ill-dressed, inelegant woman.

DOWNGYRED *adj.* Let down in circular wrinkles.

DOWNSITTING *n.* Rest, repose. The act of sitting down. or going to rest.

DOWNFALLE *n.* adj. Ruined, fallen.

DRAB *n.* A whore; a strumpet.

DRAFFY *adj.* Worthless; dreggy.

DRAGGLE *v.* To grow dirty by being drawn along the ground.

DRAGON *n.* A kind of winged serpent, perhaps imaginary. Much celebrated in the romances of the middle age.

DRAGOON *n.* A kind of soldier that serves indifferently either on foot or horseback.

DRIBLET *n.* A small sum; odd money in a sum.

DROIL *v.* To work sluggishly and slowly; to plod.

DRONISH *adj.* Idle; sluggish; dreaming; lazy; indolent;

DROUGHTINESS *n.* The state of wanting rain.

DRUDGER *n.* A mean labourer.

DULBRAINED *adj.* Stupid; doltish, foolish.

DUNCE *n.* A dullard; a dolt; a thickskul; a stupid indocile animal.

DYSPHONY *n.* A difficulty in speaking, occasioned by an ill disposition of the organs.

E

EAGLESTONE *n.* A stone said to be found at the entrance of the holes in which eagles nest, and affirmed to have a particular virtue in defending the eagle's nest from thunder. The stones of this kind, which are most valued are flat and blackish, and found, if shaken near the ear; a lesser stone being contained in the greater.

EAME *n.* Uncle; a word still used in the wilder parts of Staffordshire.

EARTHLING *n.* An inhabitant of the earth; a mortal; a poor frail creature.

EARWITNESS *n.* One who attests or can attest anything as heard by himself.

EAVESDROP *v.* To catch what comes from the eaves; in common phrase, to listen under windows.

EBRIETY *n.* Intoxication by strong liquors.

ECLEGMA *n.* A form of medicine made by the incorporation of oils with syrups, which is to be taken upon a liquorice stick.

ECONOMY *n.* The management of a family; the government of a household.

ECSTASIED *adj.* Ravished; filled with enthusiasm.

EFFEMINATE *v.* To make womanish; to weaken; to emasculate; to unman.

EJACULATION *n.* A short prayer darted out occasionally, without solemn retirement.

ELECTRICITY *n.* A property of some bodies, whereby when rubbed so as to grow warm, they draw little bits of paper, or such like substances to them.

ELFLOCK *n.* Knots of hair twisted by elves.

ELL *n.* A measure containing forty-five inches or a yard and a quarter.

ELUMBATED *adj.* Weakened in the loins.

ELYSIUM *n.* The place assigned by the heathens to happy souls; any place exquisitely pleasant.

EMACULATION *n.* The act of freeing anything from spots and foulness.

EMBOLISM *n.* Intercalation; insertion of days or years to produce regularity and equation of time.

EMBROTHEL *v.* To inclose in a brothel.

EMMET *n.* An ant; a pismire.

ENATATION *n.* The act of escape by swimming.

ENFOULDRED *adj.* Mixed with lightening.

ENGINEER *n.* One who manages engines; one who directs the artillery of an army.

ENIGMATIST *n.* One who deals in obscure and ambiguous matters; maker of riddles.

ENNEATICAL *adj.* Every ninth day of a sickness.

ENVENOM *n.* To tinge with poison; to impregnate with venom.

ENWOMB *v.* To make pregnant.

EPHEMERA *n.* A fever that terminates in one day.

EPICURE *n.* A follower of Epicurus; a man given wholly to luxury.

EPISTLER *n.* A scribbler of letters.

EPULATION *n.* Banquet; feast.

ERENOW *adv.* Before this time.

ERKE *adj.* Idle; lazy; slothful.

ERRHINE *n.* Snuffed up the nose; occasioning sneezing.

ERUCTATION *n.* The act of belching.

ESCARGATOIRE *n.* A nursery of snails.

EUTHANASIA *n.* An easy death.

EUNUCHATE *v.* To make an eunuch.

EVAGATION *n.* The act of wandering.

EVESDROPPER *n.* Some mean fellow that skulks about a house in the night.

EVISCERATE *n.* To embowl; to draw; to deprive of the entrails; to search within the entrails.

EXANIMATION *adj.* Deprivation of life.

EXCISE *n*. A hateful tax levied upon commodities and adjudged not by the common judges of property, but by wretches hired by those to whom excise is paid.

EXCUBATION *n*. The act of watching all night.

EXCUSSION *n*. Seizure by law

EXENTERATE *v*. To embowel; to deprive of the entrails.

EXHILARATION *n*. The act of giving gaiety.

EXOMPHALOS *n*. A navel rupture.

EXOSSATED *adj*. Deprived of bones.

EXOTIC *n*. A foreign plant.

EXPILATION *n*. Robbery; the act of committing waste upon land by the loss of the heir.

EXSPUITION *n*. A discharge of saliva by spitting.

EYESERVANT *n*. A servant that works only while watched.

F

FABACEOUS *adj*. Having the nature of a bean.

FABULOSITY *n*. Lyingness; fullness of stories; fabulous invention.

FACINOROUS *adj*. Wicked; atrocious; detestably bad.

FACTORY *n*. A house or district inhabited by traders in a distant country.

FADDLE *v.* To trifle, to toy with the fingers, to play.

FAGEND *n.* The end of a web of cloth, generally made of coarser materials.

FAIN *adj.* Glad; merry; cheerful; fond. It is still retained in Scotland.

FAIRYSTONE *n.* It is found in gravelpits, being of an hemispherical figure; hath five double lines arising from the centre of its base, which meet at the pole.

FAITHED *adj.* Honest, sincere. A word not in use.

FALDSTOOL *n.* A kind of stool placed at the south side of the altar, at which the kings of England kneel at their coronation.

FAMBLE *v.* To hesitate in the speech.

FAMOSITY *n.* Renown, celebrity.

FANCYMONGER *n.* One who deals in tricks of imagination.

FANCYSICK *adj.* One whose imagination is unsound; one whose distemper is in his own mind.

FAP *adj.* Fuddled; drunk.

FARM *n.* Land let to a tenant. Ground cultivated by another man upon condition of paying part of the profit to the owner.

FARTHING *n.* The fourth of a penny; the smallest English coin.

FARTHINGALE *n.* A hoop; circles of whalebone used to spread the petticoat to a wide circumference.

FATKIDNEYED *adj.* Fat; by way of reproach or contempt.

FATWITTED *adj.* Heavy; dull; stupid.

FAUCHION *n.* A crooked sword.

FAUSSEN *n.* A sort of large eel.

FAXED *adj.* Hairy.

FEABERRY *n.* A gooseberry.

FEATHERDRIVER *n.* One who cleanses feathers by whisking them about.

FELLMONGER *n.* A dealer in hides.

FELO-DE-SE *n.* He that committeth felony by murdering himself.

FELONY *n.* A crime denounced capital by the law; an enormous crime.

FENSUCKED *adj.* Sucked out of marshes.

FERIATION *n.* The act of keeping holiday; cessation from work.

FERULA *n.* An instrument of correction with which young scholars are beaten on the hand: so named because anciently the stalks of fennel (ferula) were used for this purpose.

FEUTERER *n.* A dogkeeper; perhaps the cleaner of the kennel.

FIDDLEFADDLE *adj.* Trifling; giving trouble, or making a bustle about nothing.

FIG *v.* To insult with contemptuous motions of the fingers

FIGPECKER *n.* A bird.

FIGURE-FLINGER *n.* A pretender to astrology and prediction.

FILCHER *n.* A thief; a petty robber.

FINDY *adj.* Plump; weighty; firm; solid.

FINGLEFANGLE *n.* A trifle.

FINICALNESS *n.* Superfluous nicety; foppery.

FIRECROSS *n.* A token in Scotland for the nation to take arms, the ends thereof burnt black, and in some parts smeared in blood. It is carried like lightening from one place to another. Upon refusal to send it forward, or to rise, the last person who has it shoots the other dead.

FIZGIG *n.* A kind of dart or harpoon with which seaman strike fish.

FLAGITIOUS *adj.* Wicked; villainous; atrocious.

FLAMMIVOMOUS *adj.* Vomiting out flame.

FLAPDRAGON *n.* A play in which they catch raisins out of burning brandy and, extinguishing them by closing the mouth, eat them.

FLASHER *n.* A man of more appearance of wit than reality.

FLESHMONGER *n.* One who deals in flesh; a pimp.

FLESHQUAKE *n.* A tremor of the body in imitation of earthquake.

FLEW *n.* The large chaps of a deep-mouthed hound.

FLEXANIMOUS *adj.* Having power to change the disposition of the mind.

FLIPP *n.* A liquor much used in ships, made by mixing beer with spirits and sugar.

FLITTERMOUSE *n.* The bat.

FLUSTER *n.* To make hot and dosy with drinking; to make half drunk.

FOG *n.* Aftergrass; grass which grows in autumn after hay is mown.

FOOTPAD *n.* A highwayman that robs on foot, not on horseback.

FOPDOODLE *n.* A fool; an insignificant wretch.

FOREDO *v.* To ruin; to destroy. Opposed to making happy.

FOREWORN *adj.* Worn out; wasted by time and use.

FORNICATOR *n.* One who has commerce with unmarried women.

FORTUNETELLER *n.* One who cheats common people by pretending to the knowledge of futurity.

FOULFACED *adj.* Having an ugly or hateful visage.

FOXHUNTER *n.* A man whose chief ambition is to show his bravery in hunting foxes. A term of reproach used of country gentlemen.

FRANTICKNESS *n.* Madness; fury of passion.

FREAM *v.* To growl or grunt as a boar.

FREEBOOTER *n.* A robber; a plunderer; a pillager.

FREN *n.* A worthless woman.

FRENCHIFY *v.* To infect with the manner of France.

FRIARLIKE *adv.* Monastick; unskilled in the world.

FRIBBLER *n.* A trifler.

FRIPPERER *n.* One who deals in old things vamped up.

FRISK *n.* A frolick; a fit of wanton gaiety,

FRORNE *adj.* Frozen; congealed with cold.

FRUMP *v.* To mock; to browbeat.

FRUSH *v.* To break, bruise, or crush.

FUB *n.* A plump chubby boy.

FUDDLE *v.* To drink to excess.

FUGH *interj.* An expression of abhorrence.

FULGID *adj.* Shining; glittering; dazzling.

FULHAM *n.* False dice.

FULIMART *n.* A kind of stinking ferret.

FULL-BOTTOMED *adj.* Having a large bottom.

FUMETTE *n.* A word introduced from the French by cooks and the pupils of cooks, for the stink of meat.

FURACIOUS *adj.* Thievish; inclined to steal.

FUST *v.* To grow mouldy; to smell ill.

FUSTIAN *n.* A low fellow; a stinkard; a scoundrel.

FUTILE *adj.* Talkative; loquacious.

FUTTOCKS *n.* The lower timbers that hold the ship together.

FY *interj.* A word of blame and disapprobation.

G

GAD *v.* To ramble about without any settled purpose; to rove loosely and idly.

GAFFER *n.* A word of respect now obsolete, or applied only in contempt to a mean person.

GALAGE *n.* A shepherd's clog.

GALERICULATE *adj.* Covered as with a hat.

GALLANT *n.* A gay, sprightly airy, splendid man.
and n. A whoremaster who caresses women to debauch them.

GALLIGASKINS *n.* Large open hose.

GALLIMAUFRY *n.* A hoch-poch or hash of several sorts of broken meat.

GALLOW *v.* To terrify; to fright.

GAMBLER *n.* A knave whose practice it is to invite the unwary to game and cheat them.

GAMESOMELY *adv.* Merrily.

GANCH *v.* To drop from a high place upon hooks by way of punishment, a practice in Turkey.

GANTELOPE *n.* A military punishment in which the criminal running between the ranks receives a lash from each man.

GARBAGE *n.* The bowels; the offal; that part of the inwards which is separated and thrown away.

GARGARISE *v.* To wash the mouth with medicated liquors.

GARLICK *n.* A bulbous root with an extremely strong, and to most people, a disagreeable smell, and of an acrid and pungent taste. It is an extremely active and penetrating medicine, as may be proved by applying plaisters of garlick to the soles of the feet, which will in a very little time give a strong smell to the breath.

GARLICKEATER *n.* A mean fellow.

GAS *n.* A word invented by the chemists which seems to signify a spirit not capable of being coagulated.

GAY *adj.* Airy; cheerful; merry; frolick.

GAZEHOUND *n.* A hound that pursues not by the scent but by the eye.

GAZINGSTOCK *n.* A person gazed at with scorn or abhorrence.

GEASON *adj.* Wonderful.

GEE *v.* A term used by waggoners to their horses when they would have them go faster.

GELID *adj.* Extremely cold.

GEMELLIPAROUS *adj.* Bearing twins.

GEMMOSITY *n.* The quality of being a jewel.

GENTRY *n.* Class of people above the vulgar; those between the vulgar and the nobility.

GEOMANCER *n.* A fortuneteller; a caster of figures; a cheat who pretends to foretell futurity by other means than the astrologer.

GERMAN *adj.* Related.

GEWGAW *n.* A showy trifle, a toy; a bauble; a splendid plaything.

GIBCAT *n.* An old worn-out cat.

GIDDYBRAINED *adj.* Careless; thoughtless.

GIGGLE *v.* To laugh idly; to titter; to grin with merry levity. It is retained in Scotland.

GIGLET *n.* A wanton; a lascivious girl.

GINGERNESS *n.* Niceness; tenderness.

GIP *v.* To take out the guts of herrings.

GLABRITY *n.* Smoothness; baldness.

GLAIRE *v.* To smear with the white of an egg.

GLASSGAZING *adj.* Often contemplating himself in a mirror.

GLEEK *n.* Music; or musician.

GLIKE *n.* A sneer; a scoff; a flout.

GLOAT *v.* To cast side glances as a timorous lover.

GLOSSARY *n.* A dictionary of obscure or antiquated words.

GLOUT *v.* To pout; to look sullen. It is still used in Scotland.

GLOZE *v.* To flatter, to wheedle, to insinuate; to fawn.

GNOMONICKS *n.* To find the just proportions of shadows for the construction of all kinds of sun and moon dials and for knowing what o'clock it is.

GO-CART *n.* A machine in which children are enclosed to teach them to walk, and which they push forward without danger of falling.

GORBELLY *n.* A big paunch; a swelling belly. A term of reproach for a fat man.

GOSSIP *n.* One who answers for the child in baptism.
and n. A tippling companion.

GRABBLE *v.* To grope; to feel eagerly with the hands.

GRAVY *n.* The serous juice that runs from flesh not much dried by the fire.

GRAY *n.* A badger.

GRAYBEARD *n.* An old man, in contempt.

GREATBELLIED *adj.* Pregnant; teeming.

GREAVES *n.* Armour for the legs; a sort of boots.

GREECE *n.* A flight of steps.

GREGAL *adj.* Belonging to a flock.

GREMIAL *adj.* Pertaining to the lap.

GRICE *n.* A little pig.

GRIMALKIN *n.* Grey little woman; the name of an old cat.

GRIPLE *n.* A greedy snatcher, a griping miser.

GRISKIN *n.* The vertebrae of hog boiled.

GROAT *n.* A piece valued at four pence.

GROPE *v.* To feel where one cannot see.

GRUBBLE *n.* To feel in the dark.

GRUBSTEET *n.* Originally the name of a street in Moorfields in London, much inhabited by writers of small histories, dictionaries and poems.

GRUM *adj.* Sour; surly; severe.

GRUMLEY *adv.* Sullenly, morosely.

GRY *n.* Anything of little value; as the pairing of the nails.

GUGGLE *v.* To sound as water running with intermissions out of a narrow-mouthed vessels.

GUINEA *n.* A gold coin valued at one and twenty shillings.

GULCHIN *n.* A little glutton.

GULL *n.* A cheat; a fraud; a trick.

GUTTLE *v.* To feed luxuriously, to gormandise.

GYNECOCRASAY *n.* Petticoat government, female power.

H

HABNAB *adv.* At random; at the mercy of chance; without any rule or certainty of effect.

HACKNEY *n.* A hireling, a prostitute.

HAFT *n.* A handle; that part of any instrument that is taken into the hand.

HALCYON *n.* A bird, of which it is said that she breeds in the sea, and that there is always a calm during her incubation.

HALF-SCHOLAR *n.* Imperfectly learned.

HALLUCINATION *n.* Error; blunder; mistake; folly.

HALM *n.* Straw.

HAMATED *adj.* Hooked; set with hooks.

HANAPER *n.* A treasury; an exchequer. The clerk of the hanaper receives the fees due to the king for the seal of charters and patents.

HARLEQUIN *n.* A buffoon who plays tricks to divert the populace.

HARRIDAN *n.* A decayed strumpet.

HASTINGS *n.* Peas that come early.

HATCHET-FACE *n.* An ugly face; such, I suppose, as might be hewn out of a block by a hatchet.

HAVOCK *interj.* A word of encouragement to slaughter.

HAW *v.* To speak slowly with frequent intermission and hesitation.

HEADBOROUGH *n.* A constable; a subordinate constable.

HEART-BREAKER *n.* A woman's curls, supposed to break the heart of all her lovers.

HEAVEN-BEGOT *adj.* Begot by a celestial power.

HEDGE-BORN *adj.* Of no known birth; meanly born.

HEBDOMAD *n.* A week; a space of seven days.

HECATOMB *n.* A sacrifice of an hundred cattle.

HECTOR *n.* A bully; a blustering, turbulent, pervicacious, noisy fellow.

HEDGE-PIG *n.* A young hedge-hog.

HELL-BRED *adj.* Produced in hell.

HELL-BROTH *n.* A composition boiled up for infernal purposes.

HELL-GOVERNED *adj.* Directed by hell.

HELMINTHICK *adj.* Relating to worms.

HEMICRANY *n.* A pain that affects only one part of the brain at a time.

HEXAPOD *n.* An animal with six feet.

HIGGLER *n.* One who sells provisions by retail.

HIGH-FLIER *n.* One that carries his opinions to extravagance.

HIGH-VICED *adj.* Enormously wicked.

HINDBERRIES *n.* The same as raspberries.

HOBIT *n.* A small mortar to shoot little bombs.

HOIDEN *n.* An ill-taught awkward country girl.
and v. To romp indecently.

HOLDERFORTH *n.* An haranguer; one who speaks in publick.

HOLOGRAPH *n.* This word is used in the Scottish law to denote a deed written altogether by the granter's own hand.

HONEY-MOON *n.* The first month after marriage, when there is nothing but tenderness and pleasure.

HOOK *n.* A field sown two years running.

HOROMETRY *n.* The act of measuring hours.

HOT *adj.* Lustful; lewd.

HOTCOCKLES *n.* A play in which one covers his eyes and guesses who strikes him.

HUGGERMUGGER *n.* A hug in the dark.

HUMBLEBEE *n.* A buzzing wild bee.

HUMICUBATION *n.* The act of lying on the ground.

HUMOROUS *adj.* Full of grotesque or odd images.

HUNKS *n.* A covetous sordid wretch; a miser; a curmudgeon.

HUSSY *n.* A sorry or bad woman; a worthless wench. It is often used ludicrously in slight disapprobation.

HUSWIFE *v.* A bad manager; a sorry woman.

HYSTERICKS *n.* Fits of women, supposed to proceed from disorders in the womb.

I

IATROLEPTICK *adj.* That which cures by anointing.

ICEHOUSE *n.* A house in which ice is reposited against the warm months.

IGNIVOMOUS *adj.* Vomiting fire.

IGNOBLE *adj*. Mean of birth; not noble; not of illustrious race; worthless; not deserving honour.

ILLACHRYMABLE *adj*. Incapable of weeping.

ILLNATURE *n*. Habitual malevolence.

IMBOSOM *v*. To admit to the heart, or to affection.

IMPENNOUS *adj*. Wanting wings.

IMPIGNORATE *v*. To pawn; to pledge.

IMPLORER *n*. Solicitor.

INCEPTOR *n*. A beginner; one who is in his rudiments.

INCH *n*. A measure of length supposed equal to three grains of barley laid end to end; the twelfth part of a foot.

INCOG *adv*. Unknown; in private.

INCONTINENT *adj*. Unchaste; indulging unlawful pleasure.

INFANGTHEF *n*. A privilege or liberty granted unto lords of certain manors to judge any thief taken within their fee.

INFAUSTING *n*. The act of making unlucky.

INGANNATION *n*. Cheat; fraud; deception; juggle; delusion; imposture; tick; flight.

INGATHERING *n*. The act of getting in the harvest.

INNINGS *n*. Lands recovered from the sea.

INSECTATOR *n.* One the persecutes or harasses with pursuit.

INSPECTOR *n.* A prying examiner.

INSPISSATE *v.* To thicken; to make thick.

INSUSURRATION *n.* The act of whispering.

INTERCOMMON *v.* To feed at the same table.

INTERMARRIAGE *n.* Marriage between two families, where each takes one and gives another.

INTERWISH *v.* To wish mutually to each other.

INTONATION *n.* The act of thundering.

INURN *v.* To intomb; to bury.

IRRADIATION *n.* The act of emitting beams of light.

IRRISION *n.* The act of laughing at another.

J

JACKALENT *n.* A simple sheepish fellow.

JACKPUDDING *n.* A zani; a merry-andrew.

JADE *n.* A horse of no spirit; a hired horse; a worthless nag.
 and A sorry woman. A word of contempt noting sometimes age, but generally vice.

JANGLE *v.* To altercate, to quarrel; to bicker in words.

JANGLER *n.* A wrangling, chattering, noisy fellow.

JANNOCK *n.* Oatbread. A northern word.

JEGGET *n.* A kind of sausage.

JET *n.* A very beautiful fossil of a firm and very even structure and of a smooth surface; seldom of a great size. The ancients recommended jet in medicine but it is now used only in toys.

JETTY *adj.* Made of jet; black as a jet.

JIGGUMBOB *n.* A trinket; a knick-knack; a slight contrivance in machinery.

JOBBERNOWL *n.* Loggerhead, blockhead.

JOCUNDLY *adv.* Merrily; gaily.

JOCOSE *adj.* Merry; waggish; given to jest.

JOGGER *n.* One who moves heavily and dully.

JOLL *v.* To beat the head against anything; to clash with violence.

JOWLER *n.* A kind of hunting dog or beagle.

JUMBLE *n.* Confused mixture; violent and confused agitation.

K

KECK *v.* To heave the stomach; to reach at vomiting.

KELL *n.* A sort of pottage. It is so called in Scotland, being a soup made with shredded greens.

KENNEL *v.* To lie; to dwell; used of beasts and of man in contempt.

KICKSHAW *n.* Something uncommon; something ridiculous.
and n. A dish so changed by the cookery that it can scarcely be known.

KICKSY-WICKSEY *n.* A made word in ridicule and disdain of a wife.

KINGSEVIL *n.* A scrofulous distemper, in which the glands are ulcerated, commonly believed to be cured by the touch of the king.

KISSINGCRUST *n.* Crust formed when one loaf in the oven touches another.

KITCHENWENCH *n.* Scullion; maid employed to clean the instruments of cookery.

KNACKER *n.* A maker of small work.

KNAPPLE *v.* To break off with a sharp quick noise.

KNEED *adj.* Having knees.

KNUBBLE *v.* To beat.

KNUCKLE *v.* To submit. The custom of striking the under side of the table with the knuckles, in confession of an argumental defeat.

KNUFF *n.* A lout.

L

LABIAL *adj.* Uttered by the lips.

LACED MUTTON *n.* An old word for a whore.

LACHRYMAL *adj.* Generating tears.

LACKBRAIN *n.* One that wants wit.

LACKLINEN *adj.* Wanting shirts.

LADY *n.* A woman of high rank; the title of lady properly belongs to the wives of knights, of all degrees above them, and to the daughters of earls, and all of higher ranks.

LAMBS-WOOL *n.* Ale mixed with pulp of roasted apples.

LAMM *v.* To beat soundly with a cudgel.

LANDJOBBER *n.* One who buys and sells land for other men.

LANDLOPER *n.* A landman; a term of reproach used by seaman of those who pass their lives on shore.

LAPIDATE *v.* To kill by stoning.

LARGITION *n.* The act of giving.

LASS *n.* A girl; a maid; a young woman; used only of mean girls.

LASSLORN *n.* Forsaken by his mistress.

LATISH *adj.* Somewhat late.

LATITATION *n.* The state of lying concealed.

LATITUDINARIAN *n.* One who departs from orthodoxy.

LATRANT *adj.* Barking.

LAUDANUM *n.* A soporifick tincture.

LAVATORY *n.* A wash; something in which parts diseased are washed.

LAWN *n.* An open space between woods.

LAYSTALL *n.* An heap of dung.

LAZAR *n.* One deformed and nauseous with filthy and pestilential diseases.

LAZAR-HOUSE *n.* A house for the reception of the diseased; an hospital.

LECHER *n.* A whoremaster.

LEECH *n.* A physician; a professor of the art of healing.

LEGERDEMAIN *n.* Slight of hand; juggle; power of deceiving the eye by nimble motion; trick; deception; knack.

LEMAN *n.* A sweetheart, a gallant or a mistress.

LETHE *n.* Oblivion; a draught of oblivion.

LEVET *n.* A blast on the trumpet; probably that by which the soldiers are called in the morning.

LEWDSTER *n.* A lecher, one given to criminal pleasures.

LEXICOGRAPHER *n.* A writer of dictionaries; a harmless drudge, that busies himself in tracing the original, and detailing the significance of words.

LIBATION *n.* The act of pouring wine on the ground in honour of some deity.

LIBERTINE. *adj.* Licentious; irreligious.

LIBRARIAN *n.* One who transcribes or copies books.

LICENTIOUSNESS *n.* Boundless liberty; contempt of just restraint.

LICKERISHNESS *n.* Niceness of palate.

LIFEWEARY *adj.* Wretched; tired of living.

LIG *v.* To lie.

LIGHTFINGERED *adj.* Nimble at conveyance; thievish.

LIKING *adj.* Plump; in a state of plumpness.

LIMBO *n.* A region bordering upon hell, in which there is neither pleasure nor pain. Popularly hell.

LIMMER *n.* A mongrel.

LINKBOY *n.* A boy that carries a torch to accommodate passengers with light.

LINSTOCK *n.* A staff of wood with a match at the end of it, used by gunners in firing cannon.

LION *n.* The fiercest and most magnanimous of four footed beasts.

LIPLABOUR *n.* Action of the lips without concurrence of the mind; words without sentiments.

LIPWISDOM *n.* Wisdom in talk without practice.

LITHOMANCY *n.* Prediction by stones.

LIVERGROWN *adj.* Having a great liver.

LOB'S POUND *n.* A prison probably for idlers, or sturdy beggars.

LOCOMOTIVE *adj.* Changing place; having the power of removing or changing place.

LOGGERHEAD *n.* A dolt, a blockhead; a thickscull.

LONGIMANOUS *adj.* Long-handed, having long hands.

LOO *n.* A game of cards.

LOOM *v.* To appear at sea.

LOOVER *n.* An opening for the smoke to go out in the roof of a cottage.

LOSEL *n.* A scoundrel; a sorry worthless fellow.

LOUSY *adj.* Swarming with lice.
  and adj. Mean; low born; bred on the dunghill.

LOVETHOUGHT *n.* Amorous fancy.

LOVETOY *n.* Small presents given by lovers.

LOWBELL *n.* A kind of fowling in the night, in which the birds are wakened by a bell and lured by a flame into a net.

LUBBARD *n.* A lazy sturdy fellow.

LUCRE *n.* Gain; profit; pecuniary advantage. In an ill sense.

LURKER *n.* A thief that lies in wait.

LUXURIOUS *adj.* Delighting in the pleasures of the table.

LYCANTHROPY *n.* A kind of madness in which men have the qualities of wild beasts.

M

MACAROON *n.* A coarse, rude, low fellow.

MACILENT *adj.* Lean.

MACTATION *n.* The act of killing for sacrifice.

MAD *n.* An earth worm.

MADCAP *n.* A madman; a wild hot brained fellow.

MADGEHOWLET *n.* An owl.

MAGGOTTINESS *n.* The state of abounding with maggots.

MAFFLE *v.* To stammer.

MAIDENHEAD *n.* Virginity; virgin purity; freedom from contamination.

MAIDMARIAN *n.* A kind of dance, so called from a buffoon dressed like a man, who plays tricks to the populace.

MAKEBATE *n.* Breeder of quarrels.

MALAPERT *adj.* Saucy; quick with impudence; sprightly without respect or decency.

MAN *n.* Not a woman.

MANGLER *n.* A hacker; on that destroys bunglingly.

MANUMIT *v.* To release from slavery.

MANURE *v.* To cultivate by manual labour.

MARMALADE *n.* The pulp of quinces boiled into a consistence with sugar: it is subastringent and grateful to the stomach.

MARRIAGEABLE *adj.* Fit for wedlock.

MAUNDER *v.* To grumble; to murmur.

MAZY *v.* Perplexed; confused.

MEACOCK *n.* An uxorious or effeminate man.

MECHANICK *n.* A manufacturer; a low workman.

MEDIC *n.* A plant.

MEDITERRANEAN *adj.* Encircled with land.

MELLIFLUENT *adj.* Flowing with honey; flowing with sweetness.

MERCURIFICATION *adj.* The act of mixing anything with quicksilver.

MERETICIOUS *adj*. Whorish; such as is practiced by prostitutes; alluring by false show.

MERRY-ANDREW *n*. A buffoon; a zany; a jack-pudding.

MERRYTHOUGHT *n*. A forked bone on the body of fowls; so called because boys and girls pull in play at the two sides, the longest part broken off betokening priority of marriage.

METEOR *n*. Any bodies in the air or sky that are of a flux and transitory nature.

METEOROLOGIST *n*. A man skilled in meteors or studious of them.

MEWL *v*. To squall as a child.

MIASM *n*. Such particles or atoms as are supposed to arise from distempered, putrefying, or poisonous bodies and to affect people at a distance.

MICHER *n*. A lazy loiterer, who skulks about in corners and by-places, and keeps out of sight; a hedge creeper.

MICKLE *adj*. Much; great. In Scotland it is pronounced Muckle.

MIDNIGHT *n*. The noon of night.

MILLION *n*. A proverbial name for any great number.

MINGLER *n*. He who mingles.

MILKSOP *n*. A soft, mild effeminate, feeble-minded man.

MINUTE-WATCH *n.* A watch in which minutes are more distinctly marked than in common watches which reckon only by the hour.

MISPENDER *n.* One who spends ill or prodigally.

MISPOINT *v.* To confuse sentences by wrong punctuation.

MISS *n.* A term of honour for a young girl.
    and *n.* A strumpet; a concubine; a whore; a prostitute.

MISTION *n.* The state of being mingled.

MITTIMUS *n.* A warrant by which a justice commits an offender to prison.

MIZZY *n.* A bog; a quagmire.

MNEMONICKS *n.* The act of memory.

MOBBY *n.* An American drink made of potatoes.

MOBILE *n.* The populace; the rout; the mob.

MOHOCK *n.* The name of a cruel nation of America given to ruffians who infested, or rather were imagined to infest, the streets of London.

MOLEBAT *n.* A fish.

MOME *n.* A dull stupid blockhead.

MONSIEUR *n.* A term of reproach for a Frenchman.

MOONSTRUCK *adj.* Lunatic; affected by the moon.

MOPE-EYED *adj*. Blind of one eye.

MOPSEY *n*. Puppet made of rags.

MOREBOSE *n*. Preceeding from disease; not healthy.

MORLING *n*. Wool plucked from a dead sheep.

MOUNTEBANK *n*. A doctor that mounts a bench in the market and boasts his infallible remedies and cures.

MOUTH-FRIEND *n*. One who professes friendship without intending it.

MOUTH-HONOUR *n*. Civility outwardly expressed without sincerity.

MUCHWHAT *adv*. Nearly.

MUCID *adj*. Slimy; musty.

MUCKENDER *n*. A handkerchief.

MUCRONATED *n*. Narrowed to a sharp point.

MUGHOUSE *n*. An alehouse; a low house of entertainment.

MULCT *v*. To punish with fine or forfeiture.

MULLGRUBS *n*. Twisting of the guts.

MULSE *n*. Wine boiled and mingled with honey.

MUMPER *n*. A beggar.

MUMPS *n.* Sullenness; silent anger.

MUNDIVAGANT *adj.* Wandering through the world.

MUNDUNGUS *n.* Stinking tobacco.

MURAGE *n.* Money paid to keep walls in repair.

MURRAIN *n.* The plague in cattle.

MUTTONFIST *n.* A hand large and red.

MYNCHEN *n.* A nun.

N

NAFF *n.* A kind of tufted sea-bird.

NAKEDNESS *n.* Want of provision for defence.

NAPPINESS *n.* The quality of having a nap.

NARCOTICK *adj.* Producing torpor or stupefication.

NATATION *n.* The act of swimming.

NEAF *n.* A fist. It is retained in Scotland.

NEAT *n.* Black cattle, oxen.

NECTARINE *adj.* Sweet as nectar.

NECKBEEF *n.* The coarse flesh of the neck of cattle, sold to the poor at a very cheap rate.

NECROMANCER *n.* One who, by charms, can converse with the ghosts of the dead; a conjurer.

NEESE *v.* To sneeze; to discharge flatulencies by the nose. Retained in Scotland.

NESTEGG *n.* An egg left in the nest to keep the hen from forsaking it.

NEPENTHE *n.* A drug that drives away all pains.

NEPOTISM *n.* Fondness of nephews.

NETTLE *v.* To sting, to irritate.

NEWFANGLED *adj.* Formed with vain or foolish love of novelty.

NICTATE *v.* To wink.

NIDGET *n.* The opprobrious term with which the man was anciently branded who refused to come to the royal standard in times of exigency. A coward; a dastard.

NIDIFICATION *n.* The act of building nests.

NIGHTBRAWLER *n.* One who raises disturbances in the night.

NIGHTDOG *n.* A dog that hunts in the night. Used by deer stealers.

NIM *v.* To take. To steal.

NIMIETY *n.* The state of being too much.

NINCOMPOOP *n.* A fool; a trifler.

NINNYHAMMER *n.* A simpleton.

NIPPINGLY *adv.* With bitter sarcasm.

NITHING *n.* A coward, dastard, poltroon.

NITTY *adj.* Abounding with the eggs of lice.

NIZY *n.* A dunce; a simpleton.

NOBLESS *n.* Noblemen collectively.

NOCTAMBULO *n.* One who walks in his sleep.

NOCTIVAGANT *adj.* Wandering in the night.

NODATION *n.* The state of being knotted.

NODDY *n.* A simpleton; an idiot.

NOMBLES *n.* The entrails of a deer.

NONAGE *n.* Minority; time of life before legal maturity.

NOODLE *n.* A fool; a simpleton.

NOONING *n.* Repose at noon.

NONJURING *n.* One who conceiving James II unjustly deposed, refuses to swear allegiance to those who have succeeded him.

NOVERCAL *adj.* Having the manner of a stepmother.

NOWES *n.* The marriage knot. Out of use.

NUBBLE *v.* To bruise with handy cuffs.

NULLIBIETY *n*. The state of being nowhere.

NUMSKULL *n*. A dullard; a dunce; a dolt; a blockhead.

NUNCHION *n*. A piece of victuals eaten between meals.

O

OAF *n*. A changeling; a foolish child left by the fairies.

OATS *n*. A grain which in England is generally given to horses but in Scotland supports the people.

OBAMBULATION *n*. The act of walking about.

OBEQUITATION *n*. The act of riding about.

OBERRATION *n*. The act of wandering about.

OBESE *adj*. Fat; loaden with flesh.

OBREPTION *n*. The act of creeping on.

OBSTUPEFACTION *n*. The act of inducing stupidity.

OCCLUSION *n*. The act of shutting up.

OCTONOCULAR *adj*. Having eight eyes.

ODONTALGICK *adj*. Pertaining to the tooth-ache.

OECONOMICKS *n*. Management of household affairs.

OFF *interj*. An expression of abhorrence, or command to depart.

OGLE *v.* To view with side glances, as in fondness; or with a design not to be heeded.

OILMAN *n.* One who trades in oils and pickles.

OLITORY *n.* Belonging to the kitchen garden.

ONEIROCRITICAL *adj.* Interpretative of dreams.

OPHIOPHAGOUS *adj.* Serpent eating.

OPIATE *n.* A medicine that causes sleep.

OPTIMITY *n.* The state of being best.

ORNISCOPIST *n.* One who examines the flight of birds in order to foretell futurity.

OSCITATION *n.* The act of yawning.

OSPRAY *n.* The sea eagle, of which it is reported, that when he hovers in the air, all the fish in the water turn up their bellies, and lie still for him to seize which he pleases.

OUTKNAVE *v.* To surpass in knavery.

OUT-VILLAIN *v.* To exceed in villainy.

OUPHEN *n.* Elfish.

OVATION *n.* A lesser triumph among the Romans allowed to those commanders who had won a victory without much blood shed, or defeated some less formidable enemy.

OVERMUCHNESS *n.* Exhuberance, superabundance.

OVERYEARED *adj.* Too old.

OWLER *n.* One who carries contraband goods illicitly by night.

OXGANG *n.* Twenty acres of land.

OYSTERWENCH *n.* A woman whose business is to sell oysters. A low woman.

P

PADDER *n.* A robber; a foot highwayman.

PAIGLES *n.* Cowslips

PAILMAIL *n.* Violent; boisterous.

PALACIOUS *adj.* Royal; noble; magnificent.

PALLET *n.* A small bed, a mean bed.

PALLIARDISE *n.* Fornication; whoring.

PALLMALL *n.* A play in which the ball is struck with a mallet through an iron ring.

PALMER *n.* A pilgrim; they who returned from the holy land carried branches of palm.

PALMISTRY *n.* The cheat of foretelling fortune by the lines of the palm.

PAM *n.* The knave of clubs.

PAMPHLETEER *n.* A scribbler of small books.

PARAPHERNALIA *n.* Goods in the wife's disposal.

PARASITE *n.* One that frequents rich tables and earns his welcome by flattery.

PARBREAK *v.* To vomit.

PARIS *n.* A herb.

PARKER *n.* A park keeper.

PARNEL *n.* A punk; a slut.

PARRICIDE *n.* One who destroys his father.

PARTY-JURY *n.* A jury in some trials half foreigners and half natives.

PASH *n.* A kiss.

PASSION *n.* Violent commotion of the mind.

PASSPORT *n.* Permission of egress.

PATCHERY *n.* Botchery, bungling work, forgery.

PATHETICALLY *adv.* In such a manner as may strike the passions.

PATIBULARY *adj.* Belonging to the gallows.

PEACE *n.* Respite from war.

PEARLEYED *adj.* Having a speck in the eye.

PEDAL *adj.* Belonging to the foot.

PEDANT *n.* A schoolmaster.

PEDANTRY *n.* Awkward ostentation of needless learning.

PEDESTRIOUS *adj.* Not winged; going on foot.

PEEPER *n.* Young chickens just breaking the shell.

PENCIL *n.* A small brush of hair which painters dip in their colours.

PENCIL *v.* To paint.

PENKNIFE *n.* A knife used to cut pens.

PENSION *n.* An allowance made to anyone without an equivalent. In England it is generally understood to mean pay given to a state hireling for treason to his country.

PENTHOUSE *n.* A shed hanging out aslope from the main wall.

PEOPLE *n.* The vulgar.

PAPASTICKS *n.* Medicines which are good to help the rawness of the stomach and digest crudities.

PEPPERCORN *n.* Anything of inconsiderable value.

PEPPERMINT *n.* Mint eminently hot.

PERIAPT *n.* Amulet; charm worn as preservatives against diseases or mischief.

PERIERGY *n.* Needless caution in an operation; unnecessary diligence.

PERIWIG *n.* Hair not natural, worn by way of ornament or concealment of baldness.

PERMIXTON *n.* The act of mingling; the state of being mingled.

PERPENDER *n.* A coping stone.

PERPOTATION *n.* The act of drinking largely.

PERSPICUITY *n.* Clearness to the mind; easiness to be understood; freedom from obscurity or ambiguity.

PERTURBATOUR *n.* Raiser of commotions.

PERUKEMAKER *n.* A wig maker.

PESSARY *n.* An oblong form of medicine, made to thrust up into the uterus upon some extraordinary occasions.

PESTHOUSE *n.* An hospital for persons infected with the plague.

PESTEL *n.* A gammon of bacon.

PETECHIAL *adj.* Pestilentially spotted.

PETROL *n.* A liquid bitumen, black, floating on the water of springs.

PETTIFOGGER *n.* A petty small-rate lawyer.

PETTITOES *n.* The feet of a sucking pig.

PHASELS *n*. French beans.

PHILIPPICK *adj*. Any invective declamation.

PHILOLOGER *n*. One whose chief study is language.

PHIZ *n*. The face, in a sense of contempt.

PHYSIOGNOMY *n*. The act of discovering the temper, and foreknowing the fortune by the features of the face.

PICKTHANK *n*. An officious fellow, who does what he is not desired; a whispering parasite.

PICAROON *n*. A robber; a plunderer.

PICKLE *n*. An small parcel of land enclosed with a hedge, which in some countries is called a pringle.

PICKEREL-WEED *n*. A water plant, from which pikes are fabled to be generated.

PICT *n*. A painted person.

PIDDLE *v*. To pick at table; to feed squeamishly and without appetite.

PIGMY *n*. A small nation, fabled to be devoured by the cranes; thence anything mean or inconsiderable.

PIGSNEY *n*. A word of endearment to a girl.

PILOSITY *n*. Hairiness.

PILSER *n*. The moth or fly that runs into a candle flame.

PINK *v.* To wink with the eyes.

PINMONEY *n.* Money allowed to a wife for her private expenses without account.

PINNOCK *n.* The tom-tit.

PIQUERER *n.* A robber, a plunderer.

PIRATE *n.* Any robber; particularly a bookseller who seizes the copies of other men.

PISH *v.* To express contempt.

PITAPAT *n.* A flutter; a palpitation.

PITTANCE *n.* An allowance of meat in a monastery.

PLACKET *n.* A petticoat.

PLASH *n.* A small lake of water or puddle.

PLASTICK *adj.* Having the power to give form.

PLEDGET *n.* A small mass of lint.

PLESH *n.* A puddle; a boggy marsh.

PLUMIPEDE *n.* A fowl that has feathers on the foot.

PLUMPER *n.* Something worn in the mouth to swell out the cheeks.

POLITICIAN *n.* A man of artifice; one of deep contrivance.

POLITICKLY *adv.* Artfully, cunningly.

POLTRON *n.* The practice of cowards to cut off their thumbs, that they might not be compelled to serve in war.

PONK *n.* A nocturnal spirit. A hag.

PORRIDGE *n.* Food made by boiling meat in water.

PORWIGGLE *n.* A tadpole or young frog not yet fully shaped.

POSNET *n.* A little bason; a porringer, a skillet.

POSTER *n.* A courier; one that travels hastily.

POSTUREMASTER *n.* One who teaches or practises artificial contortions of the body.

POTATO *n.* An American word. An esculent root.

POTHER *v.* To make a blustering ineffectual effort.

POTTLE *n.* Liquid measure containing four pints.

POTSHERD *n.* A fragment of a broken pot.

POTVALIANT *adj.* Heated with courage by strong drink.

POY *n.* A ropedancer's pole.

PRASON *n.* A leek; also seaweed as green as a leek.

PRECOCIOUS *adj.* Ripe before time.

PRESSGANG *n.* A crew that strolls about the streets to force men into naval service.

PRICKLOUSE *n.* A word of contempt for a tailor.

PRIESTCRAFT *n.* Religious frauds; management of wicked priests to gain power.

PRIG *n.* A pert, conceited, saucy, pragmatical, little fellow.

PRINCOCK *n.* A coxcomb, a conceited person; a pert young rogue.

PRIVADO *n.* A secret friend.

PRIVY *n.* Place of retirement; necessary house.

PROFESSOR *n.* One who declares himself of any opinion or party.

PROFLIGATE *n.* An abandoned shameless wretch.

PROLIXNESS *n.* Tediousness.

PROMISCUOUS *adj.* Mingled; confused; undistinguished.

PROSTITUTE *n.* A public strumpet.

PROVENDER *n.* Dry food for brutes, hay and corn.

PRUDE *n.* A woman over nice and scrupulous and with false affectation.

PSEUDOLOGY *n.* A Falsehood of speech.

PSHAW *interj.* An expression of contempt.

PUBERTY *n.* The time of life in which the two sexes begin first to be acquainted.

PUBLICAN *n.* A toll gatherer.
and n. A man that keeps a house of general entertainment.

PUDDER *n.* A tumult; a turbulent and irregular bustle.

PUNDLE *n.* A short and fat woman.

PUNITION *n.* Punishment.

PUNK *n.* A whore; a common prostitute; a strumpet.

PUNSTER *n.* A low wit who endeavours at reputation by double meaning.

PUTID *adj.* Mean; low; worthless.

PUTTOCK *n.* A buzzard.

Q

QUACK *n.* A boastful pretender to arts which he does not understand.

QUAFF *v.* To drink luxuriously.

QUAFF *n.* He who quaffs.
and v. To drink; to swallow in large draughts.

QUAGGY *adj.* Boggy; soft; not solid.

QUADRIN *n.* A mite; a small piece of money, in value about a farthing.

QUAIL *v.* To languish, to sink into dejection; to lose spirit.

QUALIFICATION *n.* That which makes any person or thing fit for anything.

QUALMISH *adj.* Seized with sickly languor.

QUARTAN *n.* The fourth day ague.

QUARTERCOUSINS *n.* Not of the four first degrees of kindred, that is they are not friends.

QUEAN *n.* A worthless woman, generally a strumpet.

QUELL *n.* Murder, not in use.

QUEME *v.* To please. An old word.

QUERIST *n.* An enquirer; an asker of questions.

QUERPO *n.* A dress close to the body; a waistcoat.

QUESTERMONGER *n.* Starter of lawsuits or prosecutions.

QUESTUARY *adj.* Studious of profit.

QUIBBLER *n.* A punster.

QUICKEN *v.* To make alive.

QUIDDANY *n.* Marmalade. A confection of quinces and sugar.

QUOB *v.* To move as the embryo does in the womb; to move as the heart does when throbbing.

QUODLIBETARIAN *n.* One who talks or disputes on any subject.

QUOTIDIAN *n.* A fever which returns every day.

R

RACK-RENT *n.* Rent raised to the uttermost.

RAGINGLY *adv.* With vehement fury.

RAILER *n.* One who insults or defames by opprobrious language.

RAKEHEL *n.* A wild, worthless, dissolute, debauched, sorry-fellow.

RAMBOOZE *n.* A drink made of wine, ale, eggs and sugar in the winter time; or of wine, milk, sugar and rosewater in the summer time.

RAMMISH *adj.* Strong scented.

RAMPALLIAN *n.* A mean wretch.

RANNY *n.* The shrewmouse.

RANTIPOLE *n.* Wild; roving; rakish.

RAPPER *n.* One who strikes.

RASCALION *n.* One of the low people.

RATTLEHEADED *adj.* Giddy; not steady.

RAWHEAD *n.* The name of a spectre, mentioned to frighten children.

RAZOURABLE *adj.* Fit to be shaved.

REBELLOW *v.* To bellow in return.

RECRUDESCENT *adj.* Growing painful or violent again.

RECUBATION *n.* The act of lying or leaning.

REDCOAT *n.* A name of contempt for a soldier.

REDSHANK *n.* A contemptuous appellation for some of the people of Scotland.

REFOCILLATION *n.* Restoration of strength by refreshment.

REFUSE *adj.* That which remains disregarded when the rest is taken.

REMERCIE *v.* To thank, obsolete.

REMEMBERER *n.* One who remembers.

REPASTURE *n.* Entertainment.

REPLEVIN *v.* To take back or set at liberty any thing seized upon security given.

REPROBATE *n.* Lost to virtue; lost to grace; abandoned.

REREMOUSE *n.* A bat.

RESPERSION *n.* The act of sprinkling.

RESUPINATION *n.* The act of lying on the back.

RETROGRADATION *n.* The act of going backwards.

REVERY *n.* Loose musing, irregular thought.

REVOMIT *v.* To vomit again.

REVESTIARY *n.* Place where dresses are reposited.

RHABARBARATE *adj.* Impregnated or tinctured with rhubarb.

RHABDOMANCY *n.* Divination by a wand.

RHEUMATISM *n.* A painful distemper supposed to proceed from acrid humours.

RIBALD *n.* A loose, rough, mean, brutal wretch.

RIBROAST *v.* To beat soundly.

RIC *n.* A powerful, rich or valiant man.

RIDGLING *n.* A ram half castrated.

RIGATION *n.* The act of watering.

RIVER-DRAGON *n.* A crocodile.

RIVER-HORSE *n.* Hippopotamus.

RODOMONTADE *n.* An empty noisy bluster or boast; a rant.

ROLLYPOOLY *n.* A sort of game in which, when a ball rolls into a certain place, it wins.

ROMANCER *n.* A liar; a forger of tales.

ROMP *n.* A rude, awkward, boisterous. untaught girl.

RONION *n.* A fat bulky woman.

RORATION *n.* A falling of dew.

ROTGUT *n.* Bad beer.

ROUNDHOUSE *n.* The constable's prison in which disorderly persons, found in the street, are confined.

ROYNE *v.* To gnaw; to bite.

RUBBAGE *n.* Ruins of building, fragments of matter used in building.

RUDERARY *adj.* Belonging to rubbish.

RUGOSE *adj.* Full of wrinkles.

RUM *n.* A country parson.

RUNNION *n.* A paltry scurvy wretch.

RUSTICK *n.* A clown; a swain; an inhabitant of the country.

RUSTICATE *v.* To reside in the country.

S

SABBATHBREAKER *n.* Violator of the Sabbath by labour or wickedness.

SACRIFICABLE *adj.* Capable of being offered in sacrifice.

SALACIOUS *adj.* Lustful; lecherous. *See also Trumpery*

SALAMANDER *n.* An animal supposed to live in fire and imagined to be very poisonous.

SALAMANDER'S HAIR *n.* A kind of asbestos or mineral flax.

SALMAGUNDI *n.* A mixture of chopped meat and pickled herrings with oil, vinegar, pepper and onions.

SALTANT *adj.* Jumping; dancing.

SALTINBANCO *n.* A quack or mountebank.

SAMLET *n.* A little salmon.

SARCOPHAGUS *adj.* Flesh-eating; feeding on flesh.

SARCULATION *n.* The act of weeding; plucking up weeds.

SARN *n.* A British word for pavement or stepping stones, still used in Berkshire and Hampshire.

SATELLITE *n.* A small planet revolving round a larger. Four moons move about Jupiter and five about Saturn.

SATURN *n.* The remotest planet of the solar system. Supposed by astrologers to impress melancholy, dullness or severity of temper.

SASHOON *n.* A kind of leather stuffing put into a boot for the weaver's ease.

SAUCEBOX *n.* An impertinent or petulant fellow.

SAVEALL *n.* A small pan inserted into a candlestick to save the ends of candles.

SCALLION *n.* A kind of onion.

SCAMBLE *v.* To be turbulent and rapacious; to scramble; to get by struggling with others.

SCAMBLER *n.* A bold intruder upon one's generosity or table.

SCARAMOUCH *n.* A buffoon in motley dress.

SCATCHES *n.* Stilts to put the feet in to walk in dirty places.

SCELERAT *n.* A villain; a wicked wretch. A word introduced unnecessarily from the French by a Scottish author.

SCHOOLMAN *n.* One versed in the niceties and subtleties of academical disputation.

SCIATICA *n.* The hip gout.

SCIOMACHY *n.* Battle with a shadow.

SCION *n.* A small twig taken from one tree to be engrafted into another.

SCISSIBLE *adj.* Capable of being divided by a sharp edge.

SCOAT *v.* To stop a wheel by putting a stone or piece of wood under it.

SCOLD *n.* A clamorous, rude, mean, low, foul-mouthed woman.

SCOOPER *n.* One who scoops.

SCOTCH HOPPERS *n.* A play in which boys hop over lines or scotches in the ground.

SCRANCH *v.* To grind between the teeth. The Scots retain it.

SCREECHOWL *n.* An owl that hoots in the night and whose voice is supposed to betoken danger, misery or death.

SCROYLE *n.* A mean fellow; a rascal; a wretch.

SCUDDLE *v.* To run with a kind of affected haste or precipitation.

SCULLION *n.* The lowest domestic servant that washes the kettles and the dishes in a kitchen.

SEADOG *n.* Perhaps the shark.

SECOND SIGHT *n.* The power of seeing things future, or things distant; supposed inherent in some of the Scottish islanders.

SEDUCER *n.* One who draws aside from the right; a tempter; a corrupter.

SEEKSORROW *n.* One who contrives to give himself vexation.

SELION *n.* A ridge of land.

SEMIOPACOUS *adj.* Half dark.

SENNIGHT *n.* The space of seven nights and days; a week.

SERAGLIO *n.* A house of women kept for debauchery.

SERMOCINATION *n.* The act or practice of making speeches.

SERVING-MAN *n.* A menial servant.

SERVITUDE *n.* Slavery; state of a slave.

SEXTARY *n.* A pint and a half.

SHALLOP *n.* A small boat.

SHAMBLES *n.* The place where butchers kill or sell their meat.

SHAPESMITH *n.* One who undertakes to improve the form of the body.

SHARPER *n.* A tricking fellow; a petty thief; a rascal.

SHATTERBRAINED *adj.* Inattentive; not confident.

SHEEPBITER *n.* A petty thief.

SHIFTER *n.* One who plays tricks; a man of artifice.

SHILLING *n.* A coin of various value in different times. It is now twelve pence.

SHITTLECOCK *n.* A cork stuck with feathers and driven by players from one to another with battledoors.

SHOEING-HORN *n.* A horn used to facilitate the admission of the foot into a narrow shoe.

SHOG *n.* Violent concussion.

SHOPMAN *n.* A petty trader.

SHORTSIGHTEDNESS *n.* Defect of intellectual sight

SHORTWAISTED *adj.* Having a short body.

SHOTFREE *adj.* Clear of the reckoning.

SHOULDERSHOTTEN *adj.* Strained in the shoulder.

SHOULDERSLIP *n.* Dislocation of the shoulder.

SHREWMOUSE *n.* A mouse of which the bite is generally supposed venomous, and to which vulgar tradition assigns such malignity, that she is said to lame the foot over which she runs. I am informed that all these reports are calumnious, and that her feet and teeth are equally harmless with those of any other little mouse. Our ancestors however looked on her name with such terror that they are supposed to have given her name to a scolding woman, whom for her venom they call a shrew.

SHRIMP *n.* A little wrinkled man; a dwarf.

SIDEBOX *n.* Seat for the ladies on the side of the theatre.

SIMONY *n.* The crime of buying or selling church preferment.

SINEWSHRUNK *adj.* A horse that has been overridden.

SINGULT *n.* A sigh.

SIXPENCE *n.* A coin; half a shilling.

SKELLUM *n.* A villain; a scoundrel.

SKIMBLESKAMBLE *adj.* Wandering; wild.

SKINKER *n.* One that serves drink.

SKIPKENNEL *n.* A lackey; a footboy.

SKIPJACK *n.* An upstart.

SLABBER *v.* To let spittle fall from the mouth; to drivel.

SLATCH *n.* The middle part of a rope or cable that hangs down loose.

SLATTERN *n.* A woman negligent, not elegant or nice.

SLIDDER *v.* To slide with interruption.

SLIPSLOP *n.* Bad liquor.

SLOATS *n.* Of a cart, are those underpieces which keep the bottom together.

SLUBBERDEGULLION *n.* A paltry, dirty, sorry wretch.

SLUGGARD *n.* An idler; a drone; an inactive lazy fellow.

SLUTTERY *n.* The qualities or practice of a slut.

SLUTISH *adj.* Nasty; not nice; not cleanly; dirty; indecently negligent of cleanliness.

SMATTERER *n.* One who has a slight or superficial knowledge.

SMELLFEAST *n.* A parasite; one who haunts good tables.

SMICKET *n.* The undergarment of a woman.

SNIPSNAP *n.* Tart dialogue.

SOLIDUNGULOUS *adj.* Wholehoofed.

SOMERSET *n.* A leap by which a jumper throws himself from a beam, and turns over his head.

SONNETTEER *n.* A small poet, in contempt.

SORCERER *n.* A conjurer; an enchanter; magician.

SOSS *v.* To fit lazily on a chair; to fall at once into a chair.

SOT *v.* To tipple to stupidity.

SPADDLE *n.* A little spade.

SPANKER *n.* A small coin.

SPATTERDASHES *n.* Coverings for the legs by which the wet is kept off.

SPINDLESHANKED *adj.* Having small legs.

SPITCHCOCK *v.* To cut an eel in pieces and roast him.

SPONK *n.* A word in Edinburgh which denotes a match, or anything dipped in sulphur that takes fire.

SPRIT *v.* To throw out; to eject with force.

SPRUCEBEER *n.* Beer tinctured with branches of fir.

SPRUCENESS *n.* Neatness without elegance.

SPUNGINGHOUSE *n.* A house to which debtors are taken before commitment to prison where the bailiffs sponge upon them.

SPUTATION *n.* The act of spitting.

SPYBOAT *n.* A boat sent out for intelligence.

SQUIB *n.* Any petty fellow.

SQUALLER *n.* Screamer; one that screams

SQUINTIFEGO *adj.* Squinting.

STATESMAN *n.* A politician; one versed in the arts of government.

STATESWOMAN *n.* A woman who meddles with public affairs.

STERNUTATION *n.* The act of sneezing.

STEVEN *n.* A cry, or loud clamour.

STEW *n.* A brothel; a house of prostitution.

STICKLE *v.* To contest; to altercate; to contend rather with obstinacy that vehemence.

STICKLEBAG *n.* The smallest of fresh water fish.

STILETTO *n.* A small dagger, of which the blade is not edged but round, with a sharp point.

STINGO *n.* Old beer.

STINKARD *n.* A mean stinking paltry fellow.

STIRIOUS *adj.* Resembling icicles.

STOAT *n.* A small stinking animal.

STOCKJOBBER *n*. A low wretch who gets money by buying and selling shares in the funds.

STONEHORSE *n*. A horse not castrated.

STOUND *v*. To be in pain or sorrow.

STOUT *n*. Strong; lusty; valiant; brave; bold; intrepid; obstinate; pertinacious; resolute; proud; strong; firm.
and n. Strong beer.

STRAPPADO *n*. Chastisement by blows.

STRONGWATER *n*. Distilled spirits.

STRUT *n*. An affectation of stateliness in the walk.

STULTILOQUENCE *n*. Foolish talk.

STUM *n*. Wine yet unfermented.

STUPRATE *v*. To ravish; to violate.

STY *n*. Any place of bestial debauchery.

SUBDERISORIOUS *adj*. Scoffing or ridiculing with tenderness and delicacy.

SUBLAPSARY *adj*. Done after the fall of man.

SUBMARINE *adj*. Lying or acting under the sea. These contrivances may seem difficult because submarine navigators will want winds and tides for motion, and the sight of the heavens for direction.

SUCCUMB *v.* To yield; to sink under any difficulty. Not in use, except among the Scotch.

SUDATION *n.* Sweat.

SUDORIFICK *n.* A medicine promoting sweat.

SUGGILATE *v.* To beat black and blue; to make livid by a bruise.

SUICIDE *n.* Self-murder; the horrid crime of destroying one's self.

SUN *n.* The luminary that makes the day.

SUPERVACANEOUSNESS *n.* Needlessness.

SUPPLERLESS *adj.* Wanting supper.

SWAGGERER *n.* A blusterer; a bully; a turbulent noisy fellow.

SWAIN *n.* A pastoral youth.

SWALLOW *n.* A small bird of passage or, as some say, a bird that lies hid and sleeps in winter.

SWANSKIN *n.* A kind of soft flannel, imitating for warmth the down of a swan.

SWEEPSTAKE *n.* A man that wins all.

SWILLER *n.* A luxurious drinker.

SWINEBREAD *n.* A kind of plant; truffles.

SWINGEBUCKLER *n.* A bully; a man who pretends to feats of arms.

SWINK *v.* To overlabour.

SWOON *v.* To suffer a suspension of thought and sensation.

T

TALEBEARER *n.* One who gives officious or malignant intelligence.

TANTLING *n.* One seized with hopes of pleasure unobtainable.

TAPSTER *n.* One whose business is to draw beer in an alehouse.

TARANTULA *n.* An insect whose bite is only cured by music.

TATTERDEMALION *n.* A ragged fellow.

TATTLE *v.* To talk idly, to use many words with little meaning.

TATTOO *n.* The beat of a drum by which soldiers are warned to their quarters.

TEA *n.* A Chinese plant of which the infusion has lately been much drunk in Europe.

TEAGUE *n.* A name of contempt used for an Irishman.

TED *v.* To lay grass newly mown in rows.

TEEN *n.* Sorrow; grief.

TEMULENT *adj.* Inebriated; intoxicated as with strong liquors.

TENEBRICOSE *adj.* Dark; gloomy.

TERCE *n.* A vessel containing forty-two gallons of wine; the third part of a butt or pipe.

TERMAGANT *n.* A scold; a brawling turbulent woman.

TESTUDINEOUS *adj.* Resembling the shell of a tortoise.

THESMOTHETE *n.* A lawgiver.

THICKSKIN *n.* A coarse, gross man; a numskull.

THORAL *adj.* Relating to the bed.

THRAPPLE *n.* The windpipe of any animal. They still retain it in the Scottish dialect.

THRASONICAL *adj.* Boastful; bragging.

THRID *n.* To slide through a narrow passage.

THREEPENNY *adj.* Vulgar; mean.

THREEPILE *n.* An old name for good velvet.

THRYFALLOW *v.* To give the third ploughing in summer.

TIDDLE *v.* To use tenderly; to fondle.

TILLYFALLY *adj.* Anything said rejected as trifling or impertinent.

TIPPLE *v.* To drink luxuriously; to waste life over the cup.

TIREWOMAN *n.* A woman whose business is to make dresses for the head.

TIT *n.* A woman: in contempt.

TITUBATION *n.* The act of stumbling.

TOAD *n.* An animal resembling a frog; but the frog leaps, the toad crawls: the toad is accounted venomous, I believe truly.

TOILET *n.* A dressing table.

TOLUTATION *n.* The act of pacing or ambling.

TOMBOY *n.* A mean course fellow; sometimes a wild course girl.

TONGUEPAD *n.* A great talker.

TOOT *v.* To pry; to peep; to search narrowly and slily

TOOTHDRAWER *n.* One whose business is to extract painful teeth.

TOPSYTURVY *adv.* With bottom upward.

TORPEDO *n.* A fish which while alive, if touched even with a long stick benumbs the hand that so touches it, but when dead is eaten safely.

TORREFACTION *n.* The act of drying by the fire.

TOSSPOT *n.* A toper and drunkard.

TRANTERS *n.* Men who carry fish from the sea coast to sell in the inland countries.

TRAPE *v.* To run idly and sluttishly about. It is used only of women.

TRAVELTAINTED *adj.* Harassed; fatigued by travel.

TRAVESTY *adj.* Dressed so as to be made ridiculous; burlesqued.

TREMENDOUS *adj.* Dreadful; horrible; astonishingly terrible.

TRENCHERMATE *n.* A table companion; a parasite.

TRICKSY *adj.* Pretty. A word of endearment.

TRIPUDATION *n.* The act of dancing.

TROCHILICKS *n.* The science of rotary motion.

TROLLOP *n.* A slatternly, loose woman.

TROT *n.* An old woman. In contempt.

TROY-WEIGHT *n.* A kind of weight by which gold and bread are weighed, consisting of these denominations: a pound = 12 ounces; ounce = 20 pennyweights; pennyweight = 24 grains.

TRUBTAIL *n.* A short squat woman.

TRUCIDATION *n.* The act of killing.

TRUEPENNY *n.* A familiar phrase for an honest fellow.

TRULL *n.* A low whore; a vagrant strumpet.

TRUMPERY *n.* Something salacious; something of less value than it seems. Falsehood; empty talk. Something of no value; trifles. *See also Salacious*

TUSH *interj.* An expression of contempt.

TUZ *n.* A lock or tuft of hair.

TWANGLING *adj.* Contemptibly noisy.

TWIBIL *n.* A halbert.

TWITTLETWATTLE *n.* Tattle; gabble.

TYMPANY *n.* A kind of obstructed flatulence that swells the body like a drum.

TYRANNICIDE *n.* The Act of killing a tyrant.

U

UMPIRE *n.* A common friend who decides disputes.

UNBID *adj.* Uninvited.

UNDERFELLOW *n.* A mean man; a sorry wretch.

UNDERSTRAPPER *n.* A petty fellow; an inferior agent.

UNICORN *n.* A beast, whether real or fabulous, that has only one horn.

UNIVERSE *n.* The general system of things.

UNPREGNANT *adj.* Not prolific.

UNRAZORED *adj.* Unshaven.

UNWHIPT *adj.* Not punished; not corrected with the rod.

URCHIN *n.* A hedge-hog.

URINAL *n.* A bottle in which water is kept for inspection.

URINATOR *n.* A diver; one who searches under water.

USQUEBAUGH *n.* The water of life. A compounded, distilled, aromatic spirit; the Irish sort is particularly distinguished for its pleasant and mild flavour. The Highland sort is somewhat hotter; in Scottish they call it whisky.

USTORIOUS *adj.* Having the quality of burning.

USTION *n.* The act of burning; the state of being burned.

UXORIOUS *adj.* Submissively fond of a wife; infected with connubial dotage.

V

VACATION *n.* Leisure; freedom from trouble or perplexity.

VACCARY *n.* A cow house; a cow-pasture.

VALLANCY *n.* A large wig that shades the face.

VANCOURIER *n.* A harbinger.

VAPORER *n.* A boaster; a braggart.

VARLET *n.* A scoundrel; a rascal.

VARVELS *n.* Silver rings about the leg of a hawk, in which the owner's name is engraved.

VASTATION *n.* Waste; depopulation.

VATICIDE *n.* A murderer of poets.

VAUDEVIL *n.* A song common among the vulgar, and sung about the streets.

VAUNTER *n.* Boaster; braggart; man given to vain ostentation.

VENEFICE *n.* The practice of poisoning.

VENERY *n.* The sport of hunting.

VERECUND *n.* Modest; bashful.

VESPERTINE *adj.* Happening or coming in the evening; pertaining to the evening.

VEST *n.* An outer garment.

VIDUITY *n.* Widowhood.

VIGESIMATION *n.* The act of putting to death every twentieth man.

VINNEWED *adj.* Mouldy.

VIRAGO *n.* A female warrior; a woman with the qualities of a man.

VIRGINITY *n.* Maidenhead.

VITIOUS *adj.* Corrupt; wicked; opposite to virtuous. It is applied rather to habitual faults, than criminal actions.

VIZ *n.* To wit; that is. A barbarous form of an unnecessary word.

VOLERY *n.* A flight of birds.

VOLUPTUARY *n.* A man given up to pleasure and luxury.

VULGAR *n.* The common people.

VULPINE *adj.* Belonging to the fox.

W

WAG *n.* Anyone ludicrously mischievous; a merry droll.

WAGGLE *v.* To waddle; to move from side to side.

WAID *adj.* Crushed.

WAIR *n.* A piece of timber two yards long and a foot broad.

WALLOP *v.* To boil.

WAMBLE *v.* To roll with nausea and sickness. It is used of the stomach.

WANTWIT *n.* A fool; an idiot.

WAPED *adj.* Dejected; crushed by misery.

WARDROBE *n.* A room where clothes are kept.

WARLING *n.* One often quarrelled with.

WARLOCK *n.* A male witch; a wizard. In Scotland it is applied to a man whom the vulgar suppose to be conversant with the spirits, as a woman who carries on the same commerce is called a witch.

WARMINGSTONE *n.* Useful stones digged in Cornwall, which being once heated at the fire retains its warmth a great while, and hath been found to give ease in the internal haemorrhoids.

WARRAY *v.* To make war upon.

WARWORN *adj.* Worn with war.

WASSAIL *n.* A liquor made of apples, sugar and ale, anciently much used by English goodfellows.

WATCHET *adj.* Pale blue.

WATERMELON *n.* A plant. It hath trailing branches as the cucumber or melon and is distinguished from other cucurbitaceous plants by its leaf deeply cut and jagged and by its producing uneatable fruit.

WAWL *v.* To cry; to howl.

WEATHERSPY *n.* A star-gazer; an astrologer; one that foretells the weather.

WEED *n.* A herb noxious or useless.

WEEKDAY *n.* Any day not Sunday.

WEEN *v.* To think, to imagine, to form a notion, to fancy.

WELAWAY *interj.* Alas.

WELLWILLER *n.* One who means kindly.

WENCHER *n.* A fornicator.

WHERRET *v.* To give a box on the ear.

WHIFFLE *v.* To move inconstantly, as if driven by a puff of wind.

WHIMPLED *adj.* Distorted with crying.

WHIPSTER *n.* A nimble fellow.

WHOOBUB *n.* Hubbub.

WHORE *v.* To converse unlawfully with the other sex.

WHURR *v.* To pronounce the letter r with too much force.

WIDOWHUNTER *n.* One who courts widows for a jointure.

WIDOWMAKER *n.* One who deprives women of their husbands.

WIGHT *adj.* Swift; nimble.

WIFE *n.* A woman of low employment.

WILDGOOSECHASE *n.* A pursuit of something as unlikely to be caught as the wild goose.

WILLI *adj.* Many.

WIMBLE *adj.* Active; nimble; shifting to and fro.

WIMPLE *n.* A hood; a veil.

WINDEGG *n.* An egg not impregnated; an egg that does not contain the principles of life.

WINTERBEATEN *adj.* Harassed by severe weather.

WISEACRE *n.* A wise, or sententious man.
and n. A fool; a dunce.

WITLING *n.* A pretender to wit; a man of petty smartness.

WITTOL *n.* A man who knows the falsehood of his wife and seems contented; a tame cuckold.

WITWORM *n.* One that feeds on wit; a canker of wit.

WOEBEGONE *n.* Lost in woe; distracted in woe, overwhelmed in sorrow.

WOODNOTE *n.* Wild Music.

WORKYDAY *n.* A day not the Sabbath.

WORKHOUSE *n.* A place where idlers and vagabonds are condemned to labour.

WOT *v.* To know; to be aware.

WRETCH *n.* A miserable mortal. A worthless sorry creature.

X

X is a letter, which though found in Saxon, begins no word in the English language.

Y

YARR *v.* To growl, or snarl like a dog.

YELK *n.* The yellow part of the egg. Often written yolk.

YELLOWBOY *n.* A gold coin.

YESTERNIGHT *n.* The night before this night.

YOND *adj.* Mad furious.

YUCK *n.* Itch.

YUX *n.* The hiccough.

Z

ZANY *n.* One employed to raise laughter by his gestures, actions and speeches; a merry-andrew; a buffoon.

ZEPHYR *n.* The west wind and, poetically, any calm soft wind.

ZOOTOMIST *n.* A dissector of the bodies of brute beasts.

PART THREE
Departures

Endangered words

In Part Two we were introduced to words that most readers will never have heard before. Due to lack of care by us, the users, they have slipped away into obscurity. The hope is that, having given them a glimpse of resurgence, they may once again be lured back into a vigorous existence. Others must be prevented from suffering the indignity of rejection. Part Three is where we try and catch them before they wander off.

By remembering these wastrels of the lexicon, we hope that we may press them back into life. They are words that are no longer everyday tools of the wordsmith. Here, in this retirement home of language once inhabited by Charles Dickens and Oscar Wilde, these gems of the English language will soon be forgotten unless we give them a chance. So if you hear or read these words and know what they mean but do not write or speak them yourself then you are contributing to their demise. Please help them…

A

ABATE *v.* To beat down, to diminish. *After three days of appalling weather the storm abated.*

ABERRATION *n.* A deviation into the unexpected from the correct way particularly in regard to precision in matters of truthfulness. *After his aberration he was asked to resign.*

ABET *v.* To incite by encouragement. Aiding and abetting is a legal expression. Aiding is giving practical assistance whereas abetting is merely urging someone to do something. *She abetted her husband to apply for the manager's job.*

ABHOR *v.* To shrink back from with horror, detestation and loathing. *They abhorred his behaviour when he ran off with his neighbour's wife.*

ABJURE *v.* To renounce a previously held belief while under oath. *In the hope of receiving a lighter sentence the prisoner abjured his support for the extreme political party.*

ABRADE *v.* To wear down by friction using an abrasive material or by erosion. *The riverbank had been abraded by the ferocity of the flood water.*

ABROGATE *v.* To repeal; to annul by an authoritative act. *The Great Repeal Act in 2017 was the first step towards the abrogation of many European laws.*

ABSINTHE *n.* An intoxicating spirit flavoured with extract of wormwood. *The critics debated whether Van Gogh's dramatic brush work was due to his obsession for absinthe.*

ABSTRUSE *adj.* Remote from ordinary minds or notions; difficult to be understood. *His suggestion that they should swim across the wide river was so abstruse that no one followed him.*

ACHILLEAN *adj.* Brave, unrelenting in wrath but with a single weakness. *Achilles died when struck on the heel that being the only part of his body not immersed when his mother lowered him into the River Styx to give him invulnerability.*

ACME *n.* The highest point; the culmination of perfection in a career or the crisis in the progress of a disease. *The acme of the local football team was when they won the cup by a margin of four goals.*

ACQUIESCE *v.* To accept without opposition; to agree. *I readily acquiesce to your suggestion that we should walk to the pub for lunch.*

ACRIMONY *n.* A sharpness or severity of temper; bitterness of expression. Describes the manner rather than any forceful action. *His voice was full of acrimony as he stormed out of the room.*

ACTUATE *v.* To put into action or to incite action. *The thermostat actuates the boiler when the temperature drops.*

ADAGE *n.* An old saying imparting wisdom or experience that has obtained credit merely by being long used. *An adage says that when the holly trees are laden with berries in November there will be a harsh winter.*

ADDLE *v.* To confuse someone until they are muddled and unable to think clearly. *The insurance salesman totally addled the elderly couple.*

ADMONISH *v.* To mildly reprimand someone who has engaged in wrong practice invariably adding instruction and advice. *His mother admonished him for not standing up when his grandfather entered the room explaining that it was considered polite to do so.*

ADO *n.* Fuss and worry about a situation that is undeserving of attention. *There was much ado about the spilt glass of water.*

AFFABLE *adj.* Ease of conversation in a courteous manner. *The relaxed and affable nature of the conversation resulted in a most enjoyable evening.*

AGHAST *adj.* Stupefied with shock and horror. *They were aghast when they discovered that their house had been burgled.*

AGOG *adj.* Eagerness while waiting for something to happen. *Their horse was leading when it passed them and they were agog to see if he had won.*

AGUE *n.* An illness accompanied by shivering. *The doctor worried about the patient's ague and ordered him to rest.*

AHEM *interj.* A cough to attract attention. *The chairman brought the meeting to order with a polite ahem.*

AKIMBO *adj.* Arms outstretched often to stress the importance of a pronouncement. *The grandfather stood with arms akimbo when he told the children they were going to the pantomime.*

ALACK *n.* An exclamation of sorrow and regret. Whereas alas, often used in conjunction with alack, as in 'alas and alack', denotes concern. *She cried alack when she broke her favourite plate.*

ALEATORY *adj.* Decision making by the throw of a dice or other random activity. *After extra time they were still level so the referee had to resort to the aleatory toss of a coin.*

AMANUENSIS *n.* A literary assistant who takes dictation or handles manuscripts. *The author always thanked his amanuensis in the acknowledgement section of his books.*

AMBAGE *n.* Speech intentionally delivered in a roundabout manner. *The audience grew tired of the speaker's ambage and eventually someone called out that he should get to the point.*

AMBROSIA *n.* The fabled food of the gods which gave immortal youth and beauty to those who ate it. More recently used to describe any finely flavoured food or beverage. *He loved going home for the weekend and always praised his mother's cooking as ambrosia.*

AMELIORATE *v.* To improve and make better. *The new sewage system did much to ameliorate London's unhealthy living conditions.*

AMEN *excl.* Familiar at the end of prayers, amen also means 'so be it' or 'I agree with you'. *After an excellent meal he congratulated the cook and the other diners all said 'Amen to that'.*

AMOK *adv.* Uncontrolled violence and destruction. *The football supporters ran amok after their team slipped down the league.*

ANODYNE *n.* Treatment that reduces pain. *The medicine prescribed after his accident proved to be a pleasing anodyne.*

ANTEDILUVIAN *adj.* Literally something occurring before Noah's flood but now anything that is incredibly old fashioned. *His children described the plus four trousers he wore when gardening as antediluvian.*

APPOSITE *adj.* Suitable; well adapted for the task in hand. *Her backpack was apposite for carrying her picnic lunch when she went on long walks.*

APPROBATION *n.* The act of approving with satisfaction and pleasure. *I offer my approbation for the quality of your fish pie.*

APROPOS *prep.* The appropriate association of one item to another often to emphasise a point that is being made. *Apropos of what we decide to have for lunch, I notice the raspberries in the garden are ripe.*

ARRANT *adj.* Total. *He told the politician that he was speaking arrant nonsense.*

ARTIFICE *n.* An artful, skilful or ingenious deception. *By the use of artifice he was able to defraud the pensioner of her savings.*

ARTISAN *n.* Someone skilled in an art or trade. *The apprenticeship that he served made him an exceptionally skilled artisan.*

ASPERATE *v.* To make rough or uneven. *Before sowing the seed he asperated the soil with a garden rake.*

ASPERSE *v.* To discredit by spreading falsehoods, injurious charges and slander. *The disgruntled customer was convinced he had been short changed in the bakery so he aspersed that he had suffered food poisoning from a cake he bought there.*

ASSAIL *v.* To attack someone but, unlike assault which implies violence, with argument, censure or abuse. *After the match ended in a draw the supporters of each side assailed each other with reasons why their team should have won.*

ASSIDUOUS *adj.* Performed with the utmost diligence and devotion. *After his mother fell ill he was assiduous in the help he gave to her.*

ASSUAGE *v.* To moderate a situation; to pacify. *He assuaged her fears by saying that the repairs would not be as expensive as she had thought.*

ATTENUATE *v.* To make thin or slender. *After checking her weight she determined to attenuate her waist line.*

ATTRITION *n.* The act of wearing down the strength of a person or object. *By speaking to the bank robber the police gently applied attrition until he confessed.*

AVARICE *n.* An inordinate desire to gain and possess wealth. *His whole life seemed devoted to avarice and consequently he missed out on many of life's simple pleasures.*

AVOIRDUPOIS *n.* The pre-decimalisation system of weight. *The butcher was brought up with avoirdupois so he knew what she meant by a pound of mince.*

AVOW *v.* To publicly support a belief or sentiment. *He avowed his political beliefs at the hustings.*

AVUNCULAR *adj.* Of or pertaining to an uncle. *The children loved to ride in the open topped avuncular sports car when their mother's brother came to visit.*

B

BADINAGE *n.* Light or playful discourse. *The friendly badinage in the bar after the game echoed the sporting nature in which they had been playing.*

BAGATELLE *n.* A trifle; a thing of no importance. *When I apologised to the owner of the car for splashing muddy water on it he said I should not be concerned as it was mere bagatelle.*

BALDERDASH *n.* Senseless talk; noisy nonsense. *The constituent accused the candidate of speaking balderdash and said he would not be voting for him.*

BALK *n.* A beam of timber. *The roof of the ancient barn was constructed of massive balks able to hold the weight of the heavy slates.*

BALM *n.* Fragrant substances extracted from plants for use as medicinal treatments. *The healer prepared balms from plants she found growing wild in the hedgerows.*

BALONEY *n.* Nonsense. *He was so ignorant that most things he said were baloney.*

BAMBOOZLE *v.* To hoax; to deceive. *The playground bully attempted to bamboozle the new boy out of his pocket money.*

BANAL *adj.* Commonplace vulgarity. *His habit of engaging in banal humour was out of place in the polite surroundings of the golf club.*

BANDOG *n.* A large fierce dog. *The policeman told the owner of the bandog that he should keep it on a lead.*

BANDY *adj.* Legs far apart at the knees. *They said that he had spent so long on horseback that he had developed bandy legs.*

BANNOCK *n.* An unleavened cake of oatmeal baked on an open fire. *For their supper the campers prepared bannocks on their camp fire.*

BANTER *n.* Humorous fun made with jokes or jests. *There was plenty of playful banter after he fell into the snow.*

BASSINET *n.* A wicker basket covered at one end that is used as a cradle for babies. *The first present they were given after the birth of their son was a bassinet that had once belonged to his grandmother.*

BATHOS *n.* A ludicrous descent from the elevated to the mean in writing or speech; a sinking anticlimax. *The storyline of the film made the first half most enjoyable but the bathos of the plot towards the end made them wish they had not seen it.*

BAUBLE *n.* A trifling piece of finery. *It may have been a mere bauble but the necklace they bought on their honeymoon remained her favourite.*

BAWL *v.* To cry out loudly. *When he slipped off the bridge into the river he bawled until a passer-by was able to rescue him.*

BEAU *n.* A male sweetheart or lover. *She could not wait to introduce her new beau to her friends.*

BEDABBLE *v.* To wet by sprinkling. *She bedabbled the tiny shoots as they emerged from the ground.*

BEDAUB *v.* To soil with anything thick, slimy and dirty. *After a day working under the engine of his car his clothes were bedaubed with engine oil.*

BEDRAGGLED *adj.* Dishevelled, untidy, messy. *His bicycle had a bedraggled appearance after he rode it through the fields on a rainy day.*

BEFOG *v.* To confuse by immersing in a fog either meteorologically or mentally. *He became completely befogged by the confusing details given to him by his accountant.*

BEFOOL *v.* To make a fool of; to delude or lead into error. *I was befooled by the fast talking salesman.*

BEGUILE *v.* To delude, deceive, cheat, trick or dupe. *He beguiled me into believing that the antique was genuine but later I discovered it was a reproduction.*

BELABOUR *v.* To beat soundly. *He caught the burglar red handed and belaboured him until he dropped the stolen goods and fled.*

BELIE *v.* To speak falsely; to tell lies by false reporting. *The estate agent's description that the house was in a peaceful setting belied the truth as the busy railway line ran at the bottom of the garden.*

BELITTLE *v.* To speak disparagingly of. *She belittled his achievements on the golf course in a manner which he thought was unjustified.*

BELLICOSE *adj.* Inclined to war; pugnacious; showing warlike feelings. *The politician made bellicose speeches which did not go down well with the electorate.*

BERSERK *adj.* Extreme violence; fury. *After he was arrested he went berserk and was locked in a police cell.*

BESPANGLE *v.* To dot or sprinkle with something brilliant. *The best selling china that year was bespangled with coloured dots.*

BESPATTER *v.* To discredit with calumny; to unjustifiably soil a reputation. *After the trial the newspapers bespattered his reputation even though he had been acquitted.*

BETRUMP *v.* To deceive; to cheat; to evade by guile. *He betrumped her out of winning the election*

BIBULOUS *adj.* Excessive partiality to alcohol. *His bibulous habits infuriated his wife.*

BLARNEY *n.* Excessively persuasive language; gross flattery. *The car salesman invariably resorted to blarney when he thought a sale was likely.*

BLUNDER *v.* To err stupidly; to flounder and stumble either literally or figuratively. *He did not help himself by blundering about when careful thought might have been more helpful.*

BLURT *v.* To utter suddenly or inadvertently; to divulge inadvisably. *He later regretted that he had blurted out what a good tennis player he was.*

BOHEMIAN *n.* An artist or literary person leading a carefree often dissipated life despising conventional behaviour. *She became very bohemian after she left art school and seemed not to have a care in the world.*

BOLSTER *n.* A long pillow or cushion used to support the head. *After his accident he found it more comfortable in bed if he had a bolster under his pillow.*

BOMBASTIC *adj.* Speech unnecessarily inflated in expression. *He always spoke in such a bombastic fashion that people stopped believing what he said.*

BONHOMIE *adj.* Carefree; easy going. *His bonhomie always lifted the spirits of the people he was with.*

BOON *adj.* Jovial, merry. *Her happy and amusing outlook on life meant that she was always a boon companion at a party.*

BOOR *n.* A peasant; a rustic; rude in manners. *No one could understand why he was such a boor, it was as if he took pleasure in being rude.*

BRACKISH *adj.* Salty water. *The dog soon learnt that the brackish water in the tidal estuary did not quench his thirst.*

BRAT *n.* A contemptible child. *The brat always disrupted the lessons.*

BROSE *n.* A Scottish dish of boiling water or milk with oatmeal. *His perfect meal was a main course of haggis followed by a brose.*

BUCOLIC *adj.* Pastoral, pertaining to rural life, particularly to herdsman. *He hated commuting so he bought a farm and immersed himself in a bucolic existence.*

BUDGE *v.* To move a little. *He thought he could squeeze onto the bench so he asked his friends to budge up a bit.*

BUFFER *n.* A foolish fellow; deserving mild contempt because he is lost in the past. *His outdated attitude about pretty well everything caused him to be called a buffer by those who knew him.*

BUFFOON *n.* A man who amuses others with tricks and gestures; a term of mild contempt used by people not amused by ridiculous pranks. *The circus clown played the buffoon on a bicycle and the children all laughed.*

BUMPKIN *n.* An awkward clumsy blockhead; a lout. A term of disrespect for an uncouth countryman. *His simple manner and rural lifestyle was so different to theirs that the newcomers to the village wrote him off as a country bumpkin.*

BUMPTIOUS *adj.* Offensively self-assertive; disposed to quarrelling; domineering. *The bumptious councillor was full of his own self importance and continually demanded his own way with everything.*

BURLESQUE *adj.* Humorous entertaining; exaggeration; caricature; dramatic extravaganza. *The programme of the old style music hall evening had numerous burlesque singers and entertainers.*

C

CABAL *n.* A group of plotters intent on some secret purpose. *The dissenting directors formed a cabal determined to remove the chairman.*

CABOODLE *n.* Invariably expressed with kit. As both kit and caboodle mean a complete collection the expression means absolutely everything. *He insisted on taking the whole kit and caboodle when they went camping.*

CANDOUR *n.* Freedom from prejudice and therefore totally honest. *He expressed his views with total candour and was respected for that.*

CANT *n.* Hypocritical speech supporting the speaker's view that he is morally superior. *The club secretary was inclined to cant so they took little notice of him.*

CARD *n.* An unconventional person, strangely amusing yet harmless. *As he was always up to something humorous he was considered a bit of a card.*

CARTOMANCY *n.* Fortune telling by revealing a random sequence of playing cards. *She raised money at the fete by pretending that her cartomancy could predict the future.*

CATCHPENNY *n.* A loss leader used to encourage sales of other items. *The catchpennies in the window always drew the customers into his shop.*

CATERWAUL *n.* Inconsiderate, high pitched screaming. *She complained to the landlord of the pub when the students started caterwauling at closing time.*

CATHARTIC *adj.* Relief by expressing emotional feelings. *Talking through all her problems with her friend provided a much needed cathartic effect.*

CAVEAT *n.* A stipulation attached to an instruction. *I will lend you my car with the caveat that the tank is full on its return.*

CHANTAGE *n.* Blackmail. The extortion with threats of scandalous revelations. *Even though it was clearly chantage she paid him the money because she was terrified of what he might say.*

CHIT *n.* A piece of paper recording details of a transaction. *They gave him a chit to hand in at the warehouse.*

CHOKEY *n.* Prison. *He got two years in choky for stealing the car.*

CHRONOMETER *n.* A very accurate clock or watch. *His grandfather's pocket chronometer kept perfect time.*

CHURL *n.* An ill-bred countryman. *The churl next door to the newcomers was rude and unwelcoming.*

CIRCUMABULATE *v.* To walk slowly in a circle. *The monks circumambulated the cloisters deep in thought.*

CIRCUMLOCUTION *adj.* Unnecessary use of words to evade an issue or to be intentionally vague. *In Little Dorrit Charles Dickens described a government department as The Circumlocution Office that spent a great deal of time achieving nothing at all.*

CIRCUMSPECT *adj.* Approaching an issue with extreme caution and prudence. *The doctor was always very circumspect when discussing his patient's conditions.*

CLEAVE *v.* To forcibly divide into two parts along a natural grain. *The stonemason was expert at cleaving the sandstone in precisely the right place.*

CLIQUE *n.* A closed group of people pursuing a common purpose. *They formed a clique to tidy up the village green.*

COBBLE *v.* To use random elements to produce a useful item. *She cobbled together whatever she found in the fridge to make a delicious meal.*

CODGER *n.* An elderly man given to reminiscing about the past. *The old codgers in the pub said it was not like that in their day.*

COGITATE *v.* To give thoughtful consideration to a problem. *The judge spent much time cogitating over the issues before giving his decision.*

COMITY *n.* The courteous behaviour of one country to another. *The comity that existed between the nations ensured that each respected the other's laws.*

COMMODIOUS *adj.* Spacious. *The estate agent's particulars described the large kitchen as commodious.*

COMPOS MENTIS *adj.* Being mentally competent and in control of one's mind. *The clarity of his speech showed that the patient was totally compos mentis.*

CONDIDDLE *v.* To steal. *He was arrested for condiddling in the sweet shop.*

CONFABULATE *v.* To chat. *The neighbours spent hours confabulating over the garden fence.*

CONFLOPULATION *n.* A disparate gathering of items brought together more by chance than design. *She steered clear of the conflopulation he kept in his shed.*

CONFUTE *v.* To prove a person or theory wrong. *The speed camera confuted his assertion that he was driving within the limit.*

CONK *n.* A large nose. *Thought to be slang derived by reversing the letters in the Gypsy word for nose* knoc.

CONTRETEMPS *n.* A minor disagreement or an embarrassing occurrence. *A contretemps ensued when each thought it was the other's turn to buy the next round.*

CONUNDRUM *n.* A puzzling question. *They solved the conundrum of the missing apples when they saw a squirrel making off with one.*

CORUSCATE *v.* To sparkle. *The moonlight was coruscating on the sea.*

COUTH *adj.* Well mannered, sophisticated, refined. *She always enjoyed visits from her son's couth friend.*

CRANK *n.* A person obsessed by a particular interest at the exclusion of all else. *They thought he was a crank for spending all that time train spotting.*

CRAPULENCE *n.* Sickness caused by intemperance. *Another word for a hangover.*

CREDULOUS *adj.* Too easily persuaded. *His boss was concerned that he was over credulous when approached by visiting salesmen.*

CREPUSCULAR *adj.* Pertaining to twilight. *Badgers are crepuscular as they emerge at dusk.*

CRINOLINE *n.* A framework of horse hair, bone, starched cloth or metal worn beneath women's dresses to hold the skirt away from the body. *What a relief that young girls no longer have to wear crinolines.*

CROCODILE TEARS *n.* Insincere grief or sadness derived from a belief that crocodiles only cry when killing for food. *His show of crocodile tears when his boss was sacked was insincere as he knew it was a chance for promotion.*

CUMMERBUND *n.* A decorative waist band usually worn with formal dress. *He always wore a shot silk cummerbund when he went to the office Christmas dance.*

CUPBOARD LOVE *n.* Insincere affection intended to gain a reward. *His expression of cupboard love was purely because he wanted to borrow her car.*

CUPIDITY *n.* A lust for money or possessions. *His cupidity was the cause of his downfall.*

CURMUDGEON *n.* An ill-natured, miserly person. *The curmudgeon never had a good word to say about anyone.*

D

DAINTY *adj.* Small, elegant, delicate. *The bridesmaid's dresses were daintily edged with lace.*

DEFENESTRATE *v.* To throw an object or person out of a window. *During the revolution people were executed by defenestration.*

DELETERIOUS *adj.* A cause that has a damaging effect. *Smoking has a deleterious effect on health.*

DERRING-DO *n.* An act of extreme courage undertaken in a flamboyant manner. *The pirate leapt onto the ship in an act of derring-do that inspired his men to join the fight.*

DESHABILLE *n.* The state of being scantily clothed. *The teenagers left the bar drunk and deshabille.*

DESPERADO *n.* A bold and desperate person; a criminal prepared to engage in a violent and reckless manner. *When he realised that he was surrounded by police the desperado came out firing recklessly.*

DICHOTOMY *n.* Two parts of a situation where each is quite different to the other. *There was a dichotomy between his earnings and her credit card expenditure.*

DIDACTIC *adj.* Teaching a moral issue; lecturing in a domineering manner. *His teaching methods may have been didactic but his pupils never forgot what he said.*

DIDDLE *v.* To swindle on a minor scale. *He diddled his boss by helping himself to the petty cash.*

DILETTANTE *n.* Someone choosing to impress by appearing to be knowledgeable in a subject such as the arts when, in fact, their interest is superficial. *At first they thought highly of the dilettante but soon realised his command of the subject was limited.*

DIMINUTION *n.* A reduction in any aspect of an item. *Exercise resulted in a pleasing diminution of his waist line.*

DIPSOMANIA *n.* An irresistible craving for alcohol. *She left him when dipsomania took hold of him.*

DISAVOW *v.* To deny knowledge of something; to deny responsibility for it. *The child disavowed the broken window even though his football was among the broken glass.*

DOFF *v.* To take off. *He doffed his cap to the vicar as a mark of respect.*

DOGGEREL *n.* Comic verses written without regard for rhyme or literary content. *He could entertain them for hours with his endless supply of doggerel.*

DOGGO *adv.* To remain quite still either in sleep or to avoid detection. *He stayed doggo as the police looked for him.*

DOILY *n.* A decorative mat of paper or lace placed under a cake. *The waitress always put a doily under the cakes before putting them on the plates.*

DOLT *n.* A stupid fellow. *The dolt was not paying attention and spun his car off the road.*

DO-NOTHING *n.* Idle people. *The do-nothings hung around on the street corner all day long.*

DOTARD *n.* A stupid person showing the weakness of old age. *In 2017 Kim Jong Un of North Korea called President Trump a mentally deranged dotard.*

DRIBS AND DRABS *n.* Negligible amounts. *After the wedding there were only dribs and drabs of drink left over.*

DUDGEON *n.* Deep resentment. *He left in a state of high dudgeon when he saw that his ex-wife's boyfriend was there.*

DUMPS *n.* A gloomy state of mind. *His dismissal resulted in him being down in the dumps.*

DUTCH UNCLE *n.* An experienced person giving helpful advice. *She was comforted by her Dutch uncle's advice that it would all come right in the end.*

E

ECHELON *n.* A rank within any organisation. *His meteoric rise swiftly earned him a place in the higher echelons of the company.*

EDACIOUS *adj.* Greedy; obsessed with eating. *The doctor criticised her edacious habits.*

EFFICACIOUS *adj.* Something producing a desired result. *His policies proved efficacious and he was re-elected.*

EFFLUVIUM *n.* Disagreeable vapours and minute particles discharged from chimneys or decaying matter. *The Clean Air Act greatly reduced the effluvium levels.*

EGG *v.* To urge or encourage. *The father of the shy boy egged him on to join the rugby team.*

EGRESS *n.* The way out. *The fire officer said that only one egress was inadequate.*

EMBONPOINT *n.* Plumpness, particularly of the female form. *As she approached middle age her embonpoint became increasingly apparent.*

ENTREMET *n.* A small dish of food served between the main courses. *A lemon sorbet entremet cleared the palate before the main course.*

EON *n.* A very long period of time. *The school girl thought that the end of term sounded an eon away.*

ERE *prep.* Before. *They enjoyed the holiday so much that they were sure to return ere long.*

ERGO *adv.* Therefore and in conclusion. *They took regular exercise and ergo were very fit.*

ERR *v.* To wander from the correct way. *Her husband erred so often that she started divorce proceedings.*

ESCHEW *v.* To shun or abstain from. *In later life he eschewed alcohol.*

ESQUIRE *n.* A respectful title given to men without entitlement to another but who deserve recognition of a social standing. *John Smith Esquire.*

EXCORIATE *v.* To criticize severely. *The leader of the opposition excoriated the prime minister.*

EXEMPLAR *n.* A person or thing to be imitated by virtue of perfection. *His behaviour was upheld as an exemplar to all.*

EXIMIOUS *adj.* Excellent; the very best. *Her acting was eximious.*

EXPECTORATE *v.* To spit. *He was derided for expectorating on the pitch.*

EXPOSTULATE *v.* To protest with great enthusiasm. *The pedestrian expostulated his anger with the motorist.*

EXPUNGE *v.* To wipe an unpleasant thought or memory from the mind. *She expunged him as she started her new relationship.*

EXTIRPATE *v.* To root out; to destroy totally. *It took a long time but eventually the police extirpated the criminal gang.*

EYE-SHOT *n.* The extent of visibility. *He told the policemen that the incident occurred out of his eye-shot and he so could not describe the man.*

F

FACTOTUM *n.* An employee capable of undertaking any task. *The boss valued the young factotum who seemed capable of solving any problem that was given to him.*

FARRAGO *n.* A confused mass of thought or action. *The coach chastised the losing side by calling them a total farrago.*

FASTIDIOUS *adj.* Overly attentive; difficult or impossible to please. *They were so fastidious about the state of their lawn that they found no time to grow anything else in their garden.*

FAUCET *n.* A pipe and tap to draw liquid from a barrel. *The host hammered the faucet into the wooden beer barrel and the party started.*

FEBRILE *adj.* Showing signs of fever of unknown cause. *The doctor referred the febrile patient to a specialist in tropical medicine.*

FECUND *adj.* Able to produce offspring. *Her friends were amazed by her fecundity when her seventh child was born.*

FELICITY *n.* Happiness, delight and the ability to express it. *With eloquent felicity he thanked his hostess for the excellent meal.*

FETTER *n.* A leg iron. *The prisoner was shackled with metal fetters on his ankles.*

FETTLE *n.* A state of mind and condition. *He was in fine fettle before the exam and consequently passed with a high mark.*

FIB *n.* An mild untruth. *The parent reproached the child who fibbed that he had not taken the apple.*

FILIBUSTER *n.* The obstruction of a debate by one participant speaking for a long time. *The member of parliament was determined that the matter should not be approved and filibustered for hours on end.*

FILIGREE *n.* Decorative metallic lace work of gold or silver. *The brooch he gave her had a bright jewel held in place with intricate filigree.*

FIRMAMENT *n.* The entire universe. *The small boy asked how many stars there were in the firmament.*

FIZGIG *n.* A flippant girl prone to flirtation. *The fizgig dropped her scarf at his feet in the hope that he would pay attention to her.*

FLAPPER *n.* A young girl constantly partying with little regard for conventional behaviour. *Her mother urged her to stop being a flapper as it was time to consider a career.*

FLIPPERTIGIBBET *n.* A flighty person of no intellectual substance. *All her life she had been a flippertigibbet and consequently never held down a job for more than a few months.*

FLOUNCE *v.* To move with exaggerated motion expressing displeasure or disinterest. *She flounced around the room when the dressmaker suggested that she was a little old for that style.*

FLUMMERY *n.* A meaningless, insincere compliment. *He attempted to impress her with flummery but she saw through him.*

FLUMMOX *v.* To confuse and bewilder. *She was totally flummoxed at the end of the physics lesson.*

FLUNKEY *n.* A liveried manservant junior to a butler. *The uniformed flunkey opened the door of the car as his eminent employer returned home.*

FOLDEROL *n.* Utter nonsense of a harmless nature. *The sparse arrangement of food on the plate of nouvelle cuisine was dismissed as mere folderol.*

FRIPPERY *n.* A useless item. *She regarded the new kitchen gadget as a piece of frippery and soon reverted to the way her mother taught her.*

FUDDLE *v.* To stupefy by drinking to excess. *His brain was so fuddled that he left his coat behind in the pub.*

FUDDY DUDDY *n.* An old fashioned person determined not to embrace the modern world. *His grandchildren accused him of being a fuddy duddy because he had no interest in social media.*

FUDGE *v.* To skirt around an issue in order to divert attention. *He fudged the issue by turning the conversation away from the embarrassing situation.*

G

GADZOOKS *excl.* A loud exclamation of surprise. *Gadzooks! Do you see the huge car he is driving around in now?*

GAFFER *n.* The boss. *The workforce slackened their speed when the gaffer was out to lunch.*

GAINSAY *v.* Refusing to accept as true; to contradict. *The other members of the club had seen his speed and gainsaid his claims to have been the fastest boy at school.*

GALLIMAUFRY *n.* A confused, inconsistent jumble of items. *Her daughter thought the larder shelves were a gallimaufry but she knew where to find what she needed.*

GALLIVANT *v.* Frivolous travel pursuing pleasure. *They gallivanted all over the village looking for clues in the treasure hunt.*

GAMBOL *v.* To playfully leap or skip in dance or sport. *The children gambolled through the park on their way to the playground.*

GAUDY *adj.* Showy and tasteless appearance. *The woman's gaudy dress sense astonished the other people at the party.*

GAY *adj.* Lively, carefree and jolly. *Many neighbours envied the gay lifestyle of the young married couple.*

GIRD *v.* To prepare for a dangerous situation. *They girded themselves as they prepared for the final assault on the mountain.*

GLABROUS *adj.* Totally smooth. *She preferred his glabrous face after he shaved off his beard.*

GLIB *adj.* Insincere; simplistic. *His glib response was an inadequate apology for the chaos he had caused.*

GLOAMING *n.* Twilight. *They wandered along the beach enjoying the gloaming as the sun dipped down.*

GLUTTON *n.* Someone who eats too much. *The glutton soon had to buy new trousers.*

GOAD *v.* To provoke into action with harassment. *He goaded the horse to jump the fence with too much use of the whip.*

GODSPEED *n.* An expression of good wishes for a safe journey. *He wished her godspeed as he closed the door of the car.*

GOODWIFE *n.* The senior female member of a family. *The grandmother was undisputed goodwife of her household.*

GRANDILOQUENT *adj.* Extravagant use of pompous language intended to impress. *His grandiloquent speech was not what they expected from a senior cabinet minister.*

GRASS WIDOW *n.* A wife whose husband is away from home for prolonged periods. *The grass widow longed for her husband's return from his posting overseas.*

GREEN *adj.* Inexperienced. *The young recruit was very green but soon learnt how to be an effective salesman.*

GROG *n.* Spirit diluted with water. *The sailors enjoyed their ration of grog and a singsong.*

GROUSE *v.* To grumble; to moan. *He was always grousing about being given too much homework.*

GRUEL *n.* An unappetising liquid food of oats boiled in water. *Oliver Twist was so hungry that he asked for more despite it being gruel.*

GUBBINS *n.* Insignificant miscellaneous items. *His workshop was full of gubbins because he never threw anything away.*

GUFFAW *n.* A hearty laugh. *His friends guffawed as he told them the hilarious story.*

GUMPTION *n.* Shrewd common sense. *The village handyman's gumption solved many problems.*

H

HANDMAIDEN *n.* A female servant. *The handmaiden anticipated everything the queen might need.*

HARRIDAN *n.* An unpleasant, bossy, woman. *The harridan who ran the boarding house was disliked by everyone who stayed there.*

HARUM-SCARUM *adj.* Reckless and irresponsible. *His harum-scarum driving was punished with a heavy fine.*

HAW OR HAW-HAW *v.* Drawling, vulgar speech. *The sneering manner of William Joyce's war time broadcasts from Germany earned him the nickname Lord Haw-haw.*

HEARTSTRING *n.* Deeply amorous feelings. *She tugged at her boy friend's heartstrings until he proposed to her.*

HEDONISM *n.* The pursuit of pleasure to the exclusion of all else. *His lottery win led to a life of hedonism.*

HEFT *v.* To carry something heavy by hand. *He was exhausted after a day hefting sacks of potatoes.*

HELTER-SKELTER *adv.* Undue, confused haste. *His broken bicycle meant a helter-skelter dash to the station.*

HEM *n.* An imitation cough to attract attention. *She called the meeting to order with a hem.*

HENCHMAN *n.* A supporter or employee engaging in nefarious activities. *The car dealer's henchman prepared false invoices to reduce the mileage reading.*

HENPECKED *adj.* Domineering behaviour of a wife to her husband. *The henpecked man ignored his wife's demands to mow the lawn and took the dog for a walk.*

HERCULEAN *adj.* Requiring great mental or physical strength to complete a task. *Shifting the fallen tree proved to be a herculean task.*

HEYDAY *n.* The period within a person's life or in a thing's existence when the greatest popularity or success is achieved. *The British Empire's heyday was during the latter years of Queen Victoria's reign.*

HIATUS *n.* An unplanned and unhelpful gap in progress. *The machine breakdown caused a hiatus further down the production line.*

HIGGLEDY-PIGGLEDY *adj.* Confusion and disorder caused by a muddled state of affairs. *The higgledy-piggledy layout in the shop caused bewilderment to the customers.*

HIGH-FALUTIN *adj.* Pretentious and arrogant speech chosen to overcomplicate a matter in order to impress. *The high-falutin manner in which he presented his proposal did not win him the contract.*

HIGH-JINKS *n.* Boisterous and mischievous behaviour. *The high-jinks of the stag night were soon forgotten.*

HINTERLAND *n.* A remote area of countryside that remains largely out of sight and out of mind. *The explorer preferred the solitude of the hinterland to the overcrowded city.*

HIRSUTE *adj.* Hairy. *His unkempt beard made the girls giggle at his hirsute appearance.*

HOBBLEDEHOY *n.* An awkward youth experiencing a difficult transition from childhood to manhood. *His mother was delighted when her hobbledehoy son eventually started to make friends.*

HOCK *n.* An item taken to a pawnshop. *After a run of bad luck his gold wedding ring ended up in hock.*

HOCUS-POCUS *n.* Meaningless words intended to deflect attention. *The opposition accused the minister of hocus-pocus when he attempted to cover up the failure of his policies.*

HOITY-TOITY *adj.* Behaviour that is arrogant and pretentious. *Her hoity-toity airs and graces did little to convince her colleagues that she was better than them.*

HOODLUM *n.* A violent person involved in rowdy and often criminal behaviour. *After he smashed the barstool the hoodlum was banned from the pub.*

HOODWINK *v.* To deceive or trick. *The conjuror hoodwinked the children with his sleight of hand.*

HOSE *n.* Socks or stockings *When the ugly sister danced the cancan the outrageous colours of her hose made the pantomime audience roar with laughter.*

HOTCHPOTCH *adj.* A mass of ingredients mixed together such as a stew or any assortment of unconnected items. *The hotchpotch of meat and vegetables made a casserole that was ideal on the wintery day.*

HOVE *v.* To appear; to become visible. *After a long wait his friend eventually hove into view.*

HUBBUB *n.* A confusion of noise or speech. *The hubbub in the market made it difficult to think.*

HUCKSTER *n.* A retailer resorting to devious behaviour. *Pensioners were warned of the huckster's attempts to sell double glazing.*

HULLABALOO *n.* A furore caused by people who are irritated or angry. *The increased fares resulted in a hullabaloo that caused a delay in the train's departure.*

I

IGNOMINY *n.* Public disgrace and the loss of one's good name. *The ignominy caused by his dalliance with his secretary marked the end of a promising career.*

IGNORAMUS *n.* An ignorant person. *A lack of understanding made the ignoramus quite unsuited to high office.*

IMBECILE *n.* A stupid person. *His job application was rejected as he was clearly an imbecile.*

IMBIBE *v.* To absorb alcohol by drinking or knowledge by learning. *At university he imbibed his subject with enthusiasm.*

IMBROGLIO *n.* A perplexing state of affairs; a complicated misunderstanding within the plot of a drama. *Readers of her detective stories loved unravelling the imbroglios she devised.*

IMMUTABLE *adj.* Unchangeable for all time. *The immutable actions of the tide could surely be harnessed to generate power.*

IMPECUNIOUS *adj.* Without money or the ability to earn any. *His impecunious life style lost him friends in the pub.*

IMPERIOUS *adj.* Assuming a domineering, haughty and often tyrannical command. *The imperious attitudes of the chairman won him few friends.*

IMPERTURBABLE *adj.* The ability of remaining calm even in dire circumstances. *His imperturbable determination brought hope to the flooded community.*

IMPORTUNE *v.* To make persistent demands for something often in a manner considered harassing. *The constant importuning for sweets usually resulted in the bully being given them.*

IMPUGN *v.* To call into question the validity of a pronouncement. *The customer impugned the salesman's claim that his product was the best.*

IMPUTE *v.* To attribute responsibility for an undesirable action to someone. *The jury's verdict imputed the theft of the car to the accused.*

INALIENABLE *adj.* The undisputed right of a person to ownership of a possession or the right to a freedom. *The inalienable right of free speech is a corner stone of the nation's constitution.*

INAMORATA *n.* The woman with whom a man is in love. *His wedding to his inamorata was the happiest day of his life.*

INCIPIENT *adj.* The start of a process. *The incipient hard work was the foundation of his eventual success.*

INCONDITE *adj.* Crudely put together or badly constructed thought or speech. *She received little applause after her incondite address to the meeting.*

INCULCATE *v.* To enforce a belief in someone's mind by persistent and forceful instruction. *The politician won the election after constantly inculcating his policies to the electorate.*

INDECOROUS *adj.* Unseemly conduct that does not conform to the usually accepted standards of good taste. *His indecorous behaviour at the smart party was entirely due to his love of alcohol.*

INDOLENT *adj.* Indisposed to exertion or effort. *The grandfather despaired at the indolent behaviour of his idle grandson.*

INDUBITABLE *adj.* That which cannot be denied, doubted or questioned. *It is an indubitable fact that two plus two makes four.*

INEFFABLE *adj.* Beyond words or description; incapable of being expressed. *Her ineffable beauty left him speechless.*

INESTIMABLE *adj.* Unable to be valued due to incalculable desirability or benefit. *The inestimable education she received served her career well.*

INFATUATED *adj.* The obsessive passion for a person, object or belief. *The aspiring politician was infatuated with all aspects of the European Union.*

INIMITABLE *adj.* So utterly perfect that copying would be impossible. *The critic praised the inimitable paintings of the English countryside by John Constable.*

INSCRUTABLE *adj.* Possessing qualities that are impossible to understand. *Winston Churchill found the intentions of Joseph Stalin to be inscrutable.*

INSIDIOUS *adj.* Action that may appear harmless but is intended to be harmful. *When he asked his friend's girl to dance he had insidious intentions.*

INURE *v.* To accept a frequently occurring unpleasant condition or custom. *The sad faces of the refugee children showed that they were inured to sights of violence and conditions of poverty.*

INVECTIVE *n.* A critical attack delivered in words. *The cyclist shouted a mass of invective at the motorist who had knocked him to the ground.*

INVEIGLE *v.* To seduce with cunning. *He inveigled her into his flat on the pretence of showing off his art collection.*

INVIDIOUS *adj.* Likely to provoke anger or ill-will. *His unhelpful remarks were regarded as being invidious and did nothing to secure an agreement.*

IOTA *n.* A very small amount. *His barrister told the court that there was not an iota of evidence that he had committed the crime.*

IRASCIBLE *adj.* Likely to be unduly angry when provoked. *She became irascible when the football landed in her garden again.*

J

JABBER *v.* To talk nonsense excitedly. *She jabbered on about her new boyfriend.*

JAPE *v.* To jest or joke *He loved to jape with his friends and they were always playing practical jokes on each other.*

JEMMY *n.* A crowbar favoured by burglars. *The detective realised that the door had been forced with a jemmy.*

JIFFY *n.* An instant. *She called down the stairs to her husband that she would be ready in a jiffy.*

JIGGERED *excl.* Explanation of great surprise that frequently takes the place of an unacceptable choice of words. *When he heard they were to be married he exclaimed 'Well I am totally jiggered'.*

JINGOIST *n.* A person who believes that his country is by far the best. *His jingoist view of the country's football team was not always supported by the final score.*

JOSTLE *v.* To bump into in a crowd. *She hated being jostled by strangers on the train.*

JOURNEYMAN *n.* A worker who is dependable but not outstanding. *His plodding yet reliable attitude to work made him an ideal journeyman to work in the shop.*

JUGGINS *n.* A gullible person. *What a juggins you have been to pay so much for that.*

JUNKET *n.* An extravagant entertainment of prominent figures at the expense of someone wishing to impress. *The members of parliament were given an expenses paid junket by the foreign government.*

K

KEMPT *adj.* The appearance of a person or place that is neat, tidy and clean. *Her appearance and that of her home was always well kempt.*

KICKSHAW *n.* Something previously unseen which therefore has no name. *Her originality in the kitchen often resulted in what they called a kickshaw dinner.*

KITH *n.* Friends and acquaintances whereas kin refers to people to whom you are related. *Her kith and kin were all at her funeral.*

KNAVE *n.* A minor villain. *The knave of hearts he stole the tarts and took them clean away.*

KUDOS *n.* Admiration and respect given for a job well done. *The vicar received well deserved kudos for organising a successful village fete.*

L

LACHRYMOSE *adj.* The shedding of tears. *Although her daughter's wedding was a very happy day she was lachrymose when the party was over.*

LACKADAISICAL *adj.* Lacking enthusiasm; lazy. *His lackadaisical approach to gardening resulted in a jungle.*

LACONIC *adj.* The use of few words. *He was known for his laconic replies even to complex questions.*

LAMPOON *v.* To satire with wit. *The comedians lampooned the politicians.*

LASCIVIOUS *adj.* Lustful. *She complained to their boss that his manner towards her was lewd and lascivious.*

LAX *adj.* Slack and inappropriate particularly in reference to discipline and morals. *His attitude to health and safety was unacceptably lax.*

LEER *n.* A sideways look. *The sly man was often seen leering at people.*

LIBATION *n.* A measure of liquid. *When friends came to visit he offered them a libation of gin and tonic.*

LICKSPITTLE *n.* A grovelling servant or dependent. *He became a lickspittle towards his superiors and forfeited friendships as he furthered his career.*

LIMEY *n.* A person from Britain. *A slang term for a Briton arriving in the colonies derived from the practice of eating limes on board ship to prevent scurvy.*

LINGO *n.* A language. *After living abroad for a few years he was becoming more proficient with the lingo.*

LIP SERVICE *n.* Insincere speech not followed up with promised actions. *He had no intention of voting for the motion but gave it lip service to avoid the constant demands for support.*

LISSOM *adj.* Thin; graceful. *She was much admired for her lissom appearance.*

LOLL *v.* To relax lazily. *He lolled about on the beach soaking up the sunshine.*

LOQUACIOUS *adj.* Garrulous; verbose. *He was loquacious in his praise of the performance.*

LOTHARIO *n.* A man who behaves irresponsibly with the women he seduces. *The lothario cared little for the feelings of the young girls.*

LUGUBRIOUS *adj.* Unhappy; mournful. *His misfortunes in business led to his lugubrious expression.*

M

MAGNILOQUENT *adj.* Speech in a pompous or bombastic style. *Despite addressing the court in a magniloquent manner, the barrister held the jury's attention.*

MALADROIT *adj.* Awkward; clumsy. *He was far too maladroit to be chosen for the village cricket team.*

MALEFACTOR *n.* A person living a life of crime and wrong doing. *The judge sentenced the persistent malefactor to another term in prison.*

MALFEASANCE *n.* Behaviour that is either illegal or dubious. *The extent of the malfeasance in the city was an increasing concern.*

MAMMON *n.* Riches and the desire of people who stop at nothing to accumulate wealth. *You cannot serve God and mammon. Matthew chap 6.*

MAR *v.* To damage the perfect appearance of an item or a reputation. *His standing in the local community was marred when his dishonest behaviour was revealed.*

MAROON *n.* A rocket that explodes with a loud noise and bright light to attract attention. *When the maroon went up the lifeboat men could be seen running towards the harbour.*

MASTICATE *v.* To chew. *The meat was tough so he spent quite a while masticating.*

MAWKISH *adj.* Tasteless sentimentality. *His mawkish and outdated dress sense was frequently laughed at.*

MEAN *n.* Central point between any two extremes regardless of the unit of measurement that defines their position. *The mean on the journey from London to Edinburgh brought them to York.*

MELEE *n.* An unruly gathering of people. *After the football match there was an unfortunate melee in the pub.*

MERCURIAL *adj.* Unpredictable and fickle changes of habit. *She left her job because she could not bear working for such a mercurial man.*

METHINKS *v.* Literally 'me thinks' as in 'it seems to me'; a passing comment, often humorous, that defines an observation. *'The lady doth protest too much, methinks' Shakespeare Hamlet.*

MIASMA *n.* Something that seems to hang in the air that can be either a revolting smell or a negative atmosphere. *The miasma hanging over the town was blamed on the chemical works.*

MIEN *n.* A person's expression that conveys a mood. *Her happy mien made it clear that she had passed her driving test.*

MINUTIAE *n.* The smallest item of detail. *The specification was very precise as every minutiae had been defined.*

MISCREANT *n.* A wrong doer. *The headmaster made it clear that the miscreant would be punished.*

MOLLYCODDLE *v.* To cosset over protectively. *He kept telling his wife to stop mollycoddling the boy.*

MONGER *n.* A trader in thought or goods. *The fruit monger had a stall in the market.*

MOOT *n.* A matter of little or even no importance but still worthy of discussion. *It was a moot point whether the recall of the product had been the cause of the company's demise.*

MOPE *v.* To be silent or dispirited. *He moped around the house after his girlfriend left him.*

MOSEY *v.* To walk around in a relaxed manner without apparent purpose. *After breakfast they decided to mosey off to the beach.*

MOTLEY *adj.* Poor quality of either people or items. *The army recruits were a motley collection but the sergeant was sure he could train them.*

MUGGINS *n.* A gullible person. *The muggins invariably found that he had to do the washing up.*

MUGGY *adj.* Warmth that is unpleasant due to high humidity. *The muggy weather sapped their enthusiasm for the walk they had planned.*

MUNIFICENT *adj.* Exceptionally generous. *Her munificent donation to the school appeal was praised by the headmaster.*

N

NAMBY-PAMBY *adj.* Indecisive, juvenile and lacking vigour. *They longed for their namby-pamby teenage son to find a job.*

NANNY *n.* A woman employed to look after a child in its own home. *When he was very young he spent more time with his nanny than he did with his parents.*

NASCENT *adj.* Commencement of a process, particularly of one that shows great promise. *The veteran environmentalist had been campaigning since the nascent days of the Green Party.*

NAUGHT *n.* Of no value; nothing. *Despite working really hard his business came to naught.*

NE'ER-DO-WELL *n.* A person who shows no promise of ever achieving anything. *The ne'er-do-well teenager exasperated his parents by rarely getting up before midday.*

NEFARIOUS *adj.* Illegal and wicked. *The townsfolk were delighted when his nefarious lifestyle was eventually halted by the judge.*

NIGGARDLY *adj.* Lacking generosity; parsimonious. *He looked for another job after the niggardly pay rise.*

NIL-DESPERANDUM *excl.* Never despair whatever the circumstances. *'Nil-desperandum, we will start again' said the businessman whose premises had burnt down.*

NINCOMPOOP *n.* A simple and incompetent person; often abbreviated to ninny. *He was a nincompoop in the kitchen and rarely produced a decent meal.*

NOB *n.* A superior person. *All the local nobs were at the wedding of the squire's daughter.*

NOBBLE *v.* To alter the course of an action; to acquire by underhand means. *He bribed the councillor in an attempt to nobble the planning committee.*

NOGGIN *n.* A small quantity of an alcoholic drink. *After the game they all went to the pub for a noggin.*

NOSEGAY *n.* A sweet-scented bunch of flowers. *She knew he was serious about her when he arrived with a nosegay of primroses.*

NOUVEAU RICHE *n.* People who have recently acquired riches. *A term of disparagement used by those whose wealth was inherited.*

O

OAF *n.* A clumsy and stupid person. *He was such an oaf that he lost his job in the pub because he was always dropping plates.*

OBDURATE *adj.* Dogged refusal to change an opinion even when the alternative view seems correct. *He was obdurate about being able to drive home.*

OBFUSCATE *v.* To intentionally confuse or detract from an issue by long winded speech. *He obfuscated when asked if he had knocked the car.*

OBLOQUY *n.* Public reproach; vilification. *The obloquy he received after his misdemeanour was sufficient to drive him from office.*

OBSEQUIOUS *adj.* Servile to an excessive and often irritating degree. *The waiter's obsequious attention kept interrupting their conversation.*

OBSTREPEROUS *adj.* Noisy and badly behaved. *The obstreperous child irritated the neighbours by riding his bicycle down the pavement.*

OGLE *v.* To glance in a lecherous manner. *She had learnt to ignore the young man in accounts who ogled her throughout the day.*

OMNIPOTENT *adj.* All powerful. *The founder of the company thought he was omnipotent but the shareholders disagreed.*

OMNIPRESENT *adj.* Constantly present. *The wasps were omnipresent in the garden until the nest had been dealt with.*

OPUS *n.* A work. *He was relieved to hand the manuscript of his opus over to the publisher.*

P

PAIL *n.* A bucket or any vessel, metal or wooden, for carrying liquid. *Jack and Jill went up the hill to fetch a pail of water.*

PALM *v.* To conceal an item in a closed hand to deceive its owner either by theft or in a magic trick. *The spectator was quite unaware that the magician had palmed his wallet.*

PANACEA *n.* A solution for all problems. *The substantial pay rise proved to be a panacea for all their financial worries.*

PANDER *v.* To appeal to people in a manner most likely to gain their support. *The politician pandered to the voters in the hope of getting their vote.*

PANJAMDRUM n. A person who has, or falsely claims to have, power over others or institutions. *The bossy panjamdrum seemed to organise all aspects of village life.*

PANOPLY *n.* An impressive gathering of people or items. *The exhibition was praised for the panoply of items on display.*

PANTRY *n.* A room in which non edible dining items are kept. *The butler at the stately home kept the silver cutlery and best china in his pantry.*

PARAGON *n.* A person or item considered to be a perfect example of its kind and a standard by which others might be judged. *All the music students strove to be as accomplished as the paragon who taught them.*

PARLOUS *adj.* Dangerous; uncertain. *The parlous state of the building meant it was closed to the public as a safety measure.*

PAROXYSM *n.* A sudden episode of an extreme action usually of pain or fear. *The paroxysms of agony he experienced were worse than anything he thought possible.*

PARSIMONY *n.* Extreme frugality in spending money. *The parsimony they had to adopt when he lost his job was regrettable but wise.*

PARVENU *n.* An inexperienced newcomer. *The ambitious parvenu worked hard to learn his trade.*

PASSÉ *adj.* Nearly out of date; no longer in fashion. *They laughed because her skirts were always a bit passé.*

PAT *n.* A small portion of something. *The owner of the tea shop always curled her pats of butter.*

PATE *n.* The crown of the head. *After he lost his hair he had to be careful to protect his pate from sunburn.*

PATERFAMILIAS *n.* The father in his position as head of the family. *As paterfamilias he always carved the Sunday joint.*

PATTER *v.* To repeat something over and over again. *His colleagues praised his sales patter as it produced results.*

PECCADILLO *n.* A trifling sin; a petty fault. *He persuaded the policemen that riding his bike on the pavement was a peccadillo and not a crime.*

PELL-MELL *adv.* Great haste; confusion. *The sheep rushed pell-mell all over the field when the dog began to chase them.*

PENANCE *n.* An act of self punishment expressing repentance for wrongdoing. *After arriving home worse for wear he took his wife out to dinner as a penance.*

PENNYWORTH *n.* A small but potent contribution to a debate. *She always tried to get her pennyworth in at the start of the meetings.*

PENURY *n.* A state of abject poverty experienced by people without income. *He was in penury following his eviction from the family home.*

PERCHANCE *adv.* Perhaps; maybe. '*To sleep perchance to dream*'. *Hamlet musing to himself about life after death.*

PERDITION *n.* A state of disaster and ruin. *The company headed rapidly towards perdition when the competitor started a price war.*

PEREGRINATE *v.* To wander from place to place. *They spent a carefree day peregrinating along the canal tow path.*

PERFIDIOUS *adj.* Unfaithful; breaching trust and confidence. *His perfidious behaviour to a fellow member saw him evicted from the golf club.*

PERIPATETIC *adj.* Travel from place to place; working in more than one place. *Her specialist subject required her to be a peripatetic teacher working at half a dozen schools.*

PERNICIOUS *adj.* Highly injurious behaviour applied with cunning. *The pernicious neighbour crept into their garden at night and poured weedkiller onto their flower beds.*

PERNICKETY *adj.* Over fastidious emphasis on detail. *Her small garden was her pride and joy and she was very pernickety about dead heading her roses.*

PERSPICACIOUS *adj.* Clarity of understanding. *His perspicacious approach to the business was awarded with swift promotion.*

PESKY *adj.* Annoying; causing trouble. *The neighbours pesky dog kept jumping the fence to chase their cat.*

PETTIFOGGING *adj.* Attaching undeserved importance to a matter or situation. *They wished the chairman of the parish council would stop pettifogging about litter and allow discussion about the excess traffic.*

PETULANT *adj.* Impudent in manner; moody and sulky. *The schoolboy showed no interest in maths and always gave petulant replies to his teacher.*

PHANTASMAGORIA *n.* An exhibition of changing optical effects and illusions created as an entertainment. *The phantasmagoria of lights, music and dancing thrilled the audience.*

PHILOLOGIST *n.* The study of language. *The philologist loved speaking to people in their own language.*

PIFFLE *n.* Nonsense talk. *She told him to stop talking piffle.*

POKE *n.* A bag or pouch. *A pig in a poke is a purchase acquired unseen and therefore of suspect value.*

POLEMIC *n.* A strongly worded statement that either attacks or defends a closely held belief. *Her polemic at the annual conference gave the delegates much food for thought.*

POLTROON *n.* A coward without courage or spirit. *The officer had to work hard to transform the conscripted poltroons into a fighting force.*

POOH-POOH *n.* An expression of distain that expresses a feeling that an opinion is not worth consideration. *She pooh-poohed the suggestion that she should take the lead role in the pantomime.*

PORTER *n.* An employee of a railway company available to assist passengers with their luggage. *She tipped the porter generously as without his assistance she would never have caught the train.*

POSER *n.* An exhibitionist or show off. *His style of dress was so over the top that his colleagues regarded him as a poser.*

POST-PRANDIAL *adj.* After dinner. *Every evening he had a post-prandial tot of whisky.*

POTTAGE *n.* A basic stew of meat and vegetables cooked in a pot. *After a cold walk on the moors they cooked a pottage for their dinner.*

POUT *v.* To push out the lips in an expression of contempt or displeasure. *She pouted her lips when her husband suggested that she had drunk too much.*

POWWOW *n.* An informal gathering to discuss a proposition. *Before the board meeting he called a powwow with colleagues.*

PRECOCIOUS *adj.* Mind or abilities fully developed at an unusually early age. *The precocious lad was in the first football team a year earlier than his contemporaries.*

PREDILECTION *n.* A choice made beforehand. *He was well aware of her predilection for champagne and poured a glass without asking her if she would like it.*

PREGNANT *adj.* Filled with suggestive meaning. *The actor was a master at attracting the audience's attention with pregnant pauses in his delivery.*

PREREQUISITE *n.* Something required beforehand to achieve a result. *Three A grades are a prerequisite of university entrance.*

PRESAGE *v.* To give warning of a future event; a foreboding. *The very cold night presaged a difficult drive to work the following day.*

PRESTIDIGITATION *n.* Sleight of hand. *The conjuror's prestidigitation had the audience gasping in disbelief.*

PRIG *n.* A person who assumes underserved airs of superiority and wisdom. *The prig said he could always complete the crossword in twenty minutes but some hours later many clues remained unsolved.*

PRINK *v.* To make minor adjustments to your appearance. *'If you spend any more time prinking your makeup we will miss the start of the play'.*

PRIVILY *adj.* Privately in great secret. *She took the letters from her lover and read them privily at the bottom of the garden.*

PROBITY *n.* Honesty and integrity that has been tested. *The salesman offered his product with great probity.*

PROCRASTINATE *v.* To put off until another time; to postpone. *He procrastinated for such a long time that the people who had offered to buy his house went elsewhere.*

PROFLIGATE *adj.* Abandoned to a dissolute life of reckless extravagance. *His profligate lifestyle inevitably led to severe financial problems.*

PROPINQUITY *n.* The state of being close to someone or some place. *The propinquity of their new home meant that they were still able to keep in touch with their former neighbours.*

PROTEAN *adj.* Versatility as the need arises. *The protean skills of the surgeon were renowned throughout the medical world.*

PROXIMATE *adj.* Nearest or next. *The proximate house was a mile away but they loved living in the remote countryside.*

PUCE *adj.* The darkest shade of red. *She thought his puce hair colour was very distinguished.*

PUCKER *v.* To gather in by making folds and contortions. *The child puckered his face when given coffee cake as he hated it.*

PULCHRITUDE *adj.* Comeliness; a person's great physical beauty. *The young man fell for her pulchritude as much as he did for her intelligence.*

PUNCTILIOUS *adj.* Attending to the finest detail particularly in matters of timing. *She was punctilious in her preparations and the meal was all prepared when the guests arrived.*

PURLOIN *v.* To take away for personal use; to steal. *He purloined fire wood from the forest when no one was looking.*

PURPORT *v.* To claim something that is false. *In his interview he purported to have more experience than he had.*

PUSILLANIMOUS *adj.* Lacking courage; timid. *The player's pusillanimous manner made him quite unsuited to being in the front row of the scrum.*

Q

QUAFF *v.* To drink in a jovial manner. *He enjoyed nothing more than quaffing ale with his friends.*

QUASH *v.* To crush. *She quashed the vegetables to make a wonderful soup.*

QUERULOUS *adj.* Complaining, discontent, quarrelsome. *The grumpy neighbour always found something to be querulous about.*

QUIBBLE *n.* A minor criticism or objection. *He always quibbled about the price he was asked to pay.*

R

RABBLE *n.* An unruly group of people. *He had a hard task converting the rabble into a team.*

RACONTEUR *n.* A person skilled in storytelling. *He was a brilliant raconteur and having travelled so widely he had many stories to tell.*

RACY *adj.* Lively, suggestive and mildly shocking. *Many people considered the length of her miniskirt to be rather racy.*

RAKE *n.* A dissolute person leading a debauched life. *His family despaired at the philandering lifestyle of their rake of a brother.*

RAMSHACKLE *adj.* Dilapidated; disorganised. *The ramshackled state of his office went a long way to explaining why his business was rarely profitable.*

RANT *n.* An outburst of violent or extravagant language. *The voters took little notice of his political rants.*

RAPSCALLION *n.* A mischievous young person. *The rapscallion was always nipping over garden walls to pick fruit when the owners were not looking.*

RAT *v.* To abandon your principals or promises. *His colleagues were appalled when he ratted on his agreement to buy the company.*

RECONDITE *adj.* Obscure, complex and consequently unknown. *Most people at the party had no understanding of the recondite subject being discussed by the scientists.*

RECTITUDE *n.* Integrity, morally correct conduct. *In everything she said and did she was governed by her strict sense of rectitude.*

REGIMEN *n.* A defined course of action to achieve an improvement. *His doctor gave a clear regimen that would restore him to good health.*

REPRISE *v.* To repeat. *He was always delighted to be asked to reprise his King Lear.*

REPROBATE *n.* Depraved; one lost to shame. *The reprobate stole the elderly couple's savings.*

RIFF-RAFF *n.* Undesirable people. *He would not have accepted the invitation to speak if he had known that the audience would be such riff-raff.*

RIGMAROLE *n.* A lengthy and tedious procedure of actions or words that achieve little. *They were bored with the rigmarole about her grandchildren's achievements.*

RIME *n.* Hoar frost formed of frozen water vapour. *The rime glistening on the trees in the morning sunlight made the perfect subject for the photographer.*

RISIBLE *adj.* Situations so ludicrous that they are laughed at. *She told him that the idea of them ever being able to afford a house in the picturesque village was risible.*

ROLY-POLY *adj.* Plump; either a pudding or a generously proportioned person. *The roly-poly school boy hated exercise.*

ROTE *n.* Learning by the frequent repetition of words without knowledge of their meaning. *He had learnt The Iliad by rote while at school but he never really understood what it was about.*

ROUSTABOUT n. An unskilled labourer. *As a lad he had worked as a roustabout on the fish dock but automation meant that he was no longer required.*

RUBICUND *adj.* Redness particularly in someone's cheeks. *His years of enjoying too much port were beginning to show in his rubicund appearance.*

RUCTION *n.* A minor disturbance or fracas. *There was a ruction when the disputed goal was allowed.*

RUFFIAN *n.* An unruly person living a life of violence and crime. *There was great relief in the neighbourhood when the ruffian was eventually sent to prison.*

RUM *adj.* Weird; questionable. *Her father despaired at her rum choice of boyfriends.*

RUMBUSTIOUS *adj.* Boisterous but seldom harmful. *The rumbustious youths were soon moved on by the local police.*

RUMPLE *v.* To crease, disarray and dishevel. *He had a very rumpled appearance after a day digging the garden.*

RUMPUS *n.* An uproar. *When their star player was sent off there was a rumpus in the stand.*

S

SAGACIOUS *adj.* Acuteness of perception; shrewdness, wisdom. *His sagacious approach to the problem enabled him to placate both sides of the debate.*

SALACIOUS *adj.* Lustful; lecherous. Showing an undue interest in sexual matters. *She loathed the salacious tittle tattle in her newspaper.*

SALUBRIOUS *adj.* Healthy; wholesome; upmarket and fashionable. *They were delighted to move house to a more salubrious village.*

SAMPLER *n.* An ornamental embroidery created by children to hone their skills. *Her grandmother's sampler took pride of place above the fireplace.*

SANCTIMONIOUS *adj.* Smugness when trying to convince others of a holier than thou character. *People who knew his dubious past regarded his preaching as sanctimonious nonsense.*

SANGFROID *n.* Composure retained despite stressful circumstances. *She always had remarkable sangfroid despite her demanding occupation.*

SARTORIAL *adj.* Pertaining to clothing and tailoring. *You could always rely on her stunning sartorial elegance.*

SCALLYWAG *n.* An amusingly mischievous child whose behaviour is harmless. *She called him a scallywag when he helped himself to a biscuit.*

SCANT *adj.* Scarcely sufficient; deficient in measure. *The loud music from the student's house showed scant regard for the neighbours.*

SCOFF *v.* To mock; to deride with scorn. *They scoffed at his claim that he had a first class degree.*

SCOOT *v.* To depart rapidly. *They soon scooted off when they saw the headmaster coming.*

SCULLERY *n.* A room separate to the kitchen where dishes and vegetables are washed. *The scullery maid longed to be promoted to work in the kitchen.*

SCURRILOUS *adj.* Underhand comments better left unsaid. *She sold the scurrilous story to the newspaper in the hope that it would damage his reputation.*

SEDATE *adj.* Serene and composed. *She swept her partner sedately onto the dance floor.*

SERRIED *adj.* Compact grouping of people or things. *The serried ranks of soldiers in their colourful uniforms was the finest sight she had ever seen.*

SESQUIPEDALIAN *adj.* Unnecessarily long words. *The comedian's sesquipedalian monologue had them rolling in the aisles.*

SETTLE *n.* A high backed, wooden bench with storage beneath the seat. *His idea of a good evening was to sit on the settle beside the fire and chat to his friends in the pub.*

SHABBY *adj.* Threadbare; in dilapidated condition. *He always wore his shabby old coat when he was gardening.*

SHAM *n.* Something bogus intended to deceive. *When he returned from the far-east with his bride they all knew it was a sham marriage.*

SHAMBLE *v.* To saunter with ungainly and clumsy steps. *He shambled about in a confused manner after the accident.*

SHEBANG *n.* Everything or everybody relating to the matter under discussion. *He decided to go for the whole shebang and ask everyone he knew to the party.*

SHILLY-SHALLY *adv.* To purposely hesitate; to hide indecision; to buy time. *The council shilly-shallied for months before they announced their decision.*

SHODDY *adj.* Badly produced; tawdry in appearance. *They took the shoddy table back to the shop when a leg fell off.*

SHORT-COMMONS *n.* An inadequate measure of something, usually food. *He always complained about the short-commons served in the swanky restaurant.*

SHOWER *n.* A group of people or items that is not fit for purpose. *The teachers at their son's school were a complete shower so they took him away.*

SINECURE *n.* An appointment that requires little or no work but awards the holder with status and an income. *The chairman of the board was criticised for awarding his inexperienced brother with a sinecure.*

SIT *v.* To recline as on a chair. *'I was sitting in the old oak chair' [A recent qualifier in a list of endangered words as people nowadays always say 'I was sat in the old oak chair'].*

SKULDUGGERY *n.* Unscrupulous behaviour; dishonest actions. *He was even prepared to resort to skulduggery to convince his customers that they needed more life assurance.*

SMITTEN *v.* To be strongly attracted to a person or an object. *Ever since his schooldays he had been smitten with the girl next door.*

SMUDGE *n.* A mark, a stain. *The waiter put the soup down carelessly and a splash smudged his tie.*

SMUG *n.* Overly satisfied; excessive, undeserved pride in achievements. *He only just won and was rather smug about it.*

SNAG *n.* An unexpected hindrance preventing a trouble free conclusion. *The woodworm in the attic was a major snag in their plans.*

SNIDE *adj.* Disapproving, disparaging and sarcastic remarks. *The teenager made snide remarks to his father when it was suggested that he found a job.*

SNITCHER *n.* A sneak; an informer who reports to an employer or person in authority. *By reporting the colleague's error to their boss the snitcher hoped for promotion.*

SNOLLYGOSTER *n.* A politician concerned more for his personal advancement than for performing the duties for which he or she was appointed. *The voters realised that he was a snollygoster and did not re-elect him.*

SNUFF *v.* To extinguish life from anything. *At the end of the party he snuffed out all the candles.*

SOLILOQUY *n.* A speech to no one in particular. *The final act in the play ended with the lead actor delivering a soliloquy.*

SOMNAMBULATE *v.* To walk when asleep. *She was worried that her somnambulating husband might fall down the stairs.*

SONOROUS *adj.* A noise created by an item being struck. *The sonorous tone of the large bell summoned them in from the playground.*

SOPORIFIC *adj.* Inducing sleep; causing drowsiness. *Listening to music in her rocking chair was always soporific.*

SOPPY *adj.* Feeble; spineless. *He was such a soppy individual that he never made much of his life.*

SO-SO *adj.* Tolerable; adequate but not remarkable; neither good nor bad. *Attendance at the theatre had been so-so but nothing as good as they had hoped for.*

SOUPCON *n.* A small measure. *He always added a soupcon of paprika to his casseroles.*

SOZZLED *adj.* Drunk to the point of intoxication. *He did himself no favours by getting sozzled at the office party.*

SPAT *n.* A minor altercation about a matter of little consequence. *The neighbours had a spat about the state of the fence between their gardens.*

SPECIOUS *adj.* Plausible but fallacious argument. *His claim that he spoke fluent French was soon revealed as being specious.*

SPURN *v.* To reject with disdain. *She could not stand the sight of him so she spurned his advances.*

SQUELCH *v.* To make a noise when a foot treads on soft ground. *The cows squelched through the mud as they wandered towards the barn.*

STET *v.* To restore to a previous state such as in a document on which an unwanted correction has been noted. *We need to stet that resolution as our constituents will never support it.*

STRATAGEM *n.* A plan for deceiving or gaining an advantage over an opponent. *The success of the D Day landings was greatly helped by the stratagem of telling the Germans that the invasion would take place elsewhere.*

STUPOR *n.* The state of being insensible or unconsciousness. *He fell off the bar stool in a drunken stupor.*

STYMIE *v.* To prevent the conclusion of a desired course of action due to unfortunate circumstances. *Their planned walk was stymied when they found that the bridge had been washed away.*

SUAVE *adj.* Pleasant; elegant; excessively polite; charming. *The suave young man turned the heads of all the girls as he swept passed in his sports car.*

SUBTERFUGE *n.* A deceitful scheme to achieve a goal. *He resorted to subterfuge and hid the other boy's boots before the team selection was made.*

SUCCINCT *adj.* Concise and well considered. *The succinct funeral address was just what the family had hoped for.*

SULLEN *adj.* Gloomy, sulky, morose. *She was exasperated by the sullen response from her teenage son.*

SUPERCILIOUS *adj.* Haughtiness in behaviour to imply superiority. *The supercilious actor swept passed the extras without even a smile.*

SUPINE *adj.* Lying prone on your back. *He spent an idle day supine in front of the television.*

SURLY *adj.* Uncivil, cantankerous and glum. *They gave up trying to be friendly to their surly neighbour.*

SWANK *adj.* Bragging; boastful exhibition of achievement. *He was always swanking about the three goals he scored.*

SWOT *v.* To study intensively. *She swotted hard before her finals.*

T

TABOO *n.* A practice that is prohibited by a commonly held social understanding. *Mentioning their new son-in-law's previous marriage was considered a taboo.*

TALISMAN *n.* A token believed by its owner to impart good luck. *Every year he gave her another talisman to add to her charm bracelet.*

TANTAMOUNT *adj.* Being virtually the same as something else. *The jury regarded his unwillingness to answer the question as being tantamount to admitting his guilt.*

TARDY *adj.* Unacceptably sluggish in action and timing. *The headmaster warned the pupil to improve his tardy habits.*

TAT *n.* Worthless rubbish; junk. *He had all sorts of useful bits and pieces in his shed but she thought it all looked like a load of tat.*

TAWDRY *adj.* Cheap, tasteless. *She thought that her dress sense was flamboyant but others considered it tawdry.*

TEMERITY *n.* Rash, audacious behaviour. Effrontery. *She had the temerity to pick the flowers when she went to the garden party.*

TENET *n.* The main principle or doctrine of a belief. *The Easter message was the tenet of his religious belief.*

THENCE *adv.* Moving onwards from a place already mentioned. *For Christmas they were going to his parents and thence to her family for New Year.*

THRICE *adv.* Three times. *He scored not once or twice but thrice.*

THWART *v.* To prevent, frustrate or obstruct a course of action. *His gambling debts thwarted their plan to move to a bigger house.*

TICK *n.* Credit; a sum owing. *The kind shopkeeper often allowed her to buy on tick until her money came in.*

TIFF *n.* A trivial quarrel. *They had a bit of a tiff when it came to deciding where they should honeymoon.*

TINCTURE *n.* A small measure of medicine or alcohol. *He always enjoyed a tincture as the sun dipped down.*

TINGLE *v.* To have a slight sensation of a sting or other irritation. *The tingle in her fingers caused by the nettles soon wore off.*

TITBIT *n.* A small but perfect morsel of food or news. *You could always rely on her for an interesting titbit of gossip.*

TITILLATE *v.* To cause a pleasant sensation. *She was titillated by wonderful aromas drifting from the kitchen.*

TODDY *n.* A sweet or alcoholic drink. *He always relied on a hot toddy of whisky and lemon juice to cure a cold.*

TORPID *adj.* Inactive, lethargic, without movement. *He lay on the sofa all day in a torpid state.*

TRADUCE *v.* To defame or slander; to damage another's reputation. *She traduced her former boyfriend by spreading rumours about his womanising.*

TRITE *adj.* Banal comment lacking imagination. *She was aware that her tights were badly laddered and objected to his trite comment pointing it out.*

TROLLOP *n.* A slovenly woman with promiscuous habits. *They never spoke to the trollop who lived next door.*

TRUANT *n.* A child who fails to attend school without good reason. *His parents were furious when they found out that their son was playing truant.*

TRUCULENT *adj.* Aggressive; easily inclined to violence. *He was a truculent boy and the teachers warned pupils to avoid him in the playground.*

TRUDGE *v.* To walk laboriously. *He trudged through the muddy field on his way home.*

TRUISM *n.* A self-evident truth that need not be mentioned but helps to make a point. *It was a truism that after his outstanding university career he would get an excellent job.*

TRUMP *v.* To deceive. *The judge threw the case out when it became clear that the charges against him were trumped up.*

TURBID *adj.* Clouded by suspended matter; a confused situation. *The heavy rainfall in the hills made the river water turbid.*

TURPITUDE *n.* Depraved action. *His turpitude convinced them that he had no sense of decency.*

TWIG *v.* To understand a situation. *She was slow on the uptake but eventually twigged what he was trying to tell her.*

U

UBIQUITY *n.* The capacity of existing everywhere. *He deplored the ubiquity of plastic and the damage it was doing to the environment.*

ULTIMO *n.* During the previous month. *The minutes of the meeting held ultimo were approved.*

UMBRAGE *n.* Offence; rudeness; upset. *She took umbrage when her friend did not notice her new hair style.*

UNDERGO *v.* To be subjected to something. *Following his accident he had to undergo a lengthy period of physiotherapy.*

UNKEMPT *adj.* Scruffy, untidy. *They arrived home from their camping holiday very unkempt.*

V

VACILLATE *v.* To be indecisive in movement or thought. *He vacillated for such a long time that the girl of his dreams went off and married someone else.*

VAGARY *n.* An unpredicted change in a situation. *The vagaries in her husband's health were a constant concern.*

VAINGLORIOUS *adj.* Excessive and ostentatious pride; vanity. *After he won the prize they soon got fed up listening to his vainglorious utterances.*

VALEDICTION *n.* A farewell oration. *Many people had tears in their eyes as they listened to the valediction.*

VAMOOSE *v.* To depart swiftly. *The boys vamoosed as soon as they saw the policeman coming.*

VAMP *v.* To enhance. *The young couple spent hours vamping their new home.*

VAUDEVILLE *n.* Theatrical entertainment comprising song, dance, comedy, magicians and acrobats. *The invention of the television heralded the demise of vaudeville.*

VEHEMENT *adj.* Passionate fury. *His vehement speech left no one in doubt about his disapproval.*

VENERABLE *adj.* Aged; worthy of honour. *The venerable old man was much loved by his ever-increasing family.*

VERSO *n.* The reverse side. *The art dealer assessed the authenticity of the painting by studying the verso of the canvas.*

VICISSITUDE *n.* An unwelcome change of situation. *She despaired at yet another vicissitude in her husband's career.*

VICTUAL *n.* Food and drink. *The ship put into port to bring on board victuals for the crew.*

VIE *v.* To strive with determination. *She vied for high grades to secure her place at university.*

VIRAGO *n.* A domineering woman. *They avoided the pub as the new landlady was a bad-tempered virago.*

VIRTUE *n.* Moral excellence; purity. *Her main virtue was her constant concern for the welfare of others.*

VITUPERATIVE *adj.* Communicating with abusive fault finding. *The parliamentary debate became a vituperative slanging match.*

W

WAD *n.* A collection of items gathered tightly together. *He clutched a wad of banknotes as he made his way to the betting shop.*

WAIF *n.* An abandoned person or animal in need of care. *She explained to her friend that the kitten was a waif in need of a home.*

WALLOP *v.* To hit. *He walloped the stray dog as it tried to grab one of his chickens.*

WAN *adj.* Lacking colour; languid and sickly. *Her wan appearance gave her family great cause for concern.*

WANTON *adj.* Deliberate, improper behaviour. *The bus shelter was destroyed by an act of wanton vandalism.*

WASSAIL *n.* A drink of mulled wine, apples and ale. *The wassail served at the village pub preceded a riotous party.*

WEATHER-EYE *n.* The keeping of a close watch on a situation to observe change. *She kept a weather eye on her husband's movements after his brief dalliance.*

WELSH *v.* To renege on a promise. *He welshed on their agreement that he should pay half the cost.*

WEND *v.* To wander without urgency. *They had time to spare so they decided to wend their way along the towpath.*

WHEEDLE *v.* To entice by patient, gentle coaxing. *He carefully wheedled the lost wedding ring from the crack in the floorboards.*

WIG *v.* To scold, rebuke. *She wigged him when he returned from the boy's night out at 2pm.*

WILLY-NILLY *adv.* Like it or not an unavoidable development of a situation. *With so many injured players they could see their team slipping willy-nilly down the league.*

WIZENED *adj.* Shrivelled, withered. *After a life tending sheep on the moor the old shepherd's face had become wizened and weather beaten.*

WREAK *v.* To cause damage by natural means. *The storm force winds wreaked havoc on the roads.*

XYZ

XENOPHOBIA *n.* An unreasonable dislike of any person or thing from another country. *The candidate's xenophobia ensured that he came bottom of the poll.*

YOKEL *n.* A country bumpkin; a rustic countryman. *When he pretended to be a yokel, tourists bought him a drink.*

YONDER *adj.* Indication of direction. *The shop is over yonder beyond the church.*

YORE *n.* Times past recalled in nostalgic conversation. *In times of yore the town square had a busy market every week.*

ZANY *adj.* Eccentricity verging on the peculiar. *His zany dress sense caused hilarity amongst his colleagues.*

ZEAL *n.* Passionate enthusiasm for a cause or activity. *Her zeal for tennis soon saw her in the village team.*

About the Author

Edward Allhusen spent forty years as a publisher, half of them founding and running his own company, Old House Books. Now retired, he fills his time by trying to remember and then doing all those things that he promised himself he would do one day, the great majority of which involve exploring the English countryside, which he regards as the most sublime place on Earth.